Commodity Finance

Commodity Finance
Principles and Practice

Second Edition

W. X. Huang

Hh

Hh Harriman House

HARRIMAN HOUSE LTD
18 College Street
Petersfield
Hampshire
GU31 4AD
GREAT BRITAIN
Tel: +44 (0)1730 233870
Email: enquiries@harriman-house.com
Website: www.harriman-house.com

This second edition published in Great Britain in 2019.
First edition, 2014
Copyright © 2019 W. X. Huang

Hardback ISBN: 978-0-85719-665-1
eBook ISBN: 978-0-85719-666-8

British Library Cataloguing in Publication Data
A CIP catalogue record for this book can be obtained from the British Library.

Cover design by Christopher Parker.

To Xinrong and Xinmin

O, troupe of little vagrants of the world, leave your footprints in my words!

Rabindranath Tagore (1861–1941)

Contents

Edition note   xiii

Praise   xv

Acknowledgements   xvii

About the author   xix

Foreword   xxi

List of abbreviations   xxiii

Introduction   xxv

    Structure and logic   xxvi
    Why and how   xxvi
    Target readers   xxvii

Chapter 1: Commodity Finance: Definition and Scope   1

Definition: commodities, commodity trade and commodity trade
finance   3

Characteristics of commodity trade   6

Commodity markets and commodity exchanges   8

Commodity trade finance   13

    Marketability of commodities   17
    Leverage finance   17
    Emerging market linked   18
    Pre-export production   19
    Production   19
    Post-production   19

Chapter 2: Commodity Finance: Commodity Flow and Emerging Markets

Chapter 2: Commodity Finance: Commodity Flow and Emerging Markets   **21**

Commodity flow: a global overview   23
    Soft commodities   24
    Hard commodities   25
    Energy   25
Financing commodity flow for the least-developed emerging markets   27
    Commodity finance: the importance and the difficulties for some less-developed emerging markets   27
    Guarantee funds for credit support in commodity finance   28
    Other instruments   32
Commodity finance for commodity dependent countries: the case of Ethiopia – why and how   34
    Background   35
    The financial sector in Ethiopia   35
    Commodity finance   37
    The role of micro-financial institutions in commodity finance   39
    Support from the government for commodity finance   40
    Some implications for the case   43
Contracts and documents behind the commodity flow   44
    The importance of contracts and documents   44
    Major parts of a commodity contract and points of attention   45

Chapter 3: Commodity Finance: The Major Financing Mechanisms and Products   **53**

Plain vanilla products: commodity finance versus trade finance   55
Commodity finance: finance under a letter of credit   56
Commodity finance facilities: pre-export finance   62
    Export receivables financing   63
    Prepayment finance   66
    Advantages for the lending bank and the borrower   67
    Related risks under pre-export finance   69
Trade finance facilities: ownership based finance   70

Ownership-based finance 70

Different forms of ownership-based finance 72

Advantages of ownership-based finance for the lending banks and the
borrowers 78

Relevant issues on ownership based finance 79

The risk issue 79

The legal registration issue 80

True sale issue 81

Liquidity of the commodities involved 82

Issues linked to a special category of commodity 83

Supply chain finance 85

Supply chain finance: the concept 85

Advantages of supply chain finance solutions for the lending banks
and the borrowers 88

Risks involved with supply chain finance 92

Supply chain finance application: a case of supply chain finance for
copper 93

Chapter 4: Country Risk and Bank Risk and Letters of Credit in Commodity Finance 97

Country risk and bank risk 99

Practical issues for country risk in a commodity finance bank 102

Assessment of the country risk 103

The bank's strategy towards that country 104

Commercial motivation 104

Bank risk in commodity finance 107

Practical issues for bank risk in commodity finance 110

Banks without external credit rating 110

Limit size and business need 111

Bank limit utilization and the speed of credit approval 111

Letters of credit in commodity finance 112

Letters of credit as a payment undertaking 113

Letters of credit as an instrument for financing 117

Bank risk for emerging market banks: payment dispute and delay 126

Chapter 5: Commodity Finance and Risk Management   131

Multiple risks and risk analysis in commodity finance   133

   Commodity finance and its multiple risks   133

   Financing commodity trading companies: multiple risk management   137

Risk management in commodity finance: the supply chain approach   142

Risk management in commodity finance: the collateral management approach   147

   Principles of collateral management   147

   Considerations on risk management for warehouse finance   154

Risk management in commodity finance: the instrumental approach   157

   Risk coverage instruments   157

Fraud risk in commodity finance   161

   Fraud risk and its impact   161

   Considerations in fraud risk management   165

Defaults and bad debts management for commodity finance   166

   Defaults and bad debts in commodity finance   166

   Case appraisal and solution search   167

   Litigation   169

   Debt sale and debt collection   171

Chapter 6: Commodity Finance and its Infrastructure   173

The organizational infrastructure of commodity finance in a bank   175

   Front desk: relationship management   177

   Credit analysis team   177

   Risk management team   177

   Commodity support group   178

   Financial institutions   178

   Credit approval department   178

   Legal department   178

   Bank analysis department   179

   Country risk analysis department   179

   Industry research department   179

   Corporate social responsibility department   179

   Commodity price hedging desk   180

Commodity finance and commodity market research 180

Commodity finance: the support group and the trade service
department 181

    Special competence for the trade service department 185

    Commodity finance, global market operation and price hedging 189

    Special competence for global financial markets department 190

Commodity finance, risk appetite and credit mentality 194

    Special competence for the credit department 195

    Commodity finance and financial institutions 198

    Special competence for the financial institution department 199

Chapter 7: Commodity Finance: Trends and Outlook   203

The future of commodity finance 205

Commodity finance and the commodity cycle 206

    Demand from Asian countries, especially China and India 207

    Population growth 208

    Export restrictions 208

    Other factors 208

Commodities and investment in commodities 211

    Investment in commodities 212

    Investment motivation 215

    Commodity finance along the supply chain 216

Commodity finance and environmental protection 219

Conclusion 224

Chapter 8: Commodity Finance Case Studies   227

Pre-export finance 229

    Executive summary 229

Case study – Bank M 231

    Executive summary 231

Haana Cocoa Board 233

    Executive summary 233

Payment blocked by a local court 236

    Executive summary 236

Commodity fraud   238
   Executive summary   238
Financing of railway bills   241
   Executive summary   241
Court decision   242
   Executive summary   242

Appendix 1: Major Commodity Futures Agencies   245

Appendix 2: Major Commodity Flows for China During Peak Years   255

Appendix 3: Top Commodity Trading Companies Worldwide   287

Bibliography   293

Index   295

Edition note

This edition is based on the 2014 Euromoney edition.

In addition to technical updates and amendments after the feedback from previous readers, a totally new chapter of real-life cases in commodity finance is added.

The discussion on cases has been most welcome in all commodity finance training sessions.

Praise

In the current turbulence in the world economy, various changes are taking place, including in the finance and trade domain.

Dr W. X. Huang's book on commodity finance is absolutely right on target in putting the spotlight on this important but often misunderstood subject. He has delivered his insight in a wide range of aspects, both practical and theoretical, together with a forward vision.

Dr W. X. Huang has extensive experience in commodity finance. This is derived from his life-long engagement in the financial sector in leading positions in banks, and in an advisory capacity on a truly global scale in educational roles. His book thus provides a distinct professional contribution to the field of commodity finance, including a much-needed focus on emerging economies.

Meinhard Gans, MSc,
Chief Executive Office of Maastricht School of Management

Acknowledgements

The book could not have been written without incorporating the knowledge others have so generously shared with me.

Writing the book has reminded me of the discussions and debates with my colleagues/ex-colleagues/friends inside and outside the bank, which have helped me and contributed to the book.

The conversations on various occasions with commodity trading companies and their insights into the subject definitely allowed me to check and cross check many of the understandings.

It is kind of Lex Kloosterman, ex-management member of Rabobank, to write his foreword.

The following list includes only some of the people with whom I have enjoyed working and to whom acknowledgements must go:

Rolf Dijkhuis

Audery Elaine

Rob Bonte

Diane Boogaard

Chen Dazou

Yang Meng

Li Shen

Migurel Ionita

Maggie Dong

Menno Meijer

Maes van Lanschot

Eeclo Wolters

Gary Collyer

Kaman Cheng

Gerjan Lagerwerf

Johnson Chan

Hu Ronghua

Joost van den Akker

Jenny Choi

Janson Jord

Peter van Iershot

Sema Zeyneloglu

Seb Princen

Theo Bettenhaussen

Amy Wang

Upon my request, Menno Meijer, Yong Meng, Rolf Dijkhuis, Eeclo Wolters Gary Collyer, have read Chapter 7, Chapter 6 and Chapter 5 and have given detailed professional comments, despite their busy schedules.

Teaching at the Maastricht School of Management and training on various occasions has given me a lot of inspiration on the subject.

It is my great honour to have Mr. Meinhard Gans, CEO of Maastricht School of Management, and my 20-year friend and colleague, write his kind recommendation on this new edition of my book.

Thanks should also go to Kaman, Charles and Migurel, who have contributed to some charts and tables in the book.

Ms Melissa Oshungbure, Managing Editor of Euromoney which first published this book, has given so much help and comments on the book, including the title and content. She is right in saying "manuscripts can feel that they are taking over your life towards the end!"

Only with the efforts from Harriman House, especially our editor, Craig Pearce, who carefully planned the publication, and Liz Bourne, who raised detailed questions to improve the text, this new edition is possible with a new face.

A special word to Robert Speelman, who inspired me to venture into a commodity finance banking career.

Last but not the least, thanks to my family for putting up with many of my days and hours at the computer. The book is also theirs.

W. X. Huang

About the author

Dr W. X. Huang is a career banker who has worked for Bank Mees Pierson, ABNAMRO (ex-Fortis) and Rabobank since 1990. He has served as Director of Trade and Commodity Finance in these banks. This background has provided him with extensive exposure to the subject of commodity finance.

He received his MA (Economics) in China and MA (Asia Studies) in Japan. His PhD was linked to his research project in Erasmus University Rotterdam which ex-Mees Pierson sponsored, and he joined the bank thereafter.

With his multidiscipline and multicultural education, Dr W. X. Huang is one of the few experts active both as a practitioner in commodity finance, and as a lecturer and trainer for banking.

As an emerging market specialist, he has also been regularly invited to speak at international conferences, and works as a consultant for the International Chamber of Commerce, World Bank, EU, Deloitte & Touché, FMO and European Savings Bank, among others.

He has published several books, of which the most recent one was *Institutional Banking for Emerging Markets* (John Wiley & Sons) which is regarded as a valuable addition to the literature for banking and finance.

As such, his lectures and books are positively commented on both in the banking industry and universities. As an adjunct professor in several universities, he teaches banking and finance for MBA/EMBA/DBA students. With his hands-on finance background he has the rare privilege of being a bridge between the academic ivory tower and the banking reality.

Foreword by Lex Kloosterman

It is with great pleasure that I recommend this book, *Commodity Finance: Principles and Practice*, expertly written by Dr W. X. Huang, not only to any trade finance professional or commodity trader sharpening his or her knowledge on the subject, but also to finance graduates, who are preparing to enter the interesting domain of trade and commodity finance.

Having spent a full professional career in trade and commodity finance at Mees Pierson, Fortis and the last eight years at Rabobank, Dr W. X. Huang will prove to be an eloquent partner, teacher or reference for each reader of his book.

Most of all you will be delighted to have found through his book, this unique mentor, who will always accompany you in resolving the complexities of our trade.

List of abbreviations

BL	Bill of Lading
BPO	Bank Payment Obligations
BOT	Build Operation and Turn Key
CBE	Commercial Bank of Ethiopia
CBOT	Chicago Board of Trade
CCO	Commodities Collateralized Obligations
CFC	Common Fund for Commodities
CME	Chicago Mercantile Exchange
CRB	Commodities Research Board Index
CSG	Commodity Support Group
CSCE	Coffee, Sugar, and Cacao Exchange
CSR	Corporate Social Responsibility
CTA	Commodities Trading Advisors
CTN	Commitment to Negotiate
DBE	Development Bank of Ethiopia
DFI	Development Finance Institutions
FAG	Fair Average Quality
FAO	Food and Agricultural Organization
FI	Financial Institutions
FOSFA	Federation of Oils, Seeds and Fats Association
GAFTA	Grain and Feed Trade Association
GSCI	Goldman Sachs Commodities Index
ICE	Intercontinental Exchange

ICO	International Coffee Organization
IPE	International Petroleum Exchange
LC	Letter of Credit
LDC	Least Developed Countries
LIFFE	London International Financial Futures and Options Exchange
LOI	Letters of Indemnity
LME	London Metals Exchange
MATIF	Marché à Terme International de France
MCR	Maximum Country Risk
MMTA	Minor Metal Trade Associate
NYBOT	New York Board of Trade
NYMEX	New York Mercantile Exchange
OBF	Ownership-based Finance
OTC	Over the Counter
SCC	Savings and Credit Cooperatives
SGS	Société Générale de Surveillance
SCF	Supply Chain Finance/Structured Commodity Finance
UCP	Uniform Customs and Practice
UNCTAD	United Nations Commissions for Trade and Development
USDA	United States Department of Agriculture
VAR	Value at Risk

Introduction

Commodity finance is a subject that used to be related to the privileged few, but now extends to almost every corner of the world.

Today, commodities represent most of the fast-growing markets worldwide. Commodities, historically misunderstood, very often understudied and underrepresented in literature, are now receiving the attention they deserve.

One of the reasons for the attention is due to the fact that price volatility in commodity markets has increased substantially in recent years, which directly influences the global market including the index of stock exchanges. Demand for commodities has led to serious competition and has built up giant trading commodity houses. Some modern war zones or territorial conflict may even have links with interests in commodities.

We have, nevertheless, barely seen any book which systematically explains and analyses commodity finance for the emerging markets. This can hardly be explained by lack of interest. Most of the books published so far, especially those from the academic world, seem to focus on hedging on the price volatility of commodity prices – an old topic, yet with many new developments.

Why this subject has scarcely been extensively covered is also due to the fact that this part of finance is a niche of which the knowledge is available within a limited number of players. There are a couple of hundred real commodity finance bankers in the world. Not many of them are interested in writing a book. Professors of finance in the universities may not have been privileged to have exposure to this part of finance.

Obviously, it is too ambitious to write a comprehensive handbook for commodity finance. This book only intends to have a systematic discussion on the principles and practice of commodity finance. On the one hand, the intention is indeed a summary of what is happening in commodity finance with a hands-on approach. On the other hand, all the relevant aspects of this topic will be covered in a systematic way, that is, the book is intended to serve both as a textbook for students as well as a reference book for practitioners.

The combination of principles and practice is always a challenge – 'principles' tend to outline a framework at a macro level, whereas 'practice' describes the daily operation and its problems at a micro level. Whether this book has achieved such a modest target is certainly subject to the judgment of the readers.

Structure and logic

It is not surprising that, up until the end of the last century, commodity finance – the knowledge and expertise of it – is limited to a couple of hundred privileged people, mainly in Europe.

Books so far published on commodities and commodity finance can be divided into two categories: the description of 'commodity markets' and the 'structured commodity finance', which is still a vague or loose concept covering subjects from tolling, advance payment finance to pre-export finance. These are, of course, part of commodity finance, but not all of it.

Ideally, a book on 'principles and practice of commodity finance' should cover commodities, commodity markets, commodity trade and the finance of the commodity trade. This is the skeleton of this book.

Why and how

An incidental interview, which was intended to find a sponsor for my PhD research, opened the door for my banking career in commodity finance. For more than 20 years, I have changed banks as an employee and the banks for which I worked have changed their names. I, however, remain in this domain.

The book starts with a bird's-eye view on commodity trade and finance as an introduction. Chapter 1 defines the concepts and scope of coverage, which will enable the discussion later to be more consistent and straightforward.

Chapter 2 gives a macro description of the three major sectors under commodity finance: soft commodities, hard commodities, and energy, as well as their global flow. This chapter develops further into a discussion of commodity finance and the emerging markets, as most commodity export countries are emerging market countries. It then shifts to a micro level for the case of Ethiopia, where commodity finance is done in special forms and via unique mechanisms. Together, these two chapters serve as a background for fundamentals.

Chapter 3 describes the special mechanisms and products of commodity finance. From plain vanilla products to the complicated structures of commodity finance, all are presented here.

As a large amount of commodity finance involves both bank and country risk, Chapter 4 particularly explores this subject.

Chapter 5 summarizes the risk management principles in commodity finance, with practical cases.

Chapter 6 is an organizational aspect of a typical commodity finance bank. From my limited reading, there is hardly any literature which can be found on this practical subject. Whereas departments and their functions within commodity banks may vary from one commodity bank to another, some common infrastructure is analyzed.

Chapter 7 ventures into the subject of a forward vision for commodity finance.

Upon the request of my readers after the first version, I have added an extra chapter – Chapter 8 – which presents a series of real-life cases in commodity finance.

Target readers

Although the sequence of chapters is organized with progress along the knowledge line, the book is written, on purpose, for separate reading and reference.

As such, the book is first intended for practitioners (bankers, traders and so on) who are interested in this subject and those financial institutions which have this business or plan to establish this business.

The book is also intended for business school students who major in finance, but have a special interest in 'niche banking'.

By presenting exhibits, the book tries to avoid difficult jargon to make it accessible to a wider readership. Most chapters are read by both experienced and non-experienced people with their comments on style and content. The current version has taken their comments.

I have, in fact, been trying to accumulate material for more than 20 years by reading documents, discussing with colleagues and summarizing the different and difficult cases I have experienced. Part of the material has been used for training purposes.

That said, the attempt on this book is really open for any critical comments and suggestions, either for the content or for the format.

It is readily admitted that some of the readers might disagree with many of my observations. If this can, however, inspire an interest in this area and ultimately help to better understand this fascinating subject, it is a blessing for all of us.

Needless to say, all the mistakes are mine and any critical comments are most welcome via email: weixinhuangdr@gmail.com

W. X. Huang

CHAPTER 1

Commodity Finance: Definition and Scope

Definition: commodities, commodity trade and commodity trade finance

Commodities are the basic generic goods traded in the international market. They are generally raw materials used in the production processes.

Defining a commodity is not that easy, as there are many kinds of commodities. It is much easier to say which product is not a commodity than to say which one is. There is in fact no uniform definition of a commodity. Strangely though, there is no lack of consensus on the understanding of a commodity. Generally speaking, commodities are things of value that are traded in large quantities. Commodities are uniform to the extent that they are considered to be equivalent and interchangeable to those of other producers.

The quality of a certain commodity is often standardized for all producers. For example, the oil that is pumped up in Saudi Arabia is assumed to be of the same quality as the oil coming from the Gulf of Mexico. This makes commodities good substitutes for one another. This also makes trading on a global market much easier than for non-commodities that do not have this uniformity in quality.

Commodities are thus defined in this book as things of value and uniform quality. This homogenous nature of commodity quality provides possibility for exchange and distribution. This homogeneous nature also provides the possibility of a standard price.

The fundamental specifications of various commodities have been standardized by a number of commodity trade exchanges and trade associations. In the strictest sense, commodities, by definition, should meet some basic criteria such as:

- they are usually used as raw materials in processing industries
- their price is in most cases transparent
- they are typically traded on commodity exchanges
- there is a futures market for price hedging purposes, and so on.

Commodities are consumption assets whose scarcity has a major impact on the world's and country-specific development.

Many believe that commodity markets have their roots in the trading of agricultural produce and livestock, but nowadays commodities go far beyond agricultural goods. As a matter of fact, commodities are traded inside and outside commodities exchanges.

Products under the 'commodity trading contract' can be classified/sub-divided as:

- agri-products: such as grain, corn, sugar, etc.

- livestock and meat: cattle, leather, fishmeal, feed meal, etc.

- base metals: copper, copper cathodes, steel, alumina, aluminium, lead, zinc, iron ore, metallurgical coke and coal

- precious metals: gold, silver, platinum

- energy products: natural gas, heating oil, unleaded gasoline, crude oil, liquid chemical, LPG, etc.

Agri-products, or simply 'agricultural' as they are sometimes called, are linked to the food and agricultural sector including tropical products. A detailed list for food and agricultural products can include dairy, fish, grain, oil seeds (corn, wheat, soybean), vegetables, fruit, cocoa, coffee, sugar, orange juice, rubber, spices, cotton, tea and mate, beverages, nuts, vanilla, bean, grains and oilseeds, cotton, fertilizer, bio-fuel and near commodities.

By their nature, the business pattern for agri-products is seasonal, and weather conditions are critical to the production.

As food and agricultural products are linked to daily life, the health regulation is particularly strict. Moreover, many countries have a subsidy system for agri-products. The prices of the soft commodities are subsidized in order to ensure sufficient supply for daily basic needs.

Energy is the largest commodity sector and is of strategic importance to the economy. This is because energy is the lifeblood of industries. It is the driving force for the economy and other commodities. Energy utilization is crucial for our daily life, and with the growth of the economy, the demand for energy is also increasing constantly.

Due to rapidly increasing oil prices, the liberalization of energy markets and climate change etc., public interest is drawn to the energy sector. On the other hand, to secure a reliable and sustainable energy supply in the light of declining resources and climate change, mitigation will be key challenges for this century.

The trade volume of energy is often the largest compared with other commodities, but the trade period is short or very short.

In the last decade, active markets have been developed for electricity products, that is, electricity futures for delivery at specific locations such as California/Oregon borders and so on. Following the deregulation of electricity prices, these markets have mushroomed. More recently, OTC markets and exchanges have introduced weather derivatives.

The metal market can be divided into base metals, minor metals and precious metals. The market is scattered but well organized.

Base metals have a futures exchange available for hedging price risk but minor metals do not. Base metals include copper, zinc, nickel, lead, tin and aluminium and so on. Producing hard commodities may need special permission. It may also need special equipment. Recently, due to environmental concerns, exploration of some metal products is restricted.

Precious metals include gold, platinum and silver. Major producers of gold are South Africa and Russia. Platinum is used more often for industrial purpose. For example, platinum is used for refining petroleum-based products. It is used in the watch industry and jewellery industry. Major producers of silver are Mexico, Peru, Canada, Australia and the USA.

As a benchmark for investment in the commodity markets and a measurement of commodity market performance, the Goldman Sachs Commodity Index (GSCI) is a broad index of commodity price performance, calculated primarily on a world-weighted basis, and comprises the principal commodities that are the subject of active, liquid futures markets, containing 49% energy products, 9% industrial/base metals, 3% precious metals, 28% agricultural products and 12% livestock products.

For agricultural products, trading in wheat, corn and livestock is said to have begun in the 19th century. But trading in soybeans is relatively new. In the energy sector, crude oil was the first form of energy widely traded, but electricity was included later. The trading in carbon dioxide or sulphur dioxide emission rights is a recent development but has potential. [1]

All companies involved in the production, origination, processing, trading and/or consumption of commodities are commodity companies, including institutional metal commodity investors.

The prices set on the London Metals Exchange (LME) provide the basis for the majority of commodity trade in non-ferrous metals. Some commodity markets are, however, struggling to establish a single common and transparent basis for pricing a commodity. This is because it is difficult for commodity market participants to judge if they are paying a reasonable price for the particular commodity. Moreover, if the price is not set and not transparent, and the pricing system is not consistent, to hedge price risk by forward, futures and options will hardly be possible. The commodity transaction contract will have to be privately negotiated or tailor-made.

---

[1] 'Solid Reporting, Sustainable Results – Risk Management and Financial Reporting for Commodities', KPMG 2008.

Commodity markets – commodity exchanges and the OTC markets are places where buyers and sellers meet and trade. They facilitate commodity flows and allow participants to exchange risk. Farmers, for example, can sell their crops at a fixed price on a future date, insuring themselves against variations in crop prices. Likewise, consumers can buy crops at a fixed price for future delivery.

Commodity finance involves the extending of credit to finance the purchase and sale of raw, semi-refined or semi-processed material of an animal, vegetable or mineral nature. Commodity finance is different from corporate finance, i.e. simple and straightforward lending to companies, as we will discuss later.

Traditionally, credits were indeed extended to commodity trading firms which acted as middlemen between producers and processors. Nevertheless, they are frequently privately owned and internationally oriented. From a financial perspective, they are characterized by extensive use of bank credit, high leverage, large volume and low profit margin. As the trader's margins are small but turnover is rapid, the liquidation of assets is expected to provide fully for serving debt. To finance the purchase and sale of a commodity becomes the core of commodity finance.

Commodity finance business in general demonstrates lower loss rates due to its secured (commodity collateral), most uncommitted, short-term and closely monitored self-liquidating nature. Commodity finance in terms of return is a cut above the average for clean corporate lending returns and offers interesting value-added low-risk financings for typical structured customers.

Recently, many of the commodity traders have become more integrated into the supply chain of commodities, i.e. either commodity producers who export themselves or traders themselves invest in fixed assets in the distribution, to secure the cheap and stable source of commodities. Traders and commodity producers even invest in port terminals, processing plants etc. Commodity traders are thus becoming commodity dealers.

Characteristics of commodity trade

Commodity trade is the trading of commodity assets. The characteristics of commodity trade can be summarised in a nutshell:

- having high volumes, large turnover
- trading many times prior to physical delivery
- often having a low profit margin
- having fast asset conversion: self-liquidating

- having a global market with emerging market countries as exporter and developed countries as importers
- being global professional players
- having a volatile price
- having ever-changing trade patterns
- having standardised terms
- having highly liquid assets
- being thinly-capitalised trading companies.

Such characteristics of commodity trade are related to the fundamentals of commodities. But commodity assets differ from financial assets in several ways.

First of all, unlike ordinary financial assets, they do not generate a cash flow. Compared with financial assets, commodities may generate a flow of benefits that are not directly measurable. For example, a company that manufactures copper pipes benefits from an inventory of copper which is used up in its production process. This is the so-called convenience yield for the holder of the commodity.

Second, whereas there is no problem at all to 'store' shares or bonds, commodities may be expensive or even impossible to store, and some agricultural products are very difficult to store as they are perishable. Metals can be stored but the cost of warehousing is high. Solar energy cannot be easily stored at all, nor can electricity.

Third, there are global professional players for commodities. Access to the commodity trade needs a threshold and knowledge.

Just like stocks and bonds, commodities have their prices. Commodity price is determined by supply and demand.

Commodity price is a critical point with which we will deal. The physical commodity price is the price that is paid for an actual physical delivery of a commodity. This price is dependent on quality (grade) of the commodity, location and its stage within the commodity supply chain. At each stage of a supply chain where value is added to the commodity (processing, transporting, storage, refining, manufacturing, etc.), costs are added to the price of the commodity. For example, for sugar the price structure is given in the figure below.

The stages of transportation are defined in the International Commercial Terms, or Incoterms 2000 and earlier versions. These terms provide an overview of all the steps involved in getting a commodity from A to B. Buyers and sellers use these universal terms to agree on responsibilities regarding transportation.

Figure 1.1: Sugar price

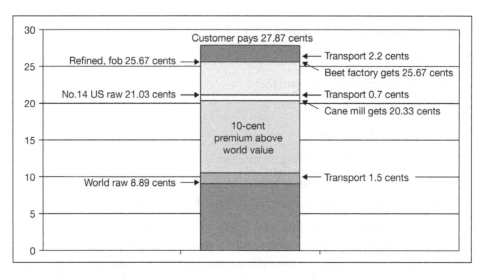

Source: *The True Story about US Sugar Prices*, Promar International, May 2007.

The price for crude oil is known for substantial price movement – a 60% p.a. price movement is no exception. Liquidity is thus extremely high, with product deliverable on active exchanges such as International Petroleum Exchange (IPE) and New York Mercantile Exchange (NYMEX). The substantial price movement can be explained by the fact that participants in this sector are reputable: the market is dominated by a large number of well-established, well-known market participants operating in a transparent market environment. Consequently, the default risk is low because historically the sector has a low default rate. Moreover, high energy prices and environmental law awareness drives the development of alternative energy sources such as liquefied natural gas, bio-fuels, etc.

Commodity markets and commodity exchanges

Without commodity markets, commodity trade and commodity finance will be of much less interest to the trading companies and commodity finance banks.

Commodity markets are platforms where commodities are traded. The uniform standard of most commodities and their quality definition facilitate the trading of commodities. Commodities can be bought and sold easily and quickly as there are established commodity markets.

Commodity markets have existed for many centuries around the world where raw commodities are traded on regulated commodity exchanges. It is here that commodities are bought and sold through standardized contracts.

'Commodities' are also active in both the spot and forward markets, traded by trading houses. At these commodity exchanges, commodity prices are officially quoted.

Commodity exchanges are de facto commodity trading markets, very similar to those markets for stocks and bonds. These markets reflect the ever-changing supply and demand of commodities and provide liquidity of commodities. Like stock exchanges, commodity exchanges provide risk takers and risk averters the platform to function.

The need for a commodity market comes from the fact that producers of commodities and buyers of commodities need a place to realize their deals. Like currency transactions, commodity markets are also served for risk hedging, by being divided into spot markets and futures markets where goods are to be delivered in the future but the price is fixed at present.

A commodity market in its early form is believed to have originated in Sumer in the mid-4th century BC. Sumer is the earliest known place in the ancient near-East and was located south-east of today's Iraq. The Sumerians used small baked clay tokens in the shape of sheep or goats as a form of commodity money. Although such deals date back to the 4th century BC, there already existed some form of futures deals. Similarly in Japan, there are records from the 17th century that show that forward contracts for the purchase of rice existed.

It is not surprising that the commodity market started with agricultural products. The first organized grain futures trading in the United States began in places such as New York, Buffalo and Chicago in the 1840s.

A significant development for commodity exchange was the establishment of the Chicago Board of Trade (CBOT) in the 1840s. Chicago was chosen due to its geographical location as a hub between Midwestern producers of agricultural products and East Coast population centres. CBOT initially served cash trading in a variety of goods and the trading of forward contracts later for flour and hay in 1849 and corn in 1851.

Nowadays there are different specialized commodity exchanges apart from CBOT: London International Financial Futures and Options Exchange (LIFFE) for coffee, Marché à Terme International de France (MATIF) for agro-commodities, LME for metals, IPE for petroleum. The New York Board of Trade (NYBOT) and NYMEX serve their relevant sectors.

There are many more commodity exchanges in the world which facilitate commodity trading. Table 1.1. shows a brief summary of major international commodity exchanges.

Table 1.1: Global commodity exchanges

Full name	Code	Description
Chicago Board of Trade	CBOT	Established in 1848, CBOT is the world's oldest futures and options exchange. It is now a part of the CME group.
Chicago Mercantile Exchange	CME	CME trades several types of financial instruments: interest rates, equities, currencies, and commodities. It also offers trading in alternative investments such as weather and real estate derivatives. CME has the largest options and futures contracts open interest of any futures exchange in the world. It is now a part of the CME group.
New York Mercantile Exchange	NYMEX	NYMEX is the world's largest physical commodity futures exchange. It is a merger between the former New York Mercantile Exchange and the Commodity Exchange of New York (COMEX). NYMEX provides markets for the trading and clearing of crude oil, gasoline, heating oil, natural gas, electricity, propane, coal, uranium, environmental commodities, softs, gold, silver, copper, aluminium, platinum, and palladium. It is now a part of the CME group.
Intercontinental Exchange US	ICE	Formerly known as New York Board of Trade (NYBOT). NYBOT is now a wholly owned subsidiary of Intercontinental Exchange (ICE). It became a unit of ICE in January 2007, and renamed ICE Futures US in September of 2007. Commodities traded include cacao, coffee, cotton and sugar.
Intercontinental Exchange Canada	ICE	Formerly known as Winnipeg Commodity Exchange (WCE), it is now renamed ICE Futures Canada. Products traded include feed wheat, western barley and canola.
Intercontinental Exchange Europe	ICE	Formerly known as the International Petroleum Exchange based in London, this is the world's largest energy futures and options exchange. It was incorporated into the ICE group in 2001. The products exchanged include UK brent crude oil, US WTI crude oil, UK natural gas, UK power, emission allowances and coal.

NYSE Euronext	LIFFE	LIFFE is a futures exchange based in London. It offers futures and options on a large range of agricultural products. LIFFE is now part of NYSE Euronext following its takeover by Euronext in January 2002, and the subsequent merger involving New York Stock Exchange in April 2007.
NYSE Euronext Paris	MATIF	Euronext Paris is France's securities market, formerly known as the Paris Bourse. It is now part of NYSE Euronext following the merger between New York Stock Exchange and Euronext in April 2007. NYSE Euronext Paris operates MATIF futures exchange for products including commodity futures and/or options on European rapeseed, rapeseed meal, rapeseed oil, milling wheat, corn and sunflower seeds.
Kansas City Board of Trade	KCBT	KCBT specializes in hard red winter wheat. Hard winter wheat constitutes the maximum of US production. KCBT prices are the benchmark for US bread wheat.
Minneapolis Grain Exchange	MGEX	MGEX provides futures and options contracts for agricultural products such as corn, wheat, barley, oats, rye, flax and soybeans.
Chicago Climate Exchange	CCX	CCX is North America's only voluntary, legally binding greenhouse gas (GHG) reduction and trading system for emission sources and offset projects in North America and Brazil.
London Metal Exchange	LME	LME is the world's largest options and futures exchange on base and other metals. It trades metals and non-ferrous metals like aluminium, copper, lead, nickel, tin and zinc.
European Climate Exchange	ECX	ECX/ICE Futures is the most liquid, pan-European platform for carbon emissions trading, with its futures contract based on the underlying EU Allowances (EUAs) and Certified Emissions Allowances (CERs) attracting over 80% of the exchange-traded volume in the European market.
European Energy Exchange	EEX	EEX is Germany's energy exchange. It is the leading energy exchange in Central Europe.
Risk Management Exchange	RMX	RMX is a futures exchange based in Hanover, Germany. Main products traded are hogs, piglets, potatoes and wheat.
Dalian Commodity Exchange	DCE	DCE is a Chinese futures exchange. It trades in corn and soybeans, and has introduced futures and options in crude oil, power, steel and plastic.

Zhengzhou Commodity Exchange	ZCE	ZCE mainly trades in futures based around agricultural and chemical products.
Shanghai Futures Exchange	SHFE	One of the biggest exchanges for copper. It also deals in industrial metals, fuel oil and rubber.
Tokyo Commodity Exchange	TOCOM	Tokyo Commodity Exchange (TOCOM) is the largest exchange in Japan and second largest commodity exchange in the world for futures and options. Crude oil, gasoline, kerosene, gas oil, gold, silver, aluminium, platinum and rubber are the commodities that are actively traded. TOCOM was formed in 1984 by mergers between the Tokyo Gold Exchange, the Tokyo Rubber Exchange, and the Tokyo Textile Exchange.
Tokyo Grain Exchange	TGE	Tokyo Grain Exchange trades in agricultural commodities such as coffee, corn, soybeans, sugar and silk.
Bursa Malaysia Derivatives Exchange	MDEX	MDEX exchange trades in crude palm oil futures, crude palm kernel oil futures, index futures and options and government securities.
Singapore Commodity Exchange	SICOM	SICOM specializes in trading rubber and agricultural outputs such as coffee.
Multi Commodity Exchange	MCX	MCX is the largest commodity exchange of India. It was established in 2003 and is based in Mumbai. Traded products include metals, precious metals, energy and chemicals.
National Multi-Commodity Exchange of India	NMCE	Trade products include metals and precious metals and agricultural outputs.
National Commodity and Derivatives Exchange	NCDEX	NCDEX is an online commodity exchange based in India. Products traded include ferrous and non-ferrous metals, energy, agricultural products and plastics.
Dubai Gold & Commodities Exchange	DGCX	DGCX mainly trades in precious metals.
Dubai Mercantile Exchange	DME	DME is a joint venture between Dubai holding and the NYMEX. It is still to be launched and is likely to be an active exchange for oil futures as it is in the centre of oil-producing nations.
Brazilian Mercantile and Futures Exchange	BMF	Products traded on the BMF include agricultural, bio-fuels and precious metals.

The South African Futures Exchange	SAFEX	SAFEX consists of a financial markets division and an agricultural markets division. Its agricultural division is Africa's only agricultural derivatives market. Products traded at the SAFEX agricultural division includes grains, corn, crude oil, gold and platinum.
Australian Securities Exchange	ASX	ASX, as it is now known, resulted from the merger of the Australian Stock Exchange with the Sydney Futures Exchange in December 2006. The products traded include agricultural, electricity, coal, and natural gas.

Commodities are traded inside, as well as outside, the commodity exchanges; they are also traded via the OTC markets. And many commodities are traded by individual contracts.

Commodity trade finance

We have already mentioned that commodity finance is different from corporate finance. In fact, it is also different from general trade finance.

There is no denying that, in general, commodity finance is trade finance – financing flows of goods – only the trade flow is linked to commodities. Commodity finance is, however, unique in the sense that it is very large in its total size compared with general trade finance, and the size of an individual deal can also be large. Commodity finance is also different from general corporate finance in that a commodity financier needs extensive knowledge and expertise about commodities and their trade flow.

Commodity finance banks and banks doing commodity finance deals are two different concepts. In Chapter 6, we discuss in detail what a fully-fledged commodity finance bank is. Some banks finance commodities and commodity traders. But they are not real commodity finance banks. And a commodity finance banker must follow the commodity market development and have commodity finance skills.

In most commodity finance banks, commodity finance is conducted by three major desks – hard commodities desk (metals etc.), soft commodities desk (agricultural products) and energy desk (oil and gas). These three sectors have different categories of commodity coverage.

- **Hard commodities** are often raw materials for industrial products. As the exploration of hard commodities is linked to mining etc., some commodity banks also involve pre-export finance and/or equipment financing.

- **Soft commodities** are agriculture linked, most of which are our daily foodstuff or materials to be used for producing foodstuff.

- **Energy commodities** refer to oil, gas, etc. This part of the market is a mature market characterized by highly developed, well-regulated futures exchange and a growing OTC hedging market. This part of the market also has price volatility and a liquid nature.

Commodity trade as a whole has more transparency than general trade, that is, the trade of textile, machinery and so on. The price of many commodities is transparent as they are listed in the commodity exchanges. Very often the major players are also well known in the business circle as they are global professional players. Names such as Bunge, Cargill, Duferco, ED & F Man, Glencore, Louis Dreyfus, Nidera, Noble Group and so on, are known for their history, volume and influence in this market, although there is 'sink and swim' in the community of commodity as well.

Figure 1.2 gives an idea of the major commodity trading houses in terms of revenue.

Figure 1.2: Largest commodities trading houses by revenue

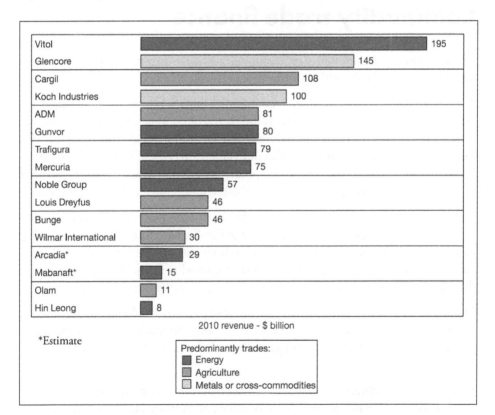

Given that a large portion of international trade is linked to commodity finance, this becomes an independent and important subject. A rough estimation of the export of primary commodities accounts for a quarter of total world trade volume. Most of them are coming from emerging countries in Africa, Asia and Latin America. Contracts for commodities can easily be worth more than a million US dollars.

In essence, commodity finance is the business of financing self-liquidating transactions and/or production of highly-liquid assets. The loan to the borrower is often self-liquidated, when the transaction proceeds recover the debt under normal circumstances. The primary repayment source of obligation is through the liquidating/ production of specific commodities. Therefore, even a long-term commitment can be justified as the financing will be utilized for an underlying trade/production circle that will self-liquidate and generate cash to repay the specific exposure. In other words, the financier is automatically reimbursed.

As a secondary security, the commodity finance bank is ensured recourse to a borrower's assets against any potential problems or default with the transaction when and if the lending contract defines such a right.

This kind of commodity finance is clearly defined under Basel II as "… structured short-term lending to finance reserves, inventories, or receivables of exchange traded commodities (for example, crude oil, metals or crops), where exposure will be repaid from the proceeds of the sale of the commodity and the borrower has no capacity to repay exposure…"[2]

Unlike traditional, unsecured corporate cash flow based credits, commodity finance obligations are typically not created unless an asset (the collateral) is freely available or is created.

Commodity finance is developed to mitigate myriad risks in giving credit exposure to companies that are typically:

- thinly capitalized
- highly leveraged
- dealing in highly volatile commodities
- in competitive industries, often based in emerging markets
- have highly liquid collateral to pledge.

As such, commodity finance is a specialised finance that requires banks to have equally specialised knowledge. This limits the number of players in this type of business.

In the meantime, the margins on profitable deals are usually smaller compared to the size of the deal. Hence if one deal goes wrong it may wipe out the profits of many successful deals. It is not surprising that some banks join in this business, but then jump out once their fingers are burnt.

---

2 'Commodity Risk Management' in *Commodities Now* Volume 11, Issue 1 March 07.

The fact of low profit margins pushes the commodity traders to a kind of package consideration – the price of the commodity, the shipping and forwarding costs, and the warehouse cost together will decide the total profits of the deal. That explains why commodity traders are now entering into the supply chain for building ports and investing in processing plants.

The origin of financing commodity trade can be traced back to the medieval age where the centre was, and perhaps still is, Europe. The involvement of banks in commodity finance is due to its nature, which makes it barely possible for a trading company to get credit based on its own balance sheet. The fixed asset size of the trading company is usually far too small compared to the turnover of the deals they are involved in.

Commodity trading companies usually have small equity bases and they work on very small margins. They make profits through the large volumes they transact. Moreover, many of the producers, processors, traders, exporters and importers are from emerging markets where credit is not easily available or accessible.

As a result, financing via banks plays an important role in facilitating commodity trade flow. In many cases, banking finance is even a must. By smartly using various banking facilities, trading companies can leverage their deals with their limited equity. By cleverly using collateral control and title to the goods under transaction, banks can finance the trade (not the trader) with limited and mitigated risk.

Commodity finance is thus to extend credit to firms in various forms of short-term loans in order to finance:

- import and export

- domestic sales or trade

- cash and carry transactions

- consignment sales.

At times, commodity finance can be quite lucrative, especially when the bank can properly mitigate its risk and have good control of collateral. By taking risks associated with top-quality customers, such as the multinational oil, grain and steel companies, commodity banks may have handsome spreads.

In daily operation, a commodity finance bank may become involved in different chains of trade flow and commodity finance may take many forms.

A commodity finance bank may be involved in trade flow management and finance one cargo several times. They can also only offer the facility for transportation costs of the shipment.

Many banks follow the chain of trade by offering finance to the counterparty (seller) of their client (buyer) to prolong involvement in the trade chain, without increasing the risk profile. This will lead to the natural expansion of their portfolio. Most commodity finance banks are active in offering the finance for the storage of commodities (floating and land). In price hedging deals, margin call financing is popular. Commodity traders require a bank that is receptive to their hedging activities and one that understands the risks involved.

As we will see in other chapters, a bulk part of commodity finance is linked to letter of credit (LC) financing: a facility to allow traders to issue LCs for the purchase, confirmation and discounting of export LCs to provide country and bank risk cover and cash flow.

Financing LCs can also be a business relationship entrance point between a commodity finance bank and a commodity trader. From here, commodity finance expands to confirm and discount corporate receivables for the same purpose as LC confirmation. Pre-export finance facilities as the 'cream on the cake' are also topics for commodity finance for those countries which are short of hard currencies.

Commodity finance banks, whenever they provide finance to facilitate commodity trade flow, must bear in mind some of the following unique characteristics of commodity finance.

Marketability of commodities

As the commodity market is a very liquid market, commodities change hands more than other assets. The existence of well-established commodity exchanges has provided liquidity. On the one hand, this helps commodity finance banks to have flexibility of their collateral, on the other hand, they may also face the change of their counterparties for financing. This is because commodities are traded many times prior to physical delivery.

Leverage finance

Commodity finance is leverage finance. It can be financing producer, consumer, or traders of commodities. But most often, it is linked to traders. As traders perform the function of a go-between for the buyer (consumer) and the seller (the producer), they have to rely on bank finance since the registered capital on their balance sheet will not be substantial compared with the size of deals, so that the commodity finance bank does not feel comfortable to give clean lending. The traders will have to leverage, by relying heavily on the possibility of a commodity finance bank to cover their (buying) position. This creates the need for financing from banks which have knowledge and experience in this field.

For commodity finance banks, their finance is, therefore, mostly asset-backed. Unconditional recourse to the trading companies to cover potential loss is hardly possible, or not realistic if it is possible. Control and management of collateral is the key to risk mitigation for commodity finance banks.

Emerging market linked

One of the most interesting aspects of working in commodity finance is dealing with the nature of the underlying collateral. The import and export of commodities are often linked to various and often multiple jurisdictions, among which many are emerging market countries.

As most of the exporters of commodities are from emerging markets, the country risk (political and economic) is relevant. Accordingly, we need country risk experts involved in financing.

The linkage to the emerging markets invites the interest of many development banks. To support export, especially from the small and medium commodity producers, regional development banks such as Asia Development Bank, African Development Bank, Inter-American Development Bank, European Bank for Development and Reconstruction or World Bank have initiated special measures and mechanisms. National development agencies are also in the picture. Commodity finance banks will work closely with them in commodity finance.

As mentioned, commodity finance is different from straightforward corporate finance. But commodity finance and corporate finance are often interlinked.

In many commodity finance banks, there are both commodity finance departments and corporate finance departments. They cooperate with each other to serve one client. For example, the commodity finance department provides a credit facility for the company to import the commodity, and helps to pay the transportation costs before selling the goods; whereas the corporate finance department helps the trading company with their issuance of corporate bonds, IPOs and overseas merger and acquisition.

If we review the supply chain of commodities, we may well notice the physical movement of commodities and the major players in the commodity supply chain:

> Raw material suppliers/producers > Producer (production) > Commodity trader (trading) > Transportation > First processor > Transportation > Second processor > Transportation > End product trader/distributor

When commodities are produced and exported, a commodity bank can offer finance on a transactional basis or offer a wide range of trade finance products. It may only offer shipping cost finance (freight cost). When the commodities have arrived at the destination, a commodity bank then discusses the warehouse finance for commodities to be processed. In the oil sector, the commodity bank can also finance refiners. When the commodity eventually comes to the final buyers, financing the final buyer is then on the agenda.

Relevant financing opportunities will be available for both corporate finance and commodity finance. But for commodity finance, the supply chain is more important.

Specifically, commodity finance products can be required in this supply chain by sellers, buyers and traders, and so on.

As a brief introductory overview, we may explore the function of a commodity finance bank in the different stages of the commodity supply chain.

Pre-export production

Pre-export loans are various. To start with, a commodity bank can finance the purchase of assets, equipment or be involved in other capital investment. Here a commodity bank can offer an advisory service to help facilitate external finance (development banks such as World Bank and other regional development banks). Under project finance, we have seen ECA finance; reserve-based lending and structured finance.

Production

Facilities are provided to cover tolling, processing, transit, etc. until storage in the port's warehouse. Front-to-back finance, back-to-back finance, short-term advances and loans are available.

Post-production

Post-production finance can be anything, including freight finance, forex facilities, and bill of lading finance, and so on. It can also be receivable financing: post-sale receivable/buyer credit, reversed receivables. LC negotiation, factoring and forfaiting are also common ways of finance in many cases. For some bigger facilities, we may see insured buyer's credit ECA, structured receivable/asset-backed pool securitization and structured note single securitization.

In this commodity supply chain, corporate bankers tend to look into the financial strength of the borrower (balance sheet, profits and losses, and so on), whereas a commodity banker will be more interested in the corporate's export link and the trade flows of the raw materials or the final products.

As commodity finance involves large amounts of payment, the LC becomes a critical instrument, to convert company payment risk into bank payment risk. Around an LC, many forms of financing can be offered by a commodity finance bank, including:

- guarantees/performance bonds
- with recourse receivable (LC) financing
- confirmation/discounting bank LCs
- standby LCs covering swap contracts

- counter signing letters of indemnity (LOIs).

We will discuss the above further in Chapter 3.

In all these phases, a bank can offer both traditional corporate finance products, including capital market products (issue debt instrument, CPs, CDs, etc.), as well as commodity finance products.

There is sometimes an overlap for products. But we have to admit that there is little difference here between corporate finance in general and corporate finance in a commodity bank: it depends on whether the finance is balance sheet lending or structured finance.

Credit facilities often seen are:

- committed facilities
- working capital facilities
- (corporate lending) margin call finance facilities
- pre-export finance facilities (performance risk)
- reserve-based lending faculties (participations)
- stock and/or receivable securitization programmers
- hedging for margin calls.

Commodity finance as a product exists in many banks. But the number is limited for banks which specialise on commodity finance – i.e. those with in-house knowledge, expertise and commitment to commodity and commodity finance, a well-established sound infrastructure for commodity finance and so on.

In commodity finance, the big names are BNP, SG, ABN-AMRO, Natexis, ex-Fortis, Standard Chartered, ING, West LB, Standard Bank and Rabobank. Given its food and agricultural root, Rabobank has been especially active in soft commodities.

Other global banks, such as HSBC and CITI, are leading service producers with transactional banking at their core. They cross-sell and reap their scale benefits rather than selling fully-fledged commodity finance products, although things are changing.

CHAPTER 2

Commodity Finance: Commodity Flow and Emerging Markets

Commodity flow: a global overview

In many ways commodities are linked to emerging markets, both for importing and exporting countries but especially as exporting countries. This is because many developing countries rely on exporting commodities as a source of hard currency. Some of the emerging markets, typically China and India, are both importing and exporting commodities, whereas Brazil and Russia are more on the export side. To discuss commodities and commodity finance, we have to get into a discussion of emerging markets.

Emerging markets are considered as those upcoming to their industrialization. Whereas this is a vague concept, the major countries in this domain are known as BRIC countries (Brazil, Russia, India, and China) or the N-11 (for the next 11 countries after BRIC, as indicated by Goldman). The N-11 are Bangladesh, Egypt, Indonesia, Iran, South Korea, Mexico, Nigeria, Pakistan, the Philippines, Turkey and Vietnam.[3]

According to *The Economist*[4], there has been a dramatic shift in recent years in the relative economic balance of 'first world' and 'third world' economies. As early as the beginning of this century, *The Economist* estimated that emerging economies produced slightly more than half of the world's output measured at purchasing-power parity calculation.

Emerging markets have also accounted for more than half of the increase in global GDP in current dollar-terms since 2005. Not only is the total production impressive, but also the speed of development. During the industrial revolutions it took America and Britain 50 years to double their real income per capita. Today, China managed

---

3   In recent years, new terms have emerged to describe the largest developing countries such as BRIC that stands for Brazil, Russia, India, China, along with BRICET (BRIC + Eastern Europe and Turkey), BRICS (BRIC + South Africa), BRICM (BRIC + Mexico), BRICK (BRIC + South Korea),'Next Eleven' (Bangladesh, Egypt, Indonesia, Iran, Mexico, Nigeria, Pakistan, Philippines, South Korea, Turkey, and Vietnam) and 'CIVETS' (Colombia, Indonesia, Vietnam, Egypt, Turkey and South Africa).

These countries do not share any common agenda, but some experts believe that they are enjoying an increasing role in the world economy and on political platforms.

4   *The Economist* January 21 2006: 'Coming of Age'.

to achieve the same in a single decade. More importantly, such a kind of shift in economic power towars emerging economies is likely to continue. Emerging markets thus become the priority on the agenda in many ways.

As far as commodity finance is concerned, the shift of economic balance is mirrored as well.

Historically, emerging markets are important as exporting countries and now as importing countries as well, although it is unknown yet which country (or countries) will replace China as a dominant importer of commodities when the China cycle is over.

The relevance of emerging markets for commodity finance can also be identified in country risk evolution, foreign reserve to their economic development, bank finance instruments and products. In some countries, commodity export is the development drive for sustainable growth. We will first have a global review on major commodity flows.

Appendix 2 gives detailed information on the import and export of commodities from 2006 to 2010, the period when China emerged as a dominating commodity country.

The picture of import and export changes, of course, year by year. Some countries which usually export one commodity may import the same commodity due to domestic shortage. India, for example, exports sugar and imports sugar as well. Some countries, such as China, usually imports steel, but it exports steel as well due to overcapacity at home. However, the supply and demand of commodities have a relatively stable list. This is summarized to best describe a global picture of countries and regions that are major exporters and importers of the different types of commodities.

Soft commodities

Table 2.1: Major commodity importers and exporters of agri. commodities

Type of commodity	Major exporters	Major importers
Grains	USA, Brazil, Argentina, Russia, Australia, Europe	South America, Africa, Indonesia, North-East Asia, Europe, Middle East
Meat	Brazil, Argentina, USA	Europe, Middle East, Japan, Russia, North-East Asia
Cocoa	Côte d'Ivoire, Ghana, Nigeria, Cameroon, Papua New Guinea, Malaysia, Colombia	Europe, USA, Russia

Coffee	Brazil, Columbia, Vietnam, Ethiopia, Uganda, Kenya, Indonesia	USA, Europe, Japan
Vegetable oils	Malaysia, Indonesia, Brazil, Argentina, Europe	Europe, Asia, USA, Russia
Rice	South-East Asia	Europe, Japan, Africa, Indonesia
Tropical Timber	South America, Indonesia, Malaysia, Philippines, West Africa	Europe, USA, China, South Korea

Hard commodities

Table 2.2: Major commodity importers and exporters of metals

Type of commodity	Major exporters	Major importers
Aluminum	Australia, Russia	Europe, USA
Copper	Chili, Peru, Australia, Russia, Zambia	Europe, Asia, USA
Iron ore	Brazil, Australia, Canada	Asia, Europe
Zinc	Peru, Bolivia, Australia	Europe, South Korea, Japan
Steel	China, Brazil, Ukraine	Mexico, Middle East

Energy

Table 2.3: Major commodity importers and exporters of energy commodities

Type of commodity	Major exporters	Major importers
Crude oil	Middle East, Venezuela, Mexico, Scandinavia, Russia, Nigeria	USA, China, Europe, Japan, South Korea
Natural Gas	Russia, Saudi Arabia, Indonesia, Nigeria	Europe, Japan, South Korea, Turkey

As Tables 2.1–2.3 show, most countries on the export side of commodity products are are emerging markets.

Traditionally, the USA and Europe are major importers of many commodities, with China now quickly entering into the picture and persistently occupying the lion's share for many commodities.

Many of the emerging market countries are traditional suppliers of commodities. Brazil and Columbia are famous for coffee, Brazil, Cuba and India for sugar, Ghana, Brazil, Côte d'Ivoire, Malaysia for cocoa, Florida and Brazil for orange juice.

Some 70 countries produce coffee of which 45 are major ones who are responsible for over 97% of world output. These countries are exporting members of the International Coffee Organization (ICO): Angola, Bolivia, Brazil, Burundi, Cuba, Ethiopia, Guatemala, Haiti, Honduras, India, Indonesia, Uganda, Rwanda, Sierra Leone, Nicaragua, El Salvador, Guatemala, Madagascar, Columbia, Tanzania, Kenya, Democratic Republic of Congo, Papua New Guinea, Costa Rica, Côte d'Ivoire, Vietnam, Dominican Republic, Cameroon, Indonesia, Thailand, Sri Lanka, Malawi, Zambia, Zimbabwe and Togo.

Big exporters of commodities in terms of volume are South America, Asia, the USA and Australia. The trade flows associated with these exports are therefore often large.

Africa is a very small player on the commodity markets. For African countries the export of commodities is often a large part of their total export, and therefore the export of commodities is a major source of foreign currency. But they are not very large in terms of volume compared to the rest of the world. The southern half of Africa depends a lot on the export of agricultural products such as coffee, tobacco and fishery commodities, base metals such as iron ore and copper, and precious metals such as gold. South Africa's export depends on 34% metals and 10% on agricultural commodities.

To maintain sustainable export is of concern both for the exporting countries as a source of their income and for the importing countries for stable supply for their consumption.

In South America, the commodities that are produced and exported the most are also agricultural products such as grains, soybeans and oils, fishery commodities and base metals such as copper and zinc.

Some commodities, such as sugar, are produced in different parts of the world. Major exporters are Brazil, Australia, Cuba, Thailand, and Mauritius. The world market prices remain highly volatile and regional and international trade negotiations exist. Around 70% of sugar is consumed where it is produced. In industrialized nations, 75% of sugar consumption is in the form of products, while only 25% is consumed in the form of sugar. But in emerging markets, the proportion is reversed. Brazil is the world's largest sugar exporter with 30% of market share; Cuba has seen a decline in production. On the importing side, Russia has emerged as the world's largest importer of sugar and Asia as a whole is an increasingly important consumer of sugar as well.

The Middle East is highly dependent on the exports of crude oil. This is the main export product which drives these economies. 90% of Saudi Arabia's exports is oil and for Iran 84%.

South East Asia exports a lot of agricultural commodities, such as tropical timber, natural rubber, tropical fruits, fishery commodities, rice, vegetable oils and fiber, and also lead. Vietnam's exports are 25% agricultural. and 25% oils. Thailand's export is 20% agricultural.

Besides commodities, many Asian countries export a lot of manufactured products, two outstanding examples being Japan and Korea. This means they are not so dependent anymore purely on commodity products.

Moody's report on the Asia Pacific region describes the commodity map in South East Asia. Malaysia is a major exporter of palm oil, liquefied natural gas, petroleum, crude oil and timber. Indonesia, which used to be a net oil exporter, is still a major oil producer. Commodities account for more than 25% of GDP in Indonesia. Vietnam is a major agricultural producer and exporter.

Former Soviet countries are big exporters of energy products such as crude oil and natural gas, and base metals such as aluminium and copper.

Financing commodity flow for the least-developed emerging markets

Commodity finance: the importance and the difficulties for some less-developed emerging markets

For less-developed economies, commodity typically referred to as primary commodities, by and large, constitute agricultural products or raw materials, as our earlier global review indicated. The agricultural sector is thus the backbone of the economy of many least-developed countries (LDCs). Hence financing production of these commodities has a unique role in their economic development.

However, agricultural producers in these countries are locked in a vicious cycle of poverty. Their revenue remains low and is vulnerable to the unstable markets and weather conditions. They are losing out on market opportunities and may no longer qualify as acceptable suppliers to the more high-value parts of the commodity sector.

In certain cases, they are locked into the production of certain commodities, even if the prices of these commodities fall below production costs. Unfortunately, farmers in these countries cannot afford to diversify.

In these countries, commodity finance has a different scenario. Both public and private initiatives work together to create chances for commodity finance. The institutions, instruments and forms of finance are, therefore, different as well. This is necessary because past experience shows that agricultural commodity finance has several difficulties, some of which include inadequate government policies and a difficult marketplace. In particular, the risk of pre-harvest finance, lack of knowledge, professionalism and collateral (sometimes land cannot be held as collateral), lack of insurance for the agricultural sector, high co-variant risk caused by weather and pest attacks, and exposure to price risk are all barriers and difficulties.

For this section of commodity exports, external support is indispensable. There are several financial institutions (such as regional development banks, commercial banks, insurance companies, investment dealers, mutual funds, savings and loan associations, and micro financial institutions) that accept grants and loan funds from the supporting external funds and disperse to the commodity producers, processors and traders, and fast-track project coordinators as well.

The local commercial banks, in connection with the above, provide commodity loans including: pre-export finance, toll finance, countertrade finance, and others to the needy through their rural branches.

Insurance companies also provide different types of insurance coverage to the individuals and groups involved in commodity production and trading at a reasonable premium. They provide marine insurance for exporters. There are also various insurance schemes for the producers and processors of commodities.

Without external support, many established organizations, such as commercial banks, are often not very active in agricultural finance for risk return consideration. To help with access to finance for commodity producers, especially the small/medium-scale agricultural producers, extra supporting forms and efforts are obviously needed.

The practice of commodity finance is different from that for more general import and export of commodities. 'Access to finance' is emphasized. Special funds are established and special commodity finance skills, such as structured commodity finance, are extensively used to achieve the supporting target.

Guarantee funds for credit support in commodity finance

Along this supporting line, guarantee funds are established in order to facilitate the commodity flow. For the same purpose, some organizations emerge either on private initiative or on public initiative or on the initiative of both. Development banks, with poverty reduction as their mission, are also involved. Some of the small-scale individual (guarantee) funds and large scale funds, such as Common Funds for Commodities, are born against such a background.

Such a guarantee fund has a special mission and structure. They do not lend out loans. They work together with local financial institutions.

The core objective of such funds is to allow commodity producers to get access to finance, or financial sector deepening, which can be defined as "increasing access to financial services for those who previously had restricted or no access; and increased provision by financial institutions to such clients of products and services relevant to their needs".[5]

Within this context, the partners in such funds aim to enhance the access of small/ medium-scale agricultural producers in developing countries to credit for production, processing and marketing of their sustainable commodities on commercial and sustainable terms.

In executing such a mission, funds may issue (partial) credit-guarantees[6] as a risk-mitigating instrument in favour of financial intermediaries. This instrument should then allow such intermediaries to offer *commercial* credit to farmers' organisations for the production and export of agricultural commodities at better terms (for example, lower interest rates and/or less restrictive conditionality) than would be possible, thus contributing to reaching a double target: a more solid economic and social base for production of the commodity and to maintain the livelihood of the smallholder producer and his family.

As such, the commodity producers are expected to enjoy improved access to formal finance at an acceptable commercial rate and/or less restrictive conditions. Such a financing arrangement is on a longer term basis, while building up a credit history and records of reliability with a local bank.

The commodity producers also enjoy improved and/or more direct access to the market for sustainable products, thus enabling producers to achieve better terms of return on investment.

Providing a guarantee (at specific conditions) offers local banks an instrument to mitigate their risks while accepting those small borrowers (and their organisations) as clients that would not be accepted without guarantee.

This kind of instrument aims at providing – against an affordable fee and under manageable conditions – credit guarantees, that enable selected (certified) sustainable producers, including cooperatives and estate farms in developing countries, to obtain

---

5   Department for International Development, Financial Sector Team, London/UK: Policy Division Working Paper 'Do Credit Guarantees Lead to Improved Access to Financial Services?', February 2005.

6   A conditional guarantee.

adequate financing through a local financial intermediary that provides finance to commodity suppliers.

Such funds are often not-for-profit entities. But they are not charity funds. Rather, it aims at – on a best-efforts basis – achieving an operating surplus that is enough to absorb credit losses, if any. Annual surpluses are added to a special account to 'protect' the subordinated loans and to maintain/expand the capacity. No distribution of profit is planned.

The operation of such funds works in the way that only credit-guarantees will be issued and no direct loans will be provided, which in itself could also be considered as another risk-mitigating factor.

Generally, such guarantee funds will not provide for complete coverage of the credit demand of its end-clients. It will play a *complementary* role, and not primarily become a competitor with existing creditors.

Next, the aim of such funds is also to introduce its clients to domestic financial institutions for regular credit facilities. Ideally, the guarantee will phase out and become redundant over a foreseeable period of time.

These clients can build up their track records through the guarantee facility and end up becoming directly bankable to the local financial institution. Capacity building of these cooperatives and estates in financial management is what such guarantee funds intend to achieve.

The guarantee fund will work with local financial institutions as a means to save or reduce costs and to contribute to developing the capacity of the financial institutions in client assessment and credit risk management.

Under the guarantee fund, there is a layer of financial institutions to execute the plan. Eligible financial intermediaries in the emerging markets are banks and other financial institutions that have experience or sincerely wish to gain experience with trade finance and meet the guarantee funds' criteria. Experience and creditworthiness of local banks will be assessed. As a matter of principle such guarantee funds usually select a maximum of one or two banks in each focus country as a preferred local counterpart, to ensure efficiency.

As an incubator, the guarantee funds will stimulate the commodity sector for sustainable growth. The impact of guarantee can be measured regularly.

Structured commodity finance: contribution and limitations

For some emerging market countries, when funding the commodity producers – especially agricultural commodity producers – emphasis has so far been given to the skill of structured commodity financing that may help mitigate the above-mentioned problems, and hence risks attached by financiers to agricultural commodity financing could also be minimized.

We will deal with structured commodity finance in Chapter 3 as a product, and in Chapter 5 as a tool for risk mitigation purposes.

Structured commodity finance allows many companies to obtain finance at reasonable terms. Sound companies in countries considered as risky by financiers can actually often get credit at lower rates than those paid by their countries' governments, simply by using structured finance solutions.

Structured finance can also be very relevant for new companies without track records. One of the first things that a bank will usually ask for in normal balance-sheet-backed, working-capital-type finance is a track record. In a structured finance transaction, such requirements count much less: what matters are the transaction and the ability of the company to perform its obligations.

The rationale used behind this is that, at first glance, the risk profile for low-income and collateral-poor borrowers seems high. However, like in large volumes of commodity finance, an important security in pre-export trade finance, which will be further discussed in various chapters in this book, is the export contract that is pledged to the local bank/guarantee fund. The main resulting risk is that of non-delivery by the producer and/or his organisation, so-called performance risk, not the credit risk of the borrower.

Take an example in the coffee sector: the non-delivery risk is mitigated by the fact that sustainable coffee commands a higher price (at export) than sold as conventional green beans in a local market. If the producer can be paid on the spot and in cash by his cooperative or by the exporter, he is likely to choose the higher price locked in the sustainability contract rather than the lower price offered by a local middlemen. Hence, in financing sustainable or fair trade coffee contracts, the non-delivery risk should be somewhat lower. Only in the case of a shortage of conventional coffee in the world market could its price soar, and producers be tempted to sell locally.

If one compares structured commodity finance with the more traditional forms of finance, which are based on the company and not on the transactions that are being financed, there are also differences in country risk and importance of the balance sheet. The role of the actual transaction is completely different in the two forms of finance. The required financing skills are different, and financing costs are different.

First, let us deal with country risks. With normal financing, no company is able to get money from banks at a rate lower than is paid by the country in which it is based. The sovereign risk factor will be the main determinant of the interest rates paid by companies within that country. With structured finance, companies can obtain rates better than those paid by their governments by shifting parts of the risks abroad.

Second, there is the question of the importance of the balance sheet. Traditionally, balance-sheet based financing has a number of weaknesses. One of them is the difficulty of knowing the real value of the balance sheet that a company presents. In many parts of the world, accounting standards are not truly satisfactory from a financier's point of view. With structured finance, the role of the balance sheet is fairly minor; what matters more are the transactions for which finance is sought – they could be financed, even if the company has a poor balance sheet.

Third and related to the above point, the transactions of the borrowing company are not very important in traditional financing. Structured finance, in contrast, enables banks to isolate the financing for sound transactions from the overall accounts of the company.

Hence, structured finance continues to play an important role, providing liquidity management and risk mitigation for the production, purchase and sale of raw, semi-refined or semi-processed materials.

Nevertheless, there are a number of obstacles to structured finance which do not exist in the case of more traditional forms of financing. In many countries, the understanding and the awareness of structured financing techniques and modalities are quite weak, and this has often resulted in legal and policy barriers to this form of finance. For example, restrictions on the use of escrow accounts, or on the transferability of export contracts, or on the ability to pledge certain assets.

Additionally, there is, for state-owned or state-controlled enterprises, a potential problem with the World Bank's negative pledge covenants (and similar covenants from other multilateral financial organizations), which do not permit such entities to pledge their assets to foreign banks, other than for transactions covering less than one year, or with a specific exemption from this organization.

Finally, there is also a difference in the transaction costs of setting up traditional financing and setting up structured financing. While leading to financing at much better conditions, structured financing is relatively labour-intensive, and is generally not worthwhile for very small transactions.

Other instruments

There are other instruments used in supporting commodity flow and financing commodities for some commodity-dependent emerging market countries.

Common fund for commodities (CFCs)

CFCs are a global-level support for commodity flow especially for those commodity dependent countries.

CFCs, like other special funds, are established to help enhance the credit of the borrower and partially or fully help direct funding. Such a fund is different from the guarantee funds we discussed earlier. The CFC's main instruments are grants and loans, which account for 84% and 16% of its overall assistance, respectively.

The CFC was established by the United Nations Commission for Trade and Development (UNCTAD), to enhance production, processing and trade in commodities. It is an autonomous inter-governmental financial organization.

The CFC has played a significant role in attracting funds from different development institutions, the private sector and civil society organizations. This has resulted in a co-financing ratio of 51%.

Since 1991, the Fund has approved more than one hundred regular projects, averaging US$3 million, and 43 fast-track projects (mainly studies and workshops). The support to commodity flow and commodity finance is extensive. The projects under CFCs fall into four broad categories, the majority of them with an emphasis on the enhancement of value addition:

- pre-harvest productivity improvement including research (35%)

- post-harvest processing, marketing and quality testing (36%)

- market expansion (26%)

- price risk management (3%)[7].

The increased demand for commodity financing by producers, processors and traders of the developing and least-developed countries of Asia and the Pacific, Latin America, East Europe and Africa has forced the CFC to focus on commodities. As a result, the CFC has concentrated on the commodity concerns of LDCs and the poorer strata of the population, including smallholders and small enterprises since 1998. The projects have operating sites in approximately one hundred countries:

- 43% in Africa

- 26% in Asia

- 27% in Latin America and the Caribbean

- 4% in industrialized countries, with an emphasis on research and technology transfer.

The CFC finances projects which seek to provide assistance to commodity producers in the poorest and neediest areas of the world. These projects cover a wide variety of commodities, such as coffee, fish, bananas, copper and non-traditional commodities such as vegetables, medicinal plants and bamboo. The overriding objective of the projects is to combat poverty and enhance the commodities, so as to remain the backbone of the majority of the economies of the developing world and have a significant impact on poverty reduction and development.

To promote the international flow of commodities, the CFC gives priorities to commodities that are exportable. 70% of the total exports of the LDCs come out

---

7   http://www.common-fund.org/download/content/CFC_Annual_Report_2012.pdf

from such commodities. They are the most important sources for government revenue, income and employment.

Some of the major regional and sub-regional export-import banks and development financial institution that work in collaboration with the CFC are Export-Import Bank of India, African Export-Import Bank, Andean Development Corporation, Export-Import Bank of Malaysia, and others.[8] This institutional arrangement by the fund is intended to increase bilateral and multilateral agreements among export-import banks and development-finance institutions (DFIs) that are operating in developing countries.

The newly established network also allowed developing countries to learn from each other and share effective practices for entering new markets, financing non-traditional goods and services, and establishing risk-sharing methods for investments.

International collaboration

Knowing the importance of commodity finance, several international and multinational organizations work together in collaboration with the United Nations Commission for Trade and Development (UNCTAD) to strengthen commodity finance. Major partners include: the 106 member states, international organizations including the World Bank, commodity-specific bodies (international commodity organizations and study groups), the private sector (in particular major corporations engaged in production, marketing and distribution of commodities), NGOs promoting action on commodity issues and the academic community researching into commodity problems and solutions.

The strong collaboration among these stakeholders has helped them to achieve significant results in integrating commodity issues in development portfolios; maximizing the mobilization of resource flows; commodity sector vulnerability and risks, and full participation of developing-country farmers in international markets.

Commodity finance for commodity dependent countries: the case of Ethiopia – why and how

To finance commodity production in Ethiopia is by no means the mainstream business of many commodity banks. It is, however, interesting to pick up this country as an example to illustrate why commodity finance is important and how commodity

---

8   UNCTAD/PRESS/IN/2006/005

finance is done for commodity-dependent countries, and how commodity finance is helping such a country.

Background

Ethiopia has a long history and it is the second largest African country in terms of population, and one of the fastest growing non-oil economies in Africa.

Ethiopia is a typical under-developed country, dependent on commodity export. The population is estimated at 100 million with an annual growth rate of about 2.75%. About 85% of the population resides in rural areas.

According to the official annual report of the Ethiopian Government, the per capita income is around US$660 (World Bank 2017) from the US$100 of 2002/03 fiscal year. The Human Development Index, which takes life expectancy, adult literacy, primary schooling and per capita income as a basis, ranked Ethiopia one of the bottom-ranked countries in the world. In 2016, it was ranked 171 among 186 countries.

Subsistence-oriented and small-holder dominated agriculture accounts for about 46.5% of the GDP, for 90% of the export commodities, and for employing over 85% of the population. Industry and services constitute 13.8% and 40.7% respectively. The investment rate has been very low, although recent trends have been quite encouraging.

Though official data is not available, the informal sector plays a vital role in the Ethiopian economy since the majority of the poor (i.e. the majority of the country's people) are engaged in this sector.

The level of development of the economy, resource endowments, policies and development strategies pursued are some of the determining factors of the export structure of a country. Being an underdeveloped economy that heavily depends on agriculture, the structure of Ethiopian export is dominated by agricultural products. This used to account for more than 84%. Coffee has been the dominant export commodity for the last five decades, making on average 40% of total exports.

The financial sector in Ethiopia

There are around 18 commercial banks operating throughout the country with around two hundred branches. A point worth noting is that there are also 26 micro financial institutions in the country.

Generally, public banks dominate the financial industry in Ethiopia. The Commercial Bank of Ethiopia (CBE) is the largest bank in the industry and accounts for nearly half of the branch networks, over 60% of the outstanding loans and about 70% of the deposits of the commercial banks. However, the development of private banks during the last ten years shows a remarkable change.

The major products of commercial banks are mainly traditional commercial banking businesses including deposit facilities, loans and advances, local transfers, foreign LC facilities, and so on. In fact, more than 60% of the income of banks in Ethiopia is generated from credit businesses. Banks also give deposit facilities. The rate on interest-bearing accounts, like savings and fixed time deposits, vary from 3–3.7%, and the average lending rate is between 8% and 10.5% per annum.

Over the last decade, the Commercial Bank of Ethiopia has extended a large amount of loans to farmers to finance fertilizer and improved seed purchase, largely on the basis of guarantees from regional governments, which in effect take the responsibility of collecting the loans and repaying the bank. However, extending loans to the sparsely settled and to farmers with limited viable collateral has not been done by any of the commercial banks, and their business, by and large, remains urban based. Even in the urban economy, good business entities and project ideas may be under-financed unless they are well backed up by collaterals.

The information on which a credit decision is based is too weak to be relied on to manage risks, and good projects with viable collateral would most likely be excluded from the formal bank financing.

In Ethiopia, a remarkable and sound legal and policy environment was laid down in 1994 during which banking business proclamation No. 84/94 was issued. This proclamation ended the mono-bank system that reigned for a decade and half, and gave a new life to the financial sector in the country. Proclamation No. 84/94 stipulates that a bank's licensing is to be established as a share company, wholly owned by Ethiopian nationals, and the National Bank of Ethiopia (NBE) should approve any share ownership transfers.

Proclamation No. 97/1998 is also worth mentioning at this juncture as it empowered the banks to foreclose collaterals and retrieve their loans without resorting to the court system and further discipline borrowers to respect contracts.

A legal framework for the establishment and operation of micro-finance institutions has also been provided by proclamation No. 40/1996. The proclamation stipulates that micro-finance institutions are to be established as share companies wholly owned by Ethiopians and should be licensed by the National Bank of Ethiopia.

Following this proclamation, about 30 micro-financial institutions have been established, and the fragmented provisions of micro credits by various NGOs and government departments have now been better streamlined.

The government of Ethiopia has played an important role in the financial sector. Maintaining a stable macroeconomic environment and a sound financial system are the key monetary policy objectives of the government. Improving the operational quality and efficiency of the financial sector are also its stated objectives.

Since 2001, the agricultural development strategy of the country has taken rural finance as one of the key factors for enhancing agricultural production and ensuring food security. For this reason, formal banks were made to provide input loans to the farmers, largely on the basis of interest spread sharing and guarantees from the regional governments. However, the performance was found unsatisfactory, especially in the area of loan dispersement and collections.

The government has since encouraged the development of micro-financial services, largely to the rural people. The focus has moved towards the development of strategies for viable rural financial institutions, namely to:

1. Replace the large rural loans so far provided via the intermediary of the regional governments by viable and reliable institutions.

2. Strengthen the rural financial system by forging a strong working relationship between the formal banks and the rural financial institutions.

3. Promote a group lending system.

4. Strengthen rural banks and expand their operational scope.

5. Directly extend credit to cooperatives with strong institutional and managerial capacity via forging a strong link between rural banks and cooperatives.

Commodity finance

In such a country as Ethiopia, to finance commodity trade is very different. Commodity production is structured in such a way that commodity producers are allowed to organize under a cooperative system to ease financial and technical supports.

As agriculture is the dominant sector in the country, most of the export commodity producers are organized under agricultural cooperatives such as Sidama Coffee Farmers Cooperative Union, Yirgacheffe Coffee Farmers Cooperatives Union and Oromia Coffee Farmers Cooperative Union. On the other hand, micro and small-scale enterprises are being organized, usually in urban centres, to produce and/or process commodities and engage in different economic activities.

Payment is usually made through the LC, calculated on the basis of current sales of average quality coffee on the auction floors. Two unions (Oromia and Sidama) once received premiums of US$100,000 and US$84,306 respectively because their coffee was classified as fair trade. Moreover, in 2004, Starbucks paid a bonus of US$91,270 to the Sidama Union for its purchase, through Volcafe, of 180 mt of washed coffee. The highest bonus payment to a single farmer was birr 14,892 (US$1,690). There may also be additional payments for organic certification.

Accordingly, commodity finance is structured in a cooperative system for savings and credit cooperatives (SCCs). The major export commodities include coffee, oil seeds, leather and leather products, meat and meat products and gold.

Among the export commodities, coffee is the main source of revenue. The country exports to 29 countries with Jordan, Djibouti, USA, France, Japan, Germany, Italy,

Israel, China, Yemen, Sudan, Kenya, Saudi Arabia, United Kingdom, Turkey, Egypt, Greece, Netherlands and Switzerland as major destinations.

The cooperative nature of the finance facilitates commodity producers to organize in systems for the ease of financial and technical support. Its main objective is to provide credit services to members, facilitating master certificates for organic and fair trade, delivering materials for coffee processing. It is also to provide international and national market information and build member capacity by training, education and management assistance.

With international aid and support in technical assistance, capacity building, promotion and marketing, four coffee cooperative unions (agricultural cooperatives) are recognized by international coffee buyers as reliable suppliers of high-quality coffee traceable back to the cooperative of origin. These coffees charge premium prices in the USA, Europe, and Japan.

In fact, Ethiopia commodity finance had been started as micro credit which was run by the government and non-government organizations. The government provided loans largely for the purchase of oxen through its Rural Finance Department of the Ministry of Agriculture and Cooperatives. During the command economic system (1974–91), the government-owned Development Bank of Ethiopia (DBE) and the Commercial Bank of Ethiopia (CBE) were involved in extending loans to cooperatives. However, lately due to massive default by the cooperatives, the CBE was forced to withdraw from rural financing through the cooperatives.

Following the change of government in 1991, the CBE has continued to provide loans for the purchase of fertilizers and improved seeds on the basis of regional government guarantees. The DBE has also been providing loans to micro and small-scale operators in some selected towns. This scheme was, however, based on donors' funds – designed in the form of a revolving fund, and essentially based on a limited scale in terms of the number of clients covered.

Funds were simply given from the DBE to clients identified and screened by the Trade and Industry Bureaux of regional governments, and the Micro and Small Scale Agency, suggesting a proper loans administration and risk management on the part of the bank was not in place, which generally led to a low loan recovery rate.

Before the formalization of the micro-finance institutions, micro credit used to be provided in a fragmented and unplanned manner even during the early 1990s. The micro credit schemes were donor driven rather than an outcome stemming from a clear policy direction and development strategy. The provision of savings facilities, which is essential for a sustained credit service delivery, was also completely ignored.

The role of micro-financial institutions in commodity finance

In countries such as Ethiopia, where agriculture is the dominant sector and from which more than 90% of export items are produced, financing agriculture is a key issue in addressing development goals.

With a view to achieve the objective of financing the poor, the government of Ethiopia launched a new proclamation regarding the operation of micro-finance institutions. "The failure of the formal banks to provide banking facilities, on the one hand, and the un-sustainability of the NGO's credit scheme on the other hand, led the government to issue out a legal framework for the establishment and operation of micro-finance institutions."

Following this proclamation, these micro-finance institutions are operating throughout the country. Micro-finance institutions are governed by the directives of the National Bank of Ethiopia (CBE). During their establishment, regional governments, local NGOs, non-profit civic organizations, associations and private individuals representing foreign NGOs constitute the shareholders of the micro-finance institutions in Ethiopia.

Micro-finance institutions are playing a significant role in expanding financial services to low-income commodity groups, entrepreneurs and traders, who are not usually reached by banks. Improvements have been witnessed, not only in terms of numbers, but also in operational efficiency as well as coverage during the past years.

At the time of writing, around 250 micro-finance institutions are operating in Africa. The financial institutions offer saving and lending services. According to UNCTAD's report, 57% of this micro finance was established within the last ten years[9].

The 250 micro-finance institutions were reported serving three times as many voluntary savers (6.3 million) as borrowers (2.4 million). However, the figure is low compared to 29.8 million savers in Asian and Pacific region with the Bank Rakyat of Indonesia. Among the 20 largest micro-finance institutes in Africa, the two largest are found in Ethiopia: Amhara Credit and Saving Institution (ACSI) and Dedebit Credit and Saving Institute[10].

So far, the major activities financed by micro-finance institutions include agriculture (crop production and cattle fattening), processing and handcrafts, services, agricultural products trading, and other petty trades.

---

9   http://www.common-fund.org/download/content/CFC_Annual_Report_2013.pdf

10   Overview of the outreach and financial performance of MFIs in Africa, April 2005.

Support from the government for commodity finance

As noted earlier, improving the coverage of micro-finance institutions is one of the objectives of the government. However, while availability of credit is important, it must be recognized that in some cases credit is not the binding constraint, and that the problem may be the capacity to utilize funds or on the demand side. For these reasons, linking markets with demand (through roads and information flows), and increasing skills and education levels, are equally important in many areas.

Several financial intermediaries with other micro-finance institutions are also actively working to enhance the commodity finance as it is the backbone of Ethiopia's economy.

Financing problems also affect the broad environment in which farmers operate. Processors do not have the funds to invest in proper equipment, which leads to unnecessarily high processing costs. Small rural traders stop buying when they run out of cash, leaving farmers stranded with their products. Low investment in warehouse facilities results in high post-harvest losses. When farmers cannot get credit against the collateral of their crop, they are forced to sell their products even if they know that market conditions are temporarily unfavorable. This generates little surplus revenue and hinders overall economic development.

By itself, better access to finance is not enough for farmers to escape their cycle of poverty. They also need access to improved seed as well as better cultivation techniques, information and market access. Solving the problem of agricultural finance is crucial to unlocking farmers' potential for growth and increasing of commodity export.

The government of Ethiopia has established an institution called Commission for Cooperatives Development, at national and regional levels. The main objective of the commission is to improve the efficiency of agricultural markets through development and promotion of modern, business-oriented agricultural cooperatives active in input supply, output marketing, and extension of credit. The commission and its regional offices are also responsible for helping the cooperatives to expand market-linkage activities with private-sector businesses and international coffee buyers. The commission encourages cooperatives and unions to expand their core businesses, to diversify into new products and services (consumer stores), and to establish Savings and Credit Cooperatives (SCCs) to support members who wished to diversify their businesses and improve their family's food security.

Cooperative unions are organized to perform at least the following major activities:

- exporting farmer-member grown quality coffees
- providing credit services to members
- facilitating master certificates for organic and fair trade
- delivering materials for coffee processing

- providing international and national market information
- building capacity for member cooperatives by training, education and management assistance.

The major supports provided to unions include credit facilities, training and internationally accepted certification of their produce.

The Ethiopian government and NGOs such as CFC and USAID are financing export commodity producers who are engaged in production, processing and trading commodities and are also organized under cooperative unions. Among the supporting financial instruments are loans, leasing, warehouse receipts, guarantees and commodity price insurance. Other support may include research, capacity-building, and the establishment and enhancement of commodity-related networks and associations, and information dissemination through conferences and ICT.

The Ethiopian government helps agricultural cooperatives to acquire finance from the CBE and assists them in establishing market linkages both nationally and with buyers overseas. Market linkages are established with processors and traders for the following exportable commodities: coffee, pulses, oil seeds, chat, and hides and skins. As a result of these linkages, commodity producers have obtained higher prices and a guaranteed market for their commodities domestically and abroad. As linkages, that are being developed at the national level, cooperative unions are beginning to cut out the traders as middlemen at the international level and deal directly with foreign buyers.

To promote export of commodities, there are commodity export incentives established including Export Credit Guarantee Scheme, Export Trade Duty Incentive Scheme, Foreign Exchange Retention Scheme, Foreign Credit Scheme, Franco Valuta Import Facility, Private Public Partnership, Investment Facilitation and Preferential Market Access.

Export credit guarantee scheme

This is to support the export sector by availing the necessary financial resources from banks for a pre- and post-shipment financing of exports. The credit is equivalent to the total value of the previous year export proceeds without any collateral requirement for existing exporters and with 20% and 30% collateral requirement for new producer exporters and new exporters respectively. Both the pre- and post-shipment guarantees are provided for a maximum of 180 days.

Export trade duty incentive scheme

The scheme is meant to give exporters access to inputs at world market prices, so that they will be able to compete on equal footing with their competitors. The system comprises three incentives schemes, including a duty drawback scheme, a voucher scheme and a bonded manufacturing warehouse scheme.

Foreign exchange retention scheme

The purpose of this scheme is to let exporters use foreign currency that they earned from their export trade. The foreign currency earned should be put in to a designated account so that it can be used for expenses related to export activity.

Foreign credit scheme

Suppliers or foreign partners' credit is an interim financing provided by a supplier or a foreign partner. It is usually short-term financing, but can include medium- and long-term financing.

Franco valuta import facility

This facility imports raw materials and other items that are important for the production of export products. To benefit from this facility the exporters should acquire an import permit from the NBE.

Private public partnership

A public private partnership forum on oilseeds and pulses – which assesses competitive strengths and weaknesses, formulates and implements competitive strategies based on incentive and structural policies, monitors the achievements, corrects policy gaps and solves pressing problems facing business, and develops future strategies based on international best practices – has been established and meets once every two months to assess developments in the sector.

Investment facilitation

To enhance investment, both foreign and local, several works have been done by the Ethiopian investment commission to provide efficient services to investors. At present therefore, the majority of investment services, such as the issuance of investment permits, are designed to be provided within a very short period – from one hour to two days.

The Federal and Regional Investment Bureaus have already prepared suitable land (with all facilities, such as electricity and water) for the establishment of strategic industries targeted to produce exportable value-added products.

Preferential market access

Ethiopia has a quota and duty free preferential market access to all export items (except arms) to the EU under 'everything but arms' (EBA) initiatives. Ethiopia is well placed to benefit from EBA. Its labour market is flexible, labour laws do not represent constraint to the exit of firms and wages for unskilled workers are amongst the lowest in the world. Also, prices of inputs such as electricity and water are low by international standards.

Some implications for the case

The export sector in Ethiopia is highly commodity-dependent; and this dependency has been aggravated by adverse trends such as declining prices for primary commodities, higher input prices, deteriorating terms of trade, and high price volatility. To reverse these adverse trends, therefore, the government should give more emphasis on value addition, particularly through agricultural processing and efficient trade in commodities.

The experience of Ethiopia shows that financiers have been successful in promoting access to finance. They often provide finance along the supply chain, including a strong emphasis on education and provision of proper technology, appropriate lending technology (use of structures that depend on the actual target public, with group lending techniques for the poorest borrowers), and inclusion of a family's overall activities in the credit decision.

Structured commodity finance (SCF) is a sophisticated commodity-based financing technique, specifically designed for commodity producers and trading companies doing business in the developing markets. Using a structured commodity financing facility, loans can be granted to commodities producers in emerging markets. The terms and conditions of these loans are primarily based on the transaction and supplier's ability to produce and/or deliver the commodity in question.

Structured finance allows sound companies to obtain finance at reasonable terms and it can also be very relevant for new companies without track records. What matters in structured commodity finance is the transaction and the ability of the company to perform its obligations. However, the understanding and the awareness of structured financing techniques and modalities are quite weak, and this has often resulted in legal and policy barriers such as restrictions on the use of escrow accounts, or on the transferability of export contracts, or on the ability to pledge certain assets.

To strengthen commodity finance in Ethiopia, government and non-government organizations, financial institutions, the private sector and the academic community will have to work together to achieve significant results in integrating commodity issues in development portfolios; maximizing the mobilization of resource flows; commodity sector vulnerability and risks; and full participation of commodity producers in international markets.

The case of Ethiopia tells us that government incentives, structured commodity finance skill, micro-finance institutions, international support and aid are all contributing factors to the success of commodity finance for a least-developed country such as Ethiopia.

Contracts and documents behind the commodity flow

When we have a macro-level overview of global commodity flow and a micro-level examination of the practice of commodity finance in some commodity-dependent countries such as Ethiopia, we come back to the basics of commodity trade: contracts and documents.

The importance of contracts and documents

Needless to say, documentation is important in every business and all sorts of trading. But in commodity trading, which is large in volume and large in terms of money, it deserves special attention. Since trading is often done with parties in emerging markets, a company wants to make sure all the aspects of the trade are covered.

A commodity contract is the legal base for the transaction. If any conflict arises later between the buyer and the seller, reference is generally made to the sales contract.

As in general trade, commodity trade is done by signing a contract between the buyer and the seller. The contract should stipulate the rights and responsibilities of each party.

Proper documentation in commodity trading is very important. When this is not done it can cause disputes between parties, which has a bad influence on the profitability of the deal. It also gives a party involved in the transaction the opportunity to get out of the deal when based on discrepancies.

In the current market situation, prices are dropping rapidly and dramatically. Buyers feel as if they are paying too much for the goods they agreed to purchase at the time that prices were still high. A point we will discuss in detail is that discrepancies are used by the buyer to negotiate a lower price when the goods are already on their way to the place of destination.

If a commodity trader has never had any dealings in the contact's past, an initial contact must be established between them. The buyer or the seller may directly contact the counterparts, or via an agent or a salesperson in-between for an offer to sell or an order requesting shipment. Usually it is legally binding for the party making the offer or placing the order. Therefore, it is important that such an order or offer contains at least the major details concerning the commodity, including its grade and quality, quantity, price, terms of sale, delivery date, payment terms and other necessary specifications.

Once a seller's written offer has been formally accepted by the buyer, and both parties are authorized to make a binding commitment, a sales contract is formed. A sales contract may also be established if the buyer gives the order and the seller agrees with the specifications in the order. If the seller considers it possible for him to comply with all the provisions, the seller may send a written and signed acknowledgement, completing a sales contract that is binding on both parties.

Commodity sales contracts are merely accepted orders or offers that may arise through early contact and correspondence between the buyer and the seller. For some commodities, a detailed contract must be carefully drawn with legal advice, to define rights and responsibilities under different scenarios.

Major parts of a commodity contract and points of attention

A commodity sales contract should contain at least the following as a minimum:

1. Names and address of the signing parties that is, the buyer and the seller.

2. Specifications of the underlying commodity, including weight, grade and quantity with or without tolerance.

3. Price per unit and the total.

4. Shipping and delivery instructions and required documentation (including quality certificate, export licenses and proof of origin of the goods, etc.).

5. Payment terms and conditions.

6. Insurance coverage and so on.

Other points for attention are:

Quantity

Usually tolerance for the exactness of the quantity delivered is set between 1% and 5%. This means the seller has to deliver a quantity between 95% and 105% of the agreed amount. Contracts will often involve a third party confirming the quantities that are delivered to the buyer.

To define quantity is often thought to be easier than to define quality. Still, confusion and misunderstanding for the measurement of weight and other quantity measures are not uncommon. The example often quoted is that a US pound is different from a European pound. A ton has a different real weight, depending on whether it is a short, metric (mt, often used in commodities), or long ton.

Price

In commodity trade, there is often a significant delay between the signing of the contract and the delivery of the products. Considering the volatility of commodity prices, price agreements are very important.

Prices can be fixed, when the contract is very short term, but often they are forward contracts, with prices depending on the price of derivative markets. A combination of spot and forward prices is also possible. For example, a price floor and ceiling can be set based on the current spot price. If the spot price at the date of delivery falls within that range, then the buyer will pay that price. If the spot price at the date of delivery exceeds that range, the parties involved will split the profit either party makes from that excessive change in price. When parties commit to multiple transactions in the future, the use of the average spot price over a certain period is also a possibility.

For metals such as copper, zinc and lead, often a quotation period is agreed on to determine the price. This means that the buyer pays the average price of the commodity during the period. This quotation period splits increases or decreases in price between parties.

Conditions of payment

As large amounts of money are involved, conditions of payment for commodity trading are very important to both sides. There are many different ways the payment can be structured.

1. Cash in advance: the seller receives the payment before shipping the goods. Usually the commodity is in good demand or the buyer needs the commodity urgently.

2. Irrevocable LC: this is often used for commodity trade, especially when the buyer and seller are doing business for the first time. With the credit issued by a prime bank of excellent standing, or confirmed by a reputable bank, the exporter feels that the payment is secured. This creates business opportunities for many commodity banks. In other chapters of the book, we will explore this way of financing in detail.

3. Documents against payment: the title documents are turned over to the importer against the payment of a sight draft for the amount due drawn on the importer by the exporter. But the buyer may refuse to accept the shipment, which will cause a demurrage fee and so on.

4. Documents against acceptance: title documents are turned over to the importer on acceptance of a time draft drawn on the importer. The tenure of the draft is for a stipulated period such as 30, 60, 90 or 180 days. The seller bears the risk that the accepted draft may not be paid at maturity.

5. Consignments: this is for the exporter to retain title to the goods while physically delivering the commodity to the buyer to allow the arrangement of sales and delivery to final customers. Once the buyer has made a final sale, there is an obligation to pay the consignor. The consignor (seller) runs the risk of non-payment from the consignee (buyer). Hence a bank guarantee may be involved.

6. Open account: the seller merely ships the commodities to the buyer and mails the title documents and invoice to the buyer demanding payment within a stipulated period of time. Such terms can only be accepted for very trustworthy parties or between units in the same group.

Quality

Although many commodities are of the same quality, or more or less the same as they are supposed to be, quality can be an issue when trading in commodities.

Grains, for example, can go bad or timber coming from the forests in Brazil can be different than that coming from the forests in Indonesia. Contracts should, therefore, specify quality levels.

For metals, quality specifications are critical. The concentration of metals is not always the same. Therefore, metal contracts have to be specific about weight, composition and purity[11]. Delivery can be in T-bars, ingots, sows etc.

Contracts will state levels of tolerance for how much the commodities may differ from the quality conditions. Figure 2.1 shows examples of what those quality specifications look like.

The track record of the commodity producer can influence the extent of the quality specifications and related payment conditions. When doing business with producers with a long track record of producing high-quality products, contracts can be less specific than when dealing with unknown small producers in a part of the world without such a track record.

---

11 www.lme.com

Table 2.4: Zinc composition specifications

Special contract rules for special high grade zinc	
Quality: zinc and zinc alloys: primary zinc. BS EN 1179:2003 (grade classi cation Z1)	
Element	**Composition as percentage**
Nominal zinc content	99.995
Pb	0.003 maximum
Cd	0.003 maximium
Fe	0.002 maximum
Sn	0.001 maximum
Cu	0.001 maximum
Al	0.001 maximum
Total of all these elements	0.005 maximum

Source: London Metal Exchange Zinc contract specifications, 2010.

Figure 2.1: Example of aluminium contract specifications

Contract/quality

a) Primary aluminium of minimum 99.7% purity with maximum permissible iron content of 0.2% and maximum permissible silicon content of 0.1% or b) P1020A

Lot size (warrant)

25 tonnes (with a tolerance of +/-2%)

Form/shape

Ingots, T-bars, Sows

Source: LME Aluminium Specifications, 2008.

Delivery conditions

The date and place of delivery are relevant for price calculation. Some of the most commonly used delivery terms are as follows:

1. Ex-factory: the seller is obliged to place the commodity at the buyer's disposal at the point of origin. But the seller must fulfill other delivery obligations such as custom house cleaning etc. The price quoted in the contract covers only the cost of making the goods available at the origin point. All other costs, such as forwarding, insurance, custom charge, etc. must be borne by the buyer.

2. FOB: free on board.

3. CIF: costs, insurance and freight.

4. DEQ: the seller's price quotation covers all costs necessary to place the commodity on the dock of the named port of importation.

Miscellaneous conditions, such as penalties in case of non-compliance with the contract, cancellation of the deal and determining responsibilities of the buyer and seller are also important to commodity trading companies in case of conflicts and disputes.

To regulate the commodity trade, there are standard rules that are generally used and accepted in commodity trading: the so-called 'Incoterms 2000' (International Commercial Terms). Those rules were issued by the International Chamber of Commerce (ICC), publication 560. There are currently 13 different Incoterms, divided into four groups. They relate to the conditions under which the seller has to deliver the goods.

The four groups are:

1. Group E. The seller has to make the goods available at the seller's premises. The only example is ex-works (EXW), where the goods are available at the disposal of the buyer, not cleared for export and not loaded in any vehicle.

2. Group F. The seller must deliver the goods to a carrier appointed by the buyer. An example is free on board (FOB), where the transfer of ownership takes place when the goods are cleared for export and loaded on the appropriate ship.

3. Group C. The seller has to arrange the carriage of the goods, but does not carry all the risk of loss or damage to the goods, or additional costs that occur after shipment. An example is cost insurance and freight (CIF), where the seller has to deliver the goods to the ship's destination and pay for the costs of the freight that are necessary to deliver to that destination. This includes insurance costs against the risk of loss or damage to the goods.

4. Group D. The seller bears all costs and risks to deliver the goods to the place of destination. An example is delivery duty paid (DDP), where the seller must also clear the goods for import, not unloaded at the destination.

For delivery between established trade partners in countries near to each other or belonging to certain trade areas, group E and F are commonly used. However, when the seller wants to have more control over the transport process, C and D are more appropriate and commonly used.

Transportation documents

In commodity trade, commodities are very often, though not always, shipped by sea. To keep track of the transportation process, certain documents are dispensed at different stages of the process. These documents are a form of security for the other party.

The most common document in the transportation of commodities is a bill of lading (BL). A BL is the evidence between the exporter and a shipping company, that the goods are being transported on a ship. It also provides details on the condition of the goods on board the ship.

The BL will state whether the goods are damaged or not. When the exporter has signed the BL, the holder has the rights to possess the goods. This title to the goods is also very important for the buyer's payment conditions.

When a company hires a ship from the owner, there might be spare cargo space on board. When the exporter uses this extra cargo space from that company, there is no contract between the exporter and the ship owner, but between the exporter and the hirer of the ship. The BL is then called a charter party BL. Banks will often not accept this kind of BL as a sufficient document for documentary credit.

Documentation used for transportation by air, is called an air waybill or air freight note. This is a BL issued by the airline company. While transporting over sea usually takes a significant amount of time, transportation by air is very fast. The problem for the exporter is that he does not want to give control over the goods before payment. To solve this problem an exporter might assign the goods to a corresponding bank in the country. This bank will release the goods only when they receive the proper documents and instructions.

When transporting goods on the road, such a document is called a truck receipt. The major difference between a BL on one side and an air waybill or truck receipt on the other, is that a BL is a document of title and the others are not. This means that the importer needs the original BL before he can collect the goods. For the other documents this is not needed.

If an exporter wants extra security that the importer will pay for the goods, then the exporter can demand the importer to sign a bill of exchange. This is an unconditional order that the importer will pay the exporter a certain amount of money on demand or at a future date.

Agricultural commodities are often shipped under Grain and Feed Trade Organization (GAFTA) regulations. These are standard contracts made for agricultural products. When deals are made under GAFTA regulation, parties involved also agree to accept ruling by the GAFTA when there are disputes.

Quality is an important aspect for agricultural products. Food can go bad or even make people sick when they eat it. The incident with milk powder from China is an example.[12]

GAFTA contracts therefore state specific conditions for the quality of products. For example, a GAFTA contract can state that the goods have to be of 'fair average quality'.

---

12 See various reports in local media.

The GAFTA issues monthly FAQ standards which determine what that average quality is. When this standard is not available, an arbitrator will decide on the FAQ.

The Federation of Oils, Seeds and Fats Associations (FOSFA) is a similar arbitral body which has different contracts under which agricultural commodities can be traded. Approximately 85% of all international trade of oils and fats is traded under FOSFA contracts.[13]

Agricultural commodity deals are much more tailor-made than energy or metal deals. Agricultural commodities come in many forms and production and distribution is much more spread over the globe. This requires specific conditions in contracts and financing.

Since everybody in the world needs to eat, distribution of agricultural commodities is worldwide. Every country is involved. This also means that storage of those commodities is done in warehouses all over the world. Warehouses are therefore an important aspect of commodity trading for agricultural products.

For the metal industry, the London Metal Exchange is the most important agency. They quote prices on most types of metals and provide standard contracts and arbitration for metals, as GAFTA and FOSFA do for agricultural commodities, as discussed in the 'Quality' section earlier in the chapter.

13   www.fosfa.org

CHAPTER 3

Commodity Finance: The Major Financing Mechanisms and Products

Plain vanilla products: commodity finance versus trade finance

Commodity finance is understood as short-term, asset-backed finance, providing finance to producers, processors and trading companies where chains of commodity supply are financed.

In essence, commodity finance is trade finance as it finances cross-border trade transactions, using products which involve documents, receivables or other instruments which represent the value of goods traded, or the obligation arising from the trade transaction.

In commodity banks, finance facility structures provided to its clients can be divided into different categories:

- Transactional finance (issuance of LCs and guarantees, freight finance, margin call finance and the with (out) recourse discounting of bank and corporate receivables (receivables under confirmed LCs, draft discounting, confirmation of corporate risk), etc.).

- Short term pre-export finance.

- Inventory finance, including borrowing-based finance and ownership-based finance.

- Finance of the commodity supply chain including short-term and long-term pre-export finance, commodity-linked export finance, commodity-infrastructure finance, etc.

Sometimes corporate lending facilities based on balance sheet strength are granted in combination with well-structured commodity finance facilities.

Plain vanilla trade finance products are used in commodity trading as well, such as bills of exchange, collection, documents against payment (DP), documents against acceptance (DA), factoring and even open account.

Financing trade receivables is the basis of the transactional facilities. A bill of exchange is a means of payment used by companies to finance trade flows. The bill, as such, can be endorsed by the drawee (or accepted payable by a bank). The obligor of this bill of exchange becomes the party endorsing this bill of exchange. The instrument is thus negotiable. Under this product, we have the drawer – exporter of the goods – and the drawee – importer or purchaser of trade goods.

Frequently, a bill of exchange will be accepted payable by a bank. The company risk is thus converted into bank risk. This kind of financial instrument is used to facilitate trade by enabling an exporter to give credit to an importer by drawing a term bill of exchange. A bill of exchange, once accepted by a bank, will give the exporter chance to cash-in an advance for his sales.

A commodity bank offers other plain vanilla short-term transactional facilities, such as back-to-back, front-to-back, cash-and-carry deals, apart from LC business, which we discuss in more detail below.

Commodity finance: finance under a letter of credit

Given the large volumes of commodity trading using letters of credit, an LC is worth some discussion in commodity finance.

An LC is particularly favored in commodity finance, and commodity finance banks are involved very much under this instrument. In fact we will come back to the same topic in Chapter 4, but from the risk perspective.

An LC as a conditional undertaking from a bank gives comfort to the seller. Traditionally, this product is widely used in commodity finance, not only to secure the payment, but also to provide a structure for finance, that is, it provides a platform for each party under the LC to either play a role of financing and/or a role of risk coverage – a point of focus in Chapter 4.

For a commodity finance bank, there are two categories of LC: one is an outbound LC – an LC used for importing commodities – the other is an inbound LC – an LC received to secure payment on exported goods.

An LC received for securing payment of exported goods can further be divided into, at least, sight and usance according to the payment period. Obviously one advantage of an LC as a payment instrument is that it is regulated by Uniform Customs and Practice as UCP 600 and the International Standard Banking Practice (ISBP). The International Chamber of Commerce (ICC) is thus a well-established, professional platform of this product.

An LC is not only a secured way of payment but also a financing instrument. Under a *sight* LC, the bank which receives the LC is requested, or is allowed, to add its confirmation to such an LC which is available by payment or negotiation. Confirmation, silent or open, is often required especially if the issuing bank is located in emerging markets. By adding its confirmation, the confirming bank commits itself to pay the beneficiary at sight when the documents required under an LC have been presented, resulting in a credit risk on the issuing bank and a country risk on the country where the issuing bank is located. The confirming bank will 'negotiate' the documents.

The concept of 'negotiation' is so important and unique that UCP 600 clearly defines the term 'negotiation':

> "Negotiation means the purchase by the nominated bank of drafts (drawn on a bank other than the nominated bank) and/or documents under a complying presentation, by advancing or agreeing to advance funds to the beneficiary on or before the banking day on which reimbursement is due to the nominated bank."

Confirmation can be *open* or *silent*. Under an open confirmation scenario, the LC is available by any bank for negotiation and confirmation, whereas silent confirmation is the confirmation added upon the request of the beneficiary and is 'silent' in the sense that the applicant may not be aware of this.

There is a difference between silent confirmation and an open one. Under a silent confirmation scenario, the confirming bank is *not* requested by the LC issuing bank to add its confirmation to an LC, which is available at the counters of the confirming bank for payment or negotiation at sight. However, the beneficiary of the LC would like to cover the bank and country risk on the issuing bank and the country where this bank is located. He, therefore, requests the confirming bank to add its confirmation. If both the risk of the LC issuing bank and that of the country where the issuing bank is located are acceptable to the confirming bank, the confirming bank will honour the payment of the LC to the beneficiary. The beneficiary will thus get funding before the issuing bank pays. That is, the seller will get paid from the issuing bank rather than having to wait until the issuing bank is ready to pay.

Silent confirmation generally involves the beneficiary's bank which honours the payment undertaking to the beneficiary despite the fact that the issuing bank does not instruct the beneficiary's bank to confirm. It is sometimes called 'commit to pay' (CTN).

Under a usance LC, the negotiating bank is requested or is allowed by the LC issuing bank to add its confirmation to an LC which is available at the counters of the negotiating bank by payment at a certain moment in the future (the maturity date), for instance, 180 days or 360 days after shipment. By adding its confirmation, the negotiation bank commits itself to pay the beneficiary when credit complying documents required under LC have been presented, resulting in a credit risk on the issuing bank and a country risk on the issuing bank's country. Under usance LC, the confirming and discounting bank provides an advance to the beneficiary. This is bundle business for many commodity banks. An LC thus becomes an instrument for finance.

For the protected rights under the LC, there is often a separate contract between the confirming bank and the beneficiary.

Other LC products often used in commodity finance include the following:

Transferable letter of credit

A transferable LC was developed to avoid the risks of back-to-back credit. A transferable LC does not involve two letters of credit. Instead, there is one straightforward LC issued by the buyer's bank in favour of the commodity trading company. The LC is, however, 'transferable' to enable the trading company (middleman) to transfer most of the credit to the ultimate supplier.

Under this structure, the credit not transferred is usually the commission for the trading company, because the transferable LC involves only one LC under which one set of documents will be presented. The risk is thus only the issuing bank's (non-payment) risk or the country risk where the LC was issued.

Back-to-back finance

The rationale for back-to-back finance is that many commodity trading companies are playing the middleman function or the function of a broker, that is, they buy from the seller and then sell to another buyer. Such a fact makes (back-to-back) finance indispensable to trading companies for dealing with super large commodity deals – they rely on banking support.

A back-to-back facility provided by a commodity bank is interesting not only to the commodity trading company but also to the financing bank. Since the middleman is generally thinly capitalized, and is often not eligible for a clean credit from the bank on his own financial strength, the bank issues an LC on behalf of the client (trader or intermediary) who has an LC issued by the house bank of the buyer. His buyer's LC is used as collateral. The bank issuing the second credit is willing to do so because of the strength of the first credit.

When the supplier, who is the beneficiary of the second credit, ships the goods and presents documents in compliance with the terms and conditions of that credit, the bank pays the credit and looks for repayment from the proceeds from payment of the first credit for which the trading company or the middleman is beneficiary. The second LC, sometimes nicknamed the 'baby LC', is often for a lesser amount than the first LC to allow the profit margin for the middleman.

One of the most significant mitigants to price risk in commodity lending is the establishment of a back-to-back structure.

An exporter may have a firm order from an overseas company. The payment of the order is secured by an LC. But this exporter himself is not the supplier. Rather, he must purchase himself from another overseas supplier. Plus, he does not have enough funds to purchase and export. Under this scenario, a trader will effectively buy and sell the commodity at the same time. As there is always a time lag, a position would be created for this brief moment. A transferable LC is a solution. But when the final supplier is willing to accept an assignment of differences by the exporter, a back-to-back credit is a good alternative.

The back-to-back credit offers rather more latitude for issuing a counter-credit in favour of the supplier of the goods on the basis of credit which has been received. It is, in fact, an ordinary documentary, under which the documents which are needed to be able to dispose of the original documentary credit (the master LC) may be presented. This is obviously a new credit granted by the bank issuing the counter-credit. Items to be back-to-backed will be discussed in Chapter 5.

The back-to-back facility and the front-to-back facility, is usually limited to some conditions among which are the following:

- The financing bank should be the advising bank so as to be the first contact party in the transaction. This is to ensure a seamless match. Any amendment or change of LC terms will be totally in the hands of the financing bank.

- The financing bank will take it that the LC issuing bank is an acceptable bank, i.e. the credit risk of the issuing bank is acceptable under the current limit to this bank. This is to ensure that the back-to-back financing bank is eventually really covered.

Without meeting the conditions the first LC, sometimes nicknamed the 'mother LC', will be of little value for the second back-to-back LC to be based on.

Although the financial position of the middleman (the beneficiary of the first LC) is less critical in the credit decision of the financing bank, under a back-to-back structure, this middleman's situation is still of importance for the financing bank. This is because if the trading company fails to submit documents in good order, payment will not be affected under the first credit. The bank that has issued and paid the second credit has recourse to an entity that is very likely not able to meet the recourse requirements.

Therefore, prior to issuing the back-to-back credit, the bank must carefully check the status of the intermediary who applies for this back-to-back facility for the following:

- Is he considered reputable?

- Does he have a good record in his field?

- Is he familiar with the type of deal for which he has requested a back-to-back credit?

- Is he used to dealing with the product in question?

Front-to-back finance

Front-to-back is similar to the back-to-back, however, the issuing bank issues the LC before the bank receives any LC at its counter.

The idea is to provide finance to the importer (trader) in the form of an LC. This credit LC facility is based on trading background and relevant documents. The facility is secured by the underlying trade flow and is more flexible than back-to-back.

Needless to say, the check for the credit worthiness of a company to qualify for a front-to-back facility is stricter than that of a back-to-back facility.

Standby credit and guarantee

Among credits used in commodity finance, the standby credit occupies a special position. Its origin is in the USA, where commercial banks are not allowed to give guarantees. In order to be able to provide such a service, the guarantee has been molded into the form of a credit: the 'standby' credit.

This credit facility is in fact a bank guarantee to give the seller comfort. Therefore, standby LCs or straightforward guarantees are used to secure payment in commodity finance.

For some energy deals, a standby LC is used to shorten the delivery time of documents. These standby LCs usually have all the content of an LC, but do not require presentation of some documents such as a BL.

Example 3.1: Sample of standby LC for energy

Irrevocable standby letter of credit no. ....

Applicant: xxx

Beneficiary: xxx

Advising bank:

At the request of the above applicant, and for its account, we – xxx – hereby issue in your favor our irrevocable standby letter of credit no. xxx.

This standby letter of credit is for an amount of USD xxx, and is available for payment at sight at the counters of advising bank against the following documents:

1. Copy of unpaid invoice.

2. Beneficiary's certificate purporting to be signed by an official of the beneficiary certifying that 'the amount demanded represents a payment which has not been made to .... By petrovietnam oil corporation (pv oil) within the terms of the contract no. .... Dated .... In respect of invoice number xxx which is legally and properly past due'.

Covering: xxx net us barrels plus/minus five (5) percent operational tolerance at seller's option of ... crude oil.

Price: xxx

We hereby agree with you that presentation of the documents in compliance with the terms of this standby letter of credit will be duly honoured on presentation to us no later than the expiry date of this credit.

This standby letter of credit is valid until (date) at the counters of advising bank.

47A: additional conditions

1. Partial and multiple drawings are permitted

2. Above documents presented in authenticated swift form are acceptable.

3. The value of this standby letter of credit may escalate/de-escalate in accordance with the price calculation formula without any amendment from our part.

4. This standyby letter of credit shall take effect in accordance with its terms but such terms shall not alter, add to or in any way affect the contract(s) between xxx and petrovietnam oil corporation (pv oil) to which this letter of credit relates.

5. The construction, validity and performance of this letter of credit shall be governed by and construed in accordance with English law.

6. Except as otherwise expressly provided herein, this standby letter of credit is subject to the uniform customs and practices for documentary credits 2007 revision (icc publication no. 600).

7. Documents presented later than 21 days after date of shipment but within the standby letter of credit validity are acceptable.

8. Spelling/typing mistakes (except in amounts, quantity and unit price) not to be considered as discrepancies.

9. Confirmation: may add

71B: charges

Banking charges at beneficiary's bank are for beneficiary's account and bank charges at applicant's bank are for applicant's account.

Payment clause:

Upon receipt at our counters in .... Of documents issued in strict conformity with the terms and conditions of this standby letter of credit, we shall cover you according to your instructions, on sight basis.

Commodity finance facilities: pre-export finance

From a risk perspective, commodity finance lending facilities, by and large, can be divided into unsecured lending and secured lending. These lending arrangements target different counterparties. Similarly, to most other commodity finance facilities, pre-export finance is very often done under a secured lending category.

Unsecured lending is typically for the largest and financially strong companies which very often have their own credit ratings. These companies have reasonable if not excellent balance sheets, with a large capital base and substantial and healthy cash flows. This will enable these companies to absorb market losses, if necessary, on their own.

Some of these commodity companies are also multinationals themselves and have long been established in different markets. These multinationals may have 10–50 'house banks' to serve them, and some of these corporates even have 'financial companies' inside their own company structure, or have a department which has the function of a finance company. The mission of their 'financial company' is to structure their total trade flow portfolio to maximise their income.

These multinational companies have a group of banks – commodity banks or non-commodity banks – as their 'house banks' to serve them, paying a very sharp margin. This is because they are companies often with good credit ratings and they have easy access to capital markets by issuing commercial paper and other debt vehicles.

Working capital finance is a typical unsecured finance which is based on the balance sheet of the company. No security documentation is in place as it is not asset-backed finance. Customers can withdraw funding under such a facility according to the pre-agreed terms and conditions. The general corporate finance techniques are used here.

Secured lending in commodity finance, on the other hand, is 'structured finance' to make the lending possible but the risks for lenders are mitigated to some extent.

Structured commodity finance is a broad concept, often referring to various lending facilities to companies with payment risk secured one way or another. Structured commodity finance arrangements are based on closed end, self-liquidating commercial transactions with procurements in these markets. To 'structure the commodity finance' is to transform non-acceptable payment risk into acceptable production risk and delivery risk.

Given such a risk mitigation concept, the structured commodity finance is often made available for emerging markets. Export driven companies in these countries have resilience to shocks (both political and economic) that allow structured lending to capture the cash flow generated by the underlying commodity flow with a higher degree of certainty.

Figure 3.1: Structured commodity finance

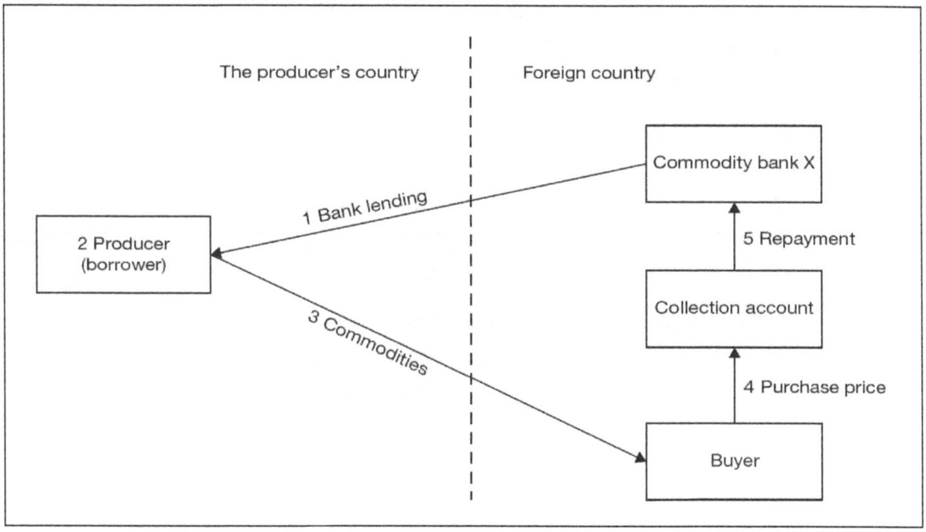

This 'asset/proceeds backed lending' rationale is the backbone for structured commodity finance. Actual individual structures may be stronger or weaker, but a basic rationale behind them is the belief that emerging market performance risk is easier to monitor than emerging market payment risk. Hence, deals with performance risk focus are targeted, and a robust attitude to securing performance must be taken.

This is done by focusing on the current assets, as the only worthwhile part of the balance sheet from the liabilities (especially third-party creditors) by preferring title to and control over the receivables, the sales contract and, ideally, the inventory (underlying commodity) as well.

We will divide the discussion on pre-export finance into export receivables finance and prepayment finance.

Export receivables financing

Structured pre-export finance refers to finance export activities that generate income in hard currencies, that is, financing provided is based on export receivables. Commodity banks have seen exports to developed countries from some emerging markets experience difficulty in paying in foreign currencies.

Pre-export finance is a product under which a borrower is a commodity producer. This financial product covers pre-crop finance (borrower is a cooperative or agricultural commodity producer), equipment purchase finance (for plant upgrade purposes) and supply chain finance (upstream/downstream integration finance). It can also simply be prepayment finance, where repayment of the loan will come from export proceeds that will be paid directly to the bank by the buyers.

Lending banks usually rely first on the ability of the borrower to perform on these transactions, that is, the ability to deliver the export. The owner of commodities may obtain finance from the lender against assignment to the bank of export sales contracts or receivables. This form is called export receivables financing.

Structured pre-export finance is especially suitable for commodities with a high export orientation. This is evidenced by our early discussion on the exports of commodity-dependent countries in emerging markets. These are cases where it is in the interest of the country where the exporter is based, that the commodities are exported to create an inflow of foreign currency.

Another important aspect is the fact that these structures always involve off-shore payments. This way, the bank is not exposed to the credit risk of the exporter but to that of the better rated (OECD) buyer, or the 'off-taker'.

Example 3.2

A mining company in an emerging market country intends to export 100 tons of copper, which still needs to be extracted, to a party that is involved in copper refining. Payment of the buyer, a refining company, is partly financed by the bank which shares performance risk with a local bank (from the country of the mining company, with a performance guarantee issued by this local bank) while the payment risk is shared with the off-taker. This way, a seemingly unacceptable risk is structured into an acceptable risk.

Such a kind of export receivables finance consists of *self-liquidating* loans that are backed by future exports proceeds. By assigning the export receivables to the lender, country risk is partly mitigated and the lenders are left with exposure to performance risk of the borrower. It is, therefore, of critical importance to collect independent information that the borrower is indeed capable of producing the goods.

Under such pre-export finance structures, country risk is mitigated but not totally offset. A part of the country risk remains as, in the case when it is suddenly difficult to move goods out of the country, the future sales proceeds might seriously be hindered, if not blocked, as a buyer needs to be found that can only be situated in the same country.

The pre-export finance facility might consist of just an existing bank limit without specific conditions or requirements in its most basic form. However, deals are often large in terms of volume and limits are easily filled, so other means might be necessary to finance the trade.

Often an export loan is granted on the basis of an LC covering a certain percentage of the deal. Another option for the exporter is to use the sales contract to obtain financing.

Figure 3.2 shows a possible structure of export receivables financing:

Figure 3.2: Export receivables financing

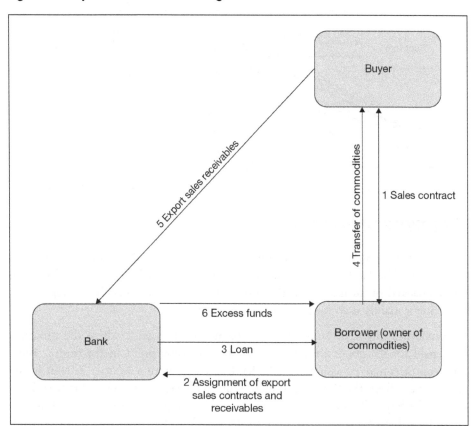

Example 3.3

A client enters into a sales contract with Company B on the sale of 100 tons of copper. The sales contract and its receivables are assigned by the client to the lending bank as security for the loan to be obtained from the bank. When the copper is exported, Company B will, upon acceptance, transfer the invoice amount into an (escrow) account controlled by the bank. This is used to cover the loan and interest after which the bank transfers any excess funds to the client.

A bank might also use a tolling structure (see Figure 3.3). In this structure the bank finances raw materials for the initial supplier and the delivery of those materials to a refining factory and is secured by the receivables created from the export to the end buyer.

Figure 3.3: Tolling

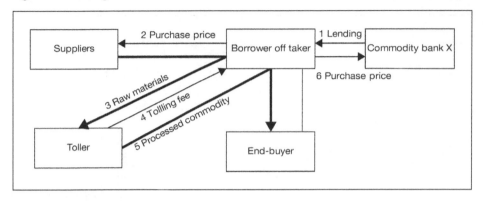

Prepayment finance

Under prepayment finance, the borrower – usually a commodity purchaser – obtains a loan from the bank and uses this to prepay the exporting producer. This loan will be backed by an interest in the commodities that are transferred. Prepayment financing is mainly used for medium to large loans.

Commodities might be sold with a prepayment agreement, where the producer is prepaid for the goods that will be exported at some point in the future. These sales contracts may be assigned to the bank (possibly with a security interest in the commodities from the time of production up to delivery to the client) that makes a loan to the buyer. This amount is then prepaid to the producer who will release the goods (possible after permission from the lending bank) to be exported to the buyer. The buyer then uses future receivables to repay the loan to the bank.

Figure 3.4: Prepayment finance

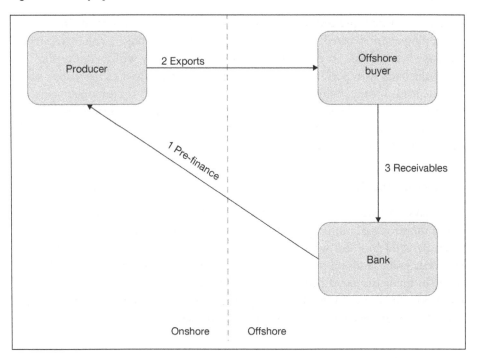

Example 3.4

A trader is looking to import 100 tons of copper from a producer in the USA. To finance this, the trader obtains a loan from its bank to prepay the exporting producer. As security, sales contracts, which the trader already entered into, are assigned to the bank together with a security interest in the copper. After the copper is transferred to the trader, the trader will repay the bank with receivables resulting from the sales contracts.

Advantages for the lending bank and the borrower

Advantages for the lending banks

To commodity banks, this type of pre-export finance can have major benefits. It can increase the range of potential clients who otherwise will not be acceptable to the bank, as well as the comfort with which facilities are (indirectly) provided by the bank to emerging-market-based exporters. Different benefits for the bank shall be discussed here.

Price risk

Under structured pre-export finance, payment risk is transferred from often developing-country-based commodity exporters to their buyers (often located in developed countries). So payment risk is shifted to a party with better credit. This leaves the bank with performance risk exposure to the exporter as repayment of the loan depends on the ability of the exporter to perform on the production needed for the transaction. As mentioned, through this structure, an unacceptable risk is turned into an acceptable risk. The price risk of the underlying commodity is on the shoulder of the buyer.

Lengthen the supply chain

Nowadays, in lengthening the commodity supply chain finance, banks can make use of the strong relationship of commodity buyers with the commodity exporters, to create extra business with those exporters. Banks may get access to them and indirectly grant funds on relatively attractive terms as this is done on the basis of the rating of the better-rated commodity buyer from, for example, an OECD country. Pre-export finance fits into this concept precisely. This benefit extends to the risk management as the bank gets collateral under the agreement.

Asset-backed

With structured pre-export finance deals, the bank obtains collateral in the form of receivables that should result from sales contracts that are assigned to the bank, that is, the lending is, at least to some extent, backed by assets – the underlying commodity to be exported. This improves security for the bank, which should give the bank more comfort in providing the facility to the client. This asset may also improve competitiveness of the bank as it can offer relatively attractive rates based on the security it has.

Advantages for the borrowers

Structured pre-export finance brings a long range of benefits for clients as well, compared with clean lending structures.

Flexible disbursement

Disbursement can be flexible, but also linked to each new contract, shipment or warehousing. This will bring two advantages to the borrower: first, structured pre-export finance deals give borrowers cheap access to long-term financing as repayment can be linked to each new contract, shipment or warehousing. Second, as the bank is repaid with the proceeds from the underlying transaction, repayment can also take place along the actual use of the commodities that are financed.

Lower interest rates

As the structured pre-export finance mitigates the risk, the bank will, more comfortably, finance a company in a structured pre-export deal than in a clean (unsecured) lending deal, because of the security obtained by the bank related to the underlying commodities. This fact will result in a lower lending interest rate. Another aspect that may lower interest rate is that exporters, with their involvement in the structure, can make use of the better credit rating as (OECD) off-takers.

Related risks under pre-export finance

Commodity finance deals, after being carefully structured, are, however, not risk free. Next to potential benefits that banks as well as their clients may obtain from this form of financing, parties remain exposed to certain risks. The most important risks include the following:

- **Performance risk**: By assigning the export receivables to the lender, country risk and credit risk to the exporter are mitigated and the lenders are left with exposure to the borrower's performance risk. Performance risk is thus the vital element in this kind of lending. This is because, when the exporter does not perform his obligation and no transaction takes place, there will be no proceeds to pay back to the bank. Under such a structure, this performance risk is the major risk. It is common that this risk is covered by a local bank's performance guarantee.

- **Country risk**: Although country risk is partially mitigated by assigning the export receivables to the lender, certain country risk remains. We highlighted that transfer of the goods, though they do readily exist in that country, may be hindered. In the case when a sudden change in government policy makes it impossible to move goods out of the country, future sales proceeds might seriously be harmed as a potential buyer, who is supposed to take over the goods, must be found in the same country. A potential buyer being located outside the country will not be allowed to take up the commodity.

- **Price risk**: With commodity price fluctuation, price risk becomes an issue when the bank which owns the commodity as security will try to sell the commodities into the market to liquidate the commodities, to recover the lending. In such a case, it might not make use of the pre-agreed price in the sales contract with the original buyer and it is exposed to any changed market prices. When prices for the secured commodities have been decreasing dramatically, the bank will have a hard time recovering the total loan with the sale of the goods.

- **Event risk**: Exporters from emerging countries may be relatively vulnerable to external events like electricity shortages, strikes, floods, etc. These events can seriously harm the production activities and therefore the ability of exporters to perform on their obligations.

Trade finance facilities: ownership-based finance

Ownership-based finance

Ownership-based finance (OBF) is a form of commodity finance whereby the bank becomes the legal owner of the commodities and the economic risk is passed on to the bank. The bank will actually own these goods, until it is paid back by the client with the proceeds of the sale of these goods. This distinguishes ownership-based finance from other forms of commodity finance where the bank lends money against a pledge of commodities.

As one of the results of the financial crisis in 2008, there was a rise in ownership structures, especially for metal deals. These deals allow banks to purchase the inventory, either to sell it back to the producers at a later date, or to sell it to its off-taker.

For producers, ownership finance is an off-balance sheet solution whereas the enhanced security allows the bank to offer cheaper financing as ownership finance structures receive improved risk weighting under Basel II than transactional security.

In an OBF structure, the bank will rarely finance the total amount of the transaction. The ratio is maintained depending on:

- the quality of the commodity

- the liquidity of the commodity

- the liquidity and transparency of the market

- counter parties involved and so on.

The valuation is either on the market value of the goods or in a mark-to-market form (that is, the market value is being assessed periodically).

The margin, or the 'haircut'[14] as it is called, in the collateral value is a very important risk mitigant as it is the cushion for potential shrinking of value and/or miscalculation of the value. Sometimes when the collateral margins fall below a certain minimum, a customer is requested to provide additional collateral to enable the lending to continue. In a deal of US$70 m/m worth of goods, for example, US$50 m/m might be financed by the bank.

This ratio for financing, or so-called 'haircut', is determined on the basis of the following factors:

- Price volatility: This volatility of the price of respective commodities is an

---

14 Difference between the market value of the commodities and the amount of loan advanced against it. It is basically the margin between a commodity dealer's buying and selling prices.

important factor related to the market value of the commodity. It can be measured, for example, by the 40 latest price observations, which could be daily, weekly, monthly, etc. depending on the type of commodity.

- The liquidity of the commodities involved: The liquidity of the commodities will give a bank a flexible position to dispose of the assets as the bank wishes. The higher the liquidity of the relevant commodity, the easier for a commodity bank to get rid of it when it is necessary. The commodity bank will be more willing to finance the ownership of that commodity.

- Price risk: The extent to which the price of commodities is hedged will have impact on the certainty of the value of the commodity owned by the bank.

- Financial strength: The financial situation of the client (and the final off-taker) is relevant in cases when recourse is necessary.

The purpose of such a 'haircut' is to give the bank some comfort against a potential decline in the value of the underlying commodities. During the life of the transaction, the bank will have a legal title to the goods, until it is paid back by the client with the proceeds of the sale of these goods. This will generally happen within 12 months, depending on the nature of the commodity, the inventory turnover of the client and the forward market structure of the underlying commodity. If in the intervening period the market price of the collateral decreases, the bank can urge the client to pay the bank a certain amount of money extra, with the alternative of selling the goods to continue the structure.

In OBF the commodities can be bought from a client or from the client's supplier and can be re-sold to the client or to a third party. As the owner of commodities, the bank has a totally different position than as a lender, requiring it to take special care over its commodities: the loss and damage of the commodities will be the loss and damage of the direct assets of the bank.

The commodities, therefore, should be stored in acceptable warehouses, clearly segregated, insured against fire and theft, quality deterioration and other damages, and managed by a reputable warehouse operator. Market risk and other risks should be fully covered by acceptable counterparts.

OBF can be beneficial to the bank as it has ownership over the goods that are traded on independent secondary markets, thereby reducing its counterpart risk and improving its legal position. However, OBF is not supposed to be used as a means of balance sheet leveraging. The bank is also able to monitor the bank's position ('marked-to-market') on a regular basis. OBF provides clients with liquidity. Under certain conditions, clients can obtain off-balance financing structures.

Most OBF deals are often booked under specifically established bank's entities. Reasons for using separate entities can be regulatory (USA), tax (Chile) or, for instance, VAT (Netherlands).

Obviously, not every commodity deal can be structured as OBF. Usually, goods under OBF facilities have to be stored in countries which have an acceptable legal environment, such as OECD countries and/or in countries where the financing bank has an office. When goods are stored in other countries, they have to be well substantiated in the credit application.

Last but not least, ownership gives the bank extra responsibilities with regard to corporate social responsibility (CSR) and the environmental impact. Hence, many banks offer this facility to soft commodities.

Different forms of ownership-based finance

Within OBF structures the distinction can be made between the purchase of receivables and the purchase of commodities. Each of these can be performed in several forms, which will be discussed here.

There are several different forms of OBF with commodity purchase, of which the forms that are used most in practice will be discussed.

- Commodity repurchase agreement

- Commodity repurchase agreement with conditional off-taker

- Three-party agreement

- Cash and carry.

There are also other forms of OBF which are less common at the time of writing. Therefore, these forms will not be covered here.

- Intervention board cash and carry

- Commodity total return swap

- Commodity total return basis swap.

Commodity repurchase agreement

A commodity repurchase agreement (commodity repo) is a form of OBF in which the bank purchases commodities from a client and at the same time agrees to sell these goods back to the client at a pre-agreed price and time in the future (see Figure 3.5).

An option may be granted to the client to terminate the transaction at an earlier stage. The deal can also be structured in the form of a put option of the bank on the client. The commodities are initially purchased at their current value minus a haircut. This haircut should protect the bank against a sudden decrease in the value of the commodities and is determined on the basis of:

- the price volatility of the goods
- the (liquidity of the) commodities involved
- the extent to which the commodities are hedged
- the financial situation of the client (and the final off-taker).

Figure 3.5: Commodity repo

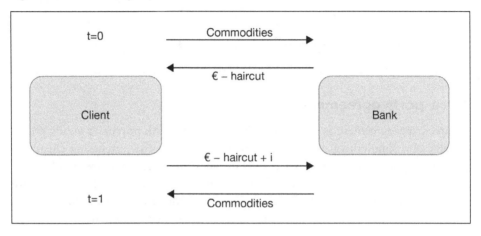

Example 3.5

Client sells to the bank 10.000 mt coffee at the current market price of US$1.600 per mt that is stored in a LIFFE warehouse. The client enters into an agreement with the bank to purchase this coffee after 180 days for US$16 m/m + cost + interest. Client will deposit US$1.6 m/m initial margin in a margin account to cover price risk exposure under the forward sale. Additional margin calls can be made. If the price of coffee increases, the initial margin may be released. However, the total funding to the client under this OBF structure will not exceed $16 m/m.

In some cases, where the credit risk of the client is considered to be too high, a conditional off-taker is added to the structure. This party will purchase the goods from the bank when the client defaults under its re-purchase obligations. In addition to the previous example, the bank would sign a conditional off-take agreement with a third party for US$1.600 per mt. If the client is unable to repurchase the goods the bank may sell the goods at a predetermined price and time to the conditional off-taker (Figure 3.6).

Figure 3.6: Commodity repo with conditional off-taker

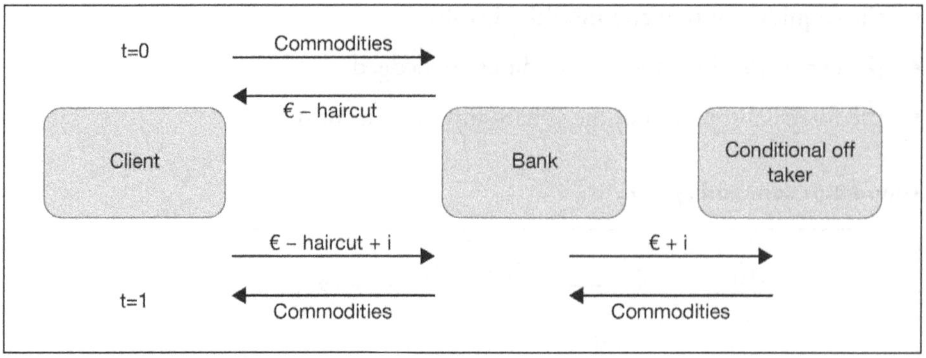

Three-party agreement

A three-party agreement is a form of OBF where the bank purchases goods from a supplier and simultaneously sells forward these goods to the purchasing client at a predefined price and at a predefined time in the future. This structure could also be reversed. In this case, the bank buys the goods from the client and sells them forward to a third party at a predefined price and at a predefined time in the future. Both structures offer the client the possibility of off balance sheet treatment.

A client may approach the bank to buy goods from his supplier and keep them on the balance sheet until they are sold to the client. In this case, the bank will know who it will sell the goods to as well as the timing of the sale. In the period that the bank is holding the goods, these are not on the balance sheet of the client.

Under OBF there is often no recourse on the client because the ownership of the goods by the bank (including the haircut margin) is supposed to be enough to cover the risk. There is no necessity to have such a condition that is disliked by the client. It is, therefore, important for the commodity finance bank to assess the ability of the third party in the transaction (supplier or off-taker) to honor its obligations.

Example 3.6

The supplier sells to the bank 10.000 mt coffee at the current market price of US$1.600 per mt that is stored in an approved warehouse in the name of the bank. The purchasing client enters into an agreement with the bank to purchase this coffee after 180 days for US$16 m/m + cost + interest. The purchasing client will deposit US$1.6 m/m initial margin in a margin account to cover price risk exposure under the forward sale. Additional margin calls can be made. If the price of coffee increases, the initial margin may be released, however the total funding to the client under this OBF structure will not exceed US$16 m/m. To avoid market risk the agreements between the supplier and the bank and between the bank and the purchasing client will be closed simultaneously.

Figure 3.7: Three-party agreement

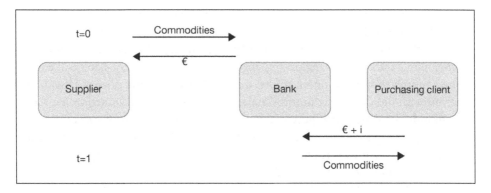

Cash and carry

Cash and carry is a form of OBF in which the bank purchases exchange traded commodities at the futures price minus the financing cost plus the cost of carry.

As in the three-party agreement structures, goods may be bought from the client as well as from the supplier of the client. The bank will then sell futures on these commodities at (acceptable) commodity exchanges. Goods will be delivered against sold futures contracts or in the market, depending on which option is more favourable. Cash and carry can be seen as an arbitrage transaction used to profit from price differences between the cash market and the futures market.

Contrary to the previous structures, the goods will need to be stored at exchange delivery warehouses and put under warrant of the respective commodity exchange. Furthermore, an independent party should confirm whether the stored goods are indeed of the quality and quantity described in the documents.

At any time during the transaction, the client may purchase the goods back at the market price. In this case, the funds received by the bank will be sufficient to cover any costs associated with closing out the bank's futures position.

If the client chooses not to exercise its option to purchase the goods back, they will be delivered into the futures exchange at the futures price. Because there is no certainty that the goods will return to the client in this structure, the client is actually able to treat the respective goods off balance sheet.

Example 3.7

> The client will sell to the bank 10.000 mt coffee at US$1.500 per mt. This price reflects the value of the goods at the LIFFE exchange, delivery in six months' time, minus the cost of warehousing, insurance and interest. The bank will enter into a futures short position for 10,000 mt of coffee at a futures price of US$1.600 per mt with delivery in six months' time. Settlement of the transaction is either six months after the initial purchase through delivery under the futures contract or through a repurchase from the client during the lifetime of the transaction at the prevailing futures price minus a reduced cost of carry, reflecting the cost of carry and margin owed to the bank.

Figure 3.8: Cash and carry

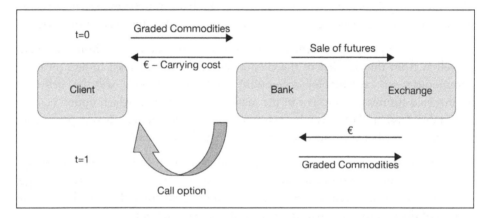

Warehouse finance

Warehouse financing is a form of inventory financing in which goods serve as collateral for the loan. The related commodities may be held in a public warehouse or stored on the premises of the borrower while controlled by a third party. Funds are granted to the borrower (for example a manufacturer), based on the goods on the warehouse receipt.

A warehouse receipt is a document that provides proof of ownership of commodities (for example, bars of copper) that are stored in a warehouse, vault, or depository for safekeeping. Warehouse receipts may be negotiable or non-negotiable. Negotiable warehouse receipts allow transfer of ownership of that commodity without having to deliver the physical commodity.

Most warehouse receipts are issued in negotiable form, making them eligible as collateral for loans. Non-negotiable receipts must be endorsed upon transfer. Warehouse receipts are regulated by the Uniform Warehouse Receipts Act.

Warehouse receipts also guarantee existence and availability of a commodity of a particular quantity, type, and quality in a named storage facility. It may also show transfer of ownership for immediate delivery or for delivery at a future date. Rather than delivering the actual commodity, negotiable warehouse receipts are used to settle expiring futures contracts.

Warehouse receipts may also indicate ownership of inventory goods and/or unfinished goods stored in a warehouse by a manufacturer or distributor.

As such, in commodity finance, warehouse receipts are actively used for commodity trade and commodity finance because it can be a negotiable document representing real commodity.

Lending with warehouse receipts as security gives comfort. This way the credit risk on the borrower is at least partially transferred to the underlying goods. Other than OBF where the main advantage was that goods could be taken off balance sheet by the borrower, warehouse finance is more about financing trade flow.

Warehouse finance, however, can also be a form of OBF. As a matter of fact, warehouse finance may be used for all transactions of (liquid) commodities that are required to be stored or remain idle for a period of time. It is a popular structure for commodities compared to other goods, because of the liquidity of most commodities.

Warehouse finance was initially used for traders who needed money to buy and sell. The goods are collateralized which should give some comfort to the bank. Every time the client wants to sell part of the goods he will have to ask the bank for permission to release part of the goods. This permission will generally only be obtained if the market price of the goods is stable or has gone up. In case the price has gone down, the borrower will usually have to pay extra when selling a part of the goods.

Example 3.8

A trader stores 100 tons of soybeans in a warehouse. The bank takes a security interest in the soybean in the form of a warehouse receipt. After the goods are inspected and found acceptable, the bank makes a loan to the trader on the basis of the stored soybean. This inspection could be performed by a collateral management agency. For every part that is sold then, the client should ask permission from the bank. If the bank regards the receivables coming from the transaction as acceptable, it will give a release order to the warehouse so the goods can be delivered to the buyer. The receivables paid by the buyer are then often paid directly to the bank after which the bank will pay out any excess funds to the borrower.

Advantages of ownership-based finance for the lending banks and the borrowers

OBF creates several advantages for the bank over other financing structures, which are discussed here.

Advantages of ownership-based finance for the lending banks

- **Actual ownership/collateral**: The first advantage of OBF is that the bank has actual ownership over the goods or receivables. This improves security as it may sell the goods or collect the receivables in the event that the client is not able to pay the bank back, i.e. the collateral is at the disposal of the lending bank. The 'haircut' further provides some margin to hold sufficient collateral even in the case of a (relatively small) decrease in the value of the goods. So there is actually relatively low credit risk on the client, as the risk is shifted to the goods that are held by the bank.

- **Economical capital**: Under the economic (regulatory) capital concept for different Basel regulations, one outstanding advantage for the bank is that OBF requires less economical capital than other financial solutions. As relatively less capital will have to be held against the facilities, this could significantly improve the return on solvency for the bank. This also has the benefit that the same solvency budget allows for higher and/or more facilities, given the fact that these facilities fit within the limits set by the bank.

- **Alternate financing possibilities**: The OBF structure creates possibilities for the bank to finance transactions, which could not have been financed in another structure due to the level of net exposure to the bank. Therefore, this structure may create room for alternative business for commodity banks, by broadening the range of clients, countries or types of transactions that may be financed. Risk related to the lending may be even further lowered in this structure when exposure is shifted to an insurance company or off-taker of the client. This risk decline is only the case when the insurance company or the final off-taker (to which exposure is shifted) has a higher credit rating than the client.

- **Downsides for the bank**: Apart from the above, OBF structures also have downsides for the bank. Most of these downsides will be discussed in the risk paragraph. Another downside, which will not be classified as a risk, is the fact that these structures often come along with intensive administrative processes. Hence, only medium or large deals are worth the effort and therefore in the interest of commodity banks.

Advantages of ownership-based finance for the borrowers

- **Off-balance sheet treatment**: The main benefit of this type of financing for the client/borrower is that the financial value of commodities may be removed from its balance sheet, which may lead to an improvement of balance sheet ratios. For this to actually happen, the transaction will have to be recognized as a true sale. An important aspect in this issue is how sure it is that the goods will be repurchased by the client at a later stage – the bank does not need the commodity anyway.

  In the coverage of several OBF structures this issue is handled as well, where a conditional off-taker is added to the structure to create the possibility that the goods are not transferred back to the client. This is still, however, an important aspect to look at when creating an OBF structure.

- **Alternate funding possibilities**: To the borrowers, OBF creates an alternate way for borrowers to obtain funds. The client has the possibility to actually obtain financing just on the basis of its inventory or receivables, although this is not the only product where this possibility is created for the client. This may also significantly improve the client's borrowing capacity and therefore the possibility to use the strength of a bank for any transactions.

Relevant issues on ownership-based finance

The risk issue

OBF, like other financial products, is not free of risks for the bank. The most important risk issues will be discussed here.

Ownership liability

As a result of the actual ownership by the bank in an OBF structure, the bank also takes on the liabilities of an owner, which is for a large part mitigated. This is because the client is supposed, in many cases, to still be responsible for storing, insuring and keeping safe the goods.

The facility/warehouse where the goods are stored needs to be safe against theft by reliable third parties, but also by the producer involved in the deal.

In practice so called 'leakage' is often a problem. The producer sends the warehouse receipts to the bank and then makes a deal with the warehouse to release the goods without the proper documents. The warehouse claims that the goods are stolen and the bank may only have worthless warehouse documents left, because the goods no longer exist.

To mitigate this risk, the bank can try to get insurance while the goods are in storage, although in practice this can be tough. A better way for banks to ensure the safety of the goods while in storage is to deal with official warehouse operators. These operators can be internationally known as collateral managers, but also state-owned or private companies. The goods stored in the warehouses are under their supervision. This increases the bank's control over the stored commodities and therefore has more security over the collateral.

Normally banks would require that the stored goods in the warehouse, used as collateral for a facility granted by the bank, are insured. Depending on the structure, this is either done by the client or the bank. In the case of insurance by the client, the bank is co-insured or the insurance policy is pawned to the bank.

Price risk

Not only may goods be stolen, perished or confiscated, there is also the risk of a significant decline in the value of the goods. When the value of the goods sinks under the level of the amount that is financed, both the level of collateral and the ability of the client to repay the bank with the proceeds will not be sufficient to cover the transaction. In this case, the bank will urge the client to pay the bank an amount of money that will partly compensate the decline in value – a kind of margin call.

If possible, this is done when the value of the goods is still sufficient to cover the transaction as the bank still has an 'escape' by selling the goods to a third party. Nonetheless, when setting up an OBF structure it is very important that the term of storage and the price volatility of the goods are taken into account and possibly hedged against and that the goods are correctly valued to start with! This risk is, of course, partly mitigated by imposing a haircut on the value of the goods that the bank is holding title to, as emphasized above.

The legal registration issue

In some cases, it may be very difficult or highly inefficient to physically manage the collateral. Lenders often settle for ownership on paper. A bank in the Netherlands, for example, which has a pledge on the inventory of a certain company located in the rainforest of Brazil, will have a hard time physically managing the collateral.

When settling ownership on paper, it is, however, very important to have clear and complete documentation. If something goes wrong in the transaction and the lending bank is not able to provide complete documentation on its rights and title, the bank will have a hard time enforcing these rights in court.

An important issue is therefore to what extent the lender can secure its title to the goods involved. The lender will need to create a 'ring fence' around the collateral. One way to further strengthen the evidence of ownership, is registering ownership certificates with a national authority. In the Netherlands, for example, registration of certificates at the Tax and Customs Administration is possible to, at least, prove its existence on the day of registration.

The lack of an appropriate legal, regulatory and institutional environment could seriously harm the security that the ownership of the goods may give to the bank. Especially in the emerging countries where such conditions might be lacking, it makes these countries unsuitable for OBF structures.

There are, indeed, much fewer OBF facilities (or none) in emerging market countries, only due to the fact that there is a lack of a good legal environment there. And even in countries with quality legislation, there is the danger of corruption. If judges can easily be bribed, a good legislation will not (necessarily) create a good legal system where property rights can effectively be enforced.

These are not the only ownership issues for this form of financing. A silo of wheat, for example, may contain a lot more wheat than you have title to. You might own 30% of what the silo contains. In some countries (like the Netherlands), however, you have to be able to show exactly what you own. In practice this means that you have to be able to show which piece of wheat is yours and which is not, otherwise the goods are owned by no one and you might have difficulty in exercising your title to the goods in the case when your client gets into trouble. In these conditions it is, therefore, very important that the goods are stored separately!

The cases described above show examples where the legislation in place makes some countries unsuitable for OBF. There are also cases where legislation actually makes OBF more suitable than other structures like a pledge. In Spain and Belgium, for example, a structure with a pledge requires very complex processes and procedures, making an OBF structure more attractive for all parties involved.

True sale issue

Another important issue around OBF is that transactions may be regarded (by the auditor or curator in the case of the bankruptcy of the client) as a normal loan instead of a 'true sale'. This has implications for both the lending bank and the client.

The client, in case of the lack of true sale recognition, may not remove the respective goods from its balance sheet, while this is one of the main benefits for the client in an OBF structure. An addition of a third party to the transaction might help in this case.

The bank could give a credit line to an independent third party which uses this credit to buy the goods from the trader. The goods will be stored in an independent warehouse and the third party receives the warehouse receipts. The bank buys the goods from the third party and receives the warehouse receipts. Finally, the trader has found a seller for the goods and buys back the goods from the bank. The seller receives the warehouse receipts and the bank gets repaid.

The lack of true sale recognition may implicate the bank when the borrower gets into trouble. In this case, the bank may want to exercise its ownership and sell the goods to cover the outstanding loan. But when the curator considers the goods as the property of the client instead of the bank, the facility is regarded as a 'normal' loan and the goods are confiscated by the curator.

There are certain precautions a bank could take to prevent such events, although legislation and treatment on these issues are constantly changing and different per country. One precaution is that the bank takes care of the insurance for the goods. This could help showing that these goods are indeed owned by the bank. A second one is that the bank has full control over the goods. This could be very impractical in some cases. When, for example, wheat is stored in large silos on the property of the client, trucks could come and go every day to pick up a part of the storage for delivery to off-takers. It would be very inefficient if every time this happens, the bank would have to give permission for release of the goods.

Liquidity of the commodities involved

To a great extent, the liquidity of a commodity depends on whether or not it is listed on a commodity exchange. When no liquid markets exist, it may be very difficult to sell the commodities and, therefore, it may not be advisable to involve the respective commodity in an OBF transaction. The lending bank might hold collateral, but when it is almost impossible to sell this, it hardly offers any security.

An important aspect, when setting up an OBF structure but also during the life of the transaction, is the level of liquidity of the commodities involved. This does not mean that unlisted commodities are not liquid at all. Frozen concentrated orange juice, for example, is less liquid than most listed commodities but still has substantial liquidity. Liquidity exists as long as there are buyers willing to take over the goods.

During the life of the transaction, liquidity could be impacted in several ways. Due to political changes, for example, it might become very difficult to get the respective goods out of the country where they are stored. This could affect the possibility of selling the goods to realize the market value and, therefore, the liquidity of the collateral for the bank.

Another example is a change of ownership of the borrowing party or a possible bankruptcy. In the case of the latter, goods might be temporarily confiscated by the curator. This would then (temporarily) remove the ability of the bank to sell the goods which may cause severe damage when the price of the goods significantly decreases in the respective period. Such a risk can be mitigated by actually renting the storage facility from the client. For example, goods might be stored in a silo, which is rented by the bank, situated on the client's property.

Issues linked to a special category of commodity

In OBF there are some issues a commodity bank must deal with. They are linked to some commodities due to their unique characteristics.

Commodities processed by the client

Holding unprocessed goods as collateral may form a significant risk, with possible consequences both for the claim of ownership and the ability to sell the goods. One reason is that unprocessed goods are more liquid than processed goods, as the range of possible uses of the goods is larger in this state. This, however, does not hold for all states of the process and for all types of commodities.

The process might be at a later stage where the goods still need to be processed by the client to be of any use. If the client holding these goods goes bankrupt, these goods might be worthless without the last step in the production phase. The bank can hardly finish this process itself and it might be difficult finding an off-taker for these goods. This might be the case for the production of cheese, for example.

The case of cheese production can also show possible consequences for a claim to ownership. A client may have a certain amount of milk stored, which serves as collateral for the facility that is granted by the bank. This is, however, turned into a completely different product – cheese. Does the bank then still hold title to the cheese, and if it does, to what amount?

More or less the same holds for the case where the bank finances receivables. Receivables may be paid out to an account that the bank cannot get to. The bank holds title to the receivables, but these actually do not exist anymore.

The warehouse may include both finished goods and raw materials or semi-finished goods. The collateral is then subject to fluctuation, in which case it is essential to be able to monitor the stored goods at any time to be able to follow any developments. A commodity bank must have commodity knowledge on the collaterals held by the bank.

Commodities that are perishable and the storage of them

In OBF, storage is obviously another key concern. Although the bank holds title documents to its collateral, there may still be uncertainty whether these goods actually are physically stored in the same quantity and quality on the agreed location during the life of the transaction.

Goods may disappear or may not preserve in the way that was agreed in the agency agreement. This risk depends on the quality and the level of independence of the warehouse where the goods are stored. To be able to monitor this, often collateral management and inspection agencies are used.

These agencies manage the whole chain from, for example, the point of harvesting to delivery to the final off-taker. The use of such agencies is less common when dealing with large traders that feel that they have sufficient knowledge and experience to deal with these issues themselves.

Instead of using these external agencies, there could also be a service agreement between the bank and the borrower (or between the bank and the warehouse), where all the responsibilities of the client with regard to the stored goods is described.

Certain types of commodities (especially soft commodities) are not good for collateral purposes because they perish rapidly, or are very sensitive to different environment conditions. When financing these goods in an OBF structure, the risk may be too high that the goods that the bank holds title to will become consequently worthless. That is why perishable goods like vegetables and fruit are unsuitable and often not financed with an OBF structure.

A question often asked is what is the difference between OBF and lending based on commodity as collateral?

In essence, OBF means that the financing bank has the legal right to possess or take possession of an asset: ownership is legal title to the goods whereas possession is physical control. The key point for OBF is to take legal title and physical control.

For the financing bank, the legal structure under ownership finance is to have a simple legal structure in place. Therefore, liquidation is quick and simple. The capital relief may be realised with certain ownership structures.

Lending with assets as security is different in the sense that security is sometimes more vulnerable to attack by a liquidator.

The legal structure must be in writing and 'perfected'. Security needs to be proved before it can be enforced.

For commodity traders, OBF may achieve off-balance sheet treatment. And risk of losses or damage to goods remains with the financing bank, whereas lending based on collateral will maintain the risk responsibility of loss or damage with the client rather than with the lending bank.

Supply chain finance

Supply chain finance: the concept

The supply chain concept is a management term used originally in logistics. When we use this in commodity finance, it is not a single product but a synthesis of many products in the commodity flow.

Supply chain finance (SCF) is a relatively new, upcoming concept of finance. Though a logistic concept, the supply chain can be approached from a financial perspective as well in commodity finance.

SCF is served for two purposes: to expand the business scope and to better mitigate the risk. The latter will be discussed more in detail in Chapter 5.

There is no uniform method of SCF, but the concept basically consists of a set of solutions for financing specific goods or activities in different parts of the supply chain of commodity.

A typical supply chain for agricultural products will start with individual farmers who would sow the seeds to grow that commodity. After the harvest season, they may store this commodity in their silos before selling to a larger trading house such as Louis Dreyfus, Cargill and Bunge. These commodity companies will then sell the soft commodity to a food producer and this food producer will use it as raw material to produce a product ready to be consumed by an end-user.

For energy products, the exploration and extraction of crude oil from an onshore or offshore location starts the supply chain. The next is the transportation and storage. Very often, the crude oil will be refined into a variety of products such as gasoline. The refined product will be delivered to a special location for a wholesale purchaser or to a gas station for the end-user to buy.

From a commodity bank's perspective, the key point here is the physical and informational control, created by a greater insight in the total supply chain. By lengthening the chain in finance, all parties in the chain may benefit when you take into account that each company's profitability is affected by the ability of its suppliers and customers.

Instead of just financing an existing, 'isolated' client – very often the 'trading company' – a bank might also serve other parties in the supply chain, upstream as well as downstream, producer of the commodity as well as the processor or the end-user of the commodity and so on.

The rationale is obvious. First of all, this broadens the network of the bank, creating new possibilities to earn money. It also provides a possibility for the bank to spread the risk it is exposed to. By being involved in a large part of the supply chain, the bank may develop a good view of the flow of goods and cash in the process and, therefore, may get a good idea of the different risks that it could be exposed to.

Figure 3.9: Expanding the service along the supply chain

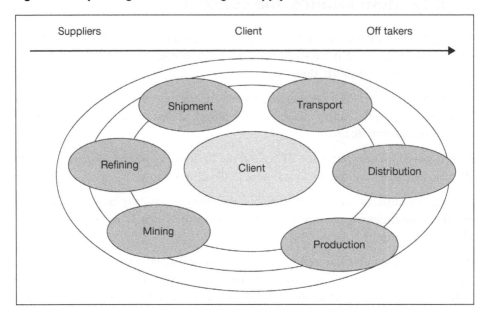

To commodity trading companies, SCF may offer financial solutions that enable them to lower costs and create financial stability in their total supply chain, while also creating deeper and broader customer relations.

Banks want to be involved from the phase where the client purchases goods and materials to the phase where it exports the goods. By doing this, the bank can finance both the buying side of a transaction and the selling side while also getting a better insight into the activities and flows within the supply chain. In this structure, a bank might act as the temporary payer of the invoice that the client receives, thereby freeing money for the supplier which may be used for further investments. Then the client will eventually pay the bank.

As noted before, some companies that can afford this due to their size may try to shift their financial risks and costs to their suppliers by negotiating more attractive payment conditions. There may be cases, however, where this is not a good solution for these companies.

Suppliers from emerging markets, for example, may have severe working capital problems when these payment terms are adjusted in favor of the buyer. To solve this, some companies, in collaboration with their banks, have created a platform which provides the following:

- All the invoices that have been approved by the company are added to the platform.

- Suppliers will have insight, through this platform, when the invoices will be paid.

- There is also an option to approach a bank to directly pay the invoice amount to the supplier (at a discount). The bank will know that the invoice is already approved by the buyer.

- The bank will then be willing to finance the invoice payment based on the credit rating of the buyer (which is often higher than the suppliers' rating in this case).

- The buyer will finally pay the bank when the payment term has expired.

In such a case, SCF spreads credit costs along the supply chain by making use of the buyer's superior credit rating to its suppliers, while taking care of a more reliable supply base and, therefore, mitigating performance risk that the buyer is exposed to. Such a difference in credit worthiness may be especially large with emerging market-based suppliers. All parties are able to benefit from this construction.

First, suppliers are quickly provided with working capital at a relatively low rate. Second, because of this benefit to the supplier, the buyer will be able to negotiate lower prices or more attractive payment terms. Third, the bank has created extra revenues. Of course, there are many other events in the process which the bank may be involved in.

A commodity bank can increase its focus on international trade flows with an emphasis on repetitive trade flows from origin to destination, lengthening involvement in the chain and increasing revenues per transaction. Ideally, activities of one client (trader) throughout the supply chain are financed by the bank, limiting the counterparties to one which should give the bank a good insight in the timing of the flows and the risks involved in the chain.

This is especially attractive within the energy sector where transactions are often in huge amounts. Commodity banks are actively seeking to expand its SCF activities for both risk and revenue purposes. The energy sector is an attractive market for commodity banks to expand. Some commodity loads are even sold seven times, which makes it highly attractive for involvement along the chain.

SCF may be offered at the different stages (chains) of commodity trade flow. The following summarizes different opportunities (relevant products) to banks to serve the different financing needs of clients at each stage:

- Finance before production
  - Chain: capital machinery > purchase of raw material/equipment
  - Finance: project finance, pre-export finance, buy backs/counter trade,

equipment leasing, and joint venture production

- Finance during production/inventory

  - Chain: production, tolling, processing

  - Finance: pre-export finance, tolling finance

  - Chain: commodity transportation, arrival in port warehouse

  - Finance: inventory finance, warehouse receipts finance, structured finance

  - Chain: post shipment

  - Finance: shipping document finance, supplier credit finance

- Finance in the post-production/post shipment period

  - Chain: the buyer has received the goods

  - Finance: reversed receivable finance, LC negotiation, factoring, forfaiting, insuring the buyer, ECA credit, asset-backed pool securitization

Advantages of supply chain finance solutions for the lending banks and the borrowers

Advantages of supply chain finance solutions for the lending bank

This type of financing can have major benefits for banks involved in commodity trading. SCF may give banks extra control in the trade process, making financing more straightforward.

Increased access to information

By being involved in a large part of the supply chain process, the commodity finance bank has access to a range of information on the timing of the flow of goods and cash. This overall view may give the bank a good insight into the performance of its counterparties and any of the risks involved in the process. Increased knowledge about the timing of trade flows of the counterparty may reduce the perceived credit risk that the bank is exposed to.

The increased access to information should give the bank some comfort in providing the funds which may result in increasing the amount of the facility while lowering the interest rates at which the funds are provided. This may give the bank a more competitive position relative to other banks that are operating by one-to-one relations in the client's sector.

The bank can also be much more flexible in granting credit to their clients. For example, the bank may rely more on an open account payment method rather than on documentary collection structures.

Expand business opportunities

Expanding the focus from the client on a stand-alone basis to its suppliers and customers creates extra business opportunities for the bank, simply because the suppliers of the customers may become qualified future clients of the bank. Extra opportunities are created through the larger network (customer base) that the bank is operating in. Moreover, the information available to the bank creates funding possibilities for deals that could otherwise not have been financed.

Given risks are better identified, they may be transformed from an unacceptable to an acceptable risk. Deals may be combined and structured over several different steps in the process, as we discussed in pre-export finance. Through these factors, SCF may help the bank to expand their business horizon to emerging markets where commodity trading is growing rapidly, with a lot of economic expansion. Especially in these markets, this SCF may be very attractive for banks as these markets are often less transparent and expose banks to higher risks than those of more developed markets.

Apart from these benefits for the bank, it could also create attractive profits. It becomes attractive in some commodity deals, as loads are repeated in this chain. A boat of oil might be sold six or seven times in some cases. The commodity bank, being involved in all these transactions, will get multiple profits.

Not only do risks decline over the whole supply chain but also the workload of due diligence done by the bank for providing finance declines. The commodity bank gets more control over the process and is more motivated to repeat financing the transaction. In the whole chain, you can make more money by financing more transactions in the chain, while basically taking the same or even a lower amount of risk.

However, in order to be able to provide all solutions and products, the commodity finance bank must be a very big bank, to successfully carry out this strategy on a continuing basis. This is because the commodity finance bank not only serves a large range of customers but also customers with a full range of products, which may well be beyond the commodity finance banks' existing activities.

Customer relationship

Compared with many other commodity finance products, SCF is more than just supplying credit on a transactional basis. It aims at a more sustainable relation between the bank and the client from which both parties are able to benefit. Involvement in the client's supply chain, upstream as well as downstream, may increase the volume of business with clients and strengthen ties with them.

First, as has been discussed before, the bank has the ability to offer funding at relatively attractive rates, which may lower costs for the client and create extra opportunities to expand his business. The client tends to stay with the finance bank. Second, by providing the client's trade partners with financial solutions, financial performance of the client may further be improved as a result of increased financial stability in the supply chain. So, not only may the current relation with the client be positively affected, it may also boost the client's performance, from which both the bank and the client may benefit in the future.

Banks could take this idea one step further by using the information on the total process within the supply chain to help its customers. For example, a bank may warn its client who is investing in a mine development, if the demand for that commodity is supposed to drop sharply.

As a result of the uncertainty of several supply chain transactions, customers might be forced to hedge this by holding extra inventory. By making the supply chain more transparent and visible for all parties, this extra inventory might not be necessary to hold and customers are more able to switch to a 'just-in-time inventory', lowering the required working capital for the business. The same holds for hedging uncertainty by holding an excess amount of cash.

Risk management

One of the most important motivations for offering SCF products is risk management. As discussed before, involvement in different parts of the supply chain may give the bank a clear insight into the performance of its counterparties and any of the risks involved in the process. Long before the supply chain concept was introduced, risk management in the bank would have been searching for information of the upstream and downstream performance anyway, to mitigate the risk of the deal financed.

Except for a better risk determination, SCF may also create a natural hedge. When you partly control extracting activities from a mine, you have more certainty about the ability of the end producer (who is a client) to obtain the respective commodities that are required as inputs.

Advantages of supply chain finance to the borrowers

Due to globalization and increased cross-border production activity, supply chains have been broadened and many companies have seen a growing need for working capital. As this affects suppliers as well, this also influences other parts of the value chain.

For example, more attractive payment terms are negotiated by companies that may afford that due to their size, partly shifting the working capital problems and increasing risk in the supply chain. SCF solutions may counter this problem by offering financial solutions to parties along the supply chain and by collecting information on activities in the total chain.

Increased funds at lower rates

Information on activities in the total chain may provide the bank with a good insight into the risk that it is exposed to. Together with possible physical control over the goods by the lender, this may positively affect the comfort at which funds are extended to their borrowers. This may first increase the amount of funds that borrowers can obtain. Second, this may also increase the negotiation power of the borrower and affect the rates at which funds are provided, in favor of the borrower.

Reliable supply base

As noted before, each company's profitability is affected by the ability of its suppliers and customers to efficiently raise funds. Therefore, involvement of the bank on both sides of the supply chain may help clients by providing their trade partners with funds or by monetizing their inventory to free money for further investments. This should create a more reliable supply (and customer) base for the client by lowering performance risk and credit risk on the one hand and simply facilitate activities of their supplier and customers on the other.

Optimize supply chain

Via SCF, clients may get access to information through their bank that otherwise would have been unobtainable to them. This information may significantly help clients with their inventory and cash management. Often, supply chain managers hedge against uncertainty in the supply chain by holding more inventory and more cash. This way, the probability that the company will get to the point where inventory is too low to be able to match demand is kept as low as possible within certain ranges of efficiency.

The lack of supply chain visibility could have a negative impact on the financial productivity of the firm. SCF may partly solve this inefficiency by providing the client with information on its pool of suppliers and customers, making the timing and reliability of trade and cash flows more transparent and predictable. This facilitates the use of 'just-in-time inventory management'.

Besides improvements in internal management, SCF structures may also help companies to get closer to their key suppliers, thereby strengthening their strategic relationship and providing a way of possibly lowering costs of capital for *both parties* involved.

Solve the lack of developed capital markets in countries of production

In the commodity community, many companies are making use of suppliers from developing countries. They import commodities from emerging market countries. In some cases, these suppliers are not able to offer favorable payment terms due to undeveloped capital markets. This may increase the production costs of the companies significantly. This problem can be countered by financing these suppliers, with credit risk on the more reliable importer. Receivables are then financed with payback from the importer directly to the bank. This may benefit the supplier, importer and the bank through respectively relatively low costs of financing, more attractive payment terms and extra business opportunities.

Risks involved with supply chain finance

As for any financial product, certain risks have to be taken in order to make any profit. The same for SCF since, apart from the benefits to all parties, the commodity bank is exposed to certain risks.

Performance risk

By being involved in different stages of the supply chain, the bank is able to spread the risk that it is exposed to. The bank is, however, still exposed to performance risk.

Performance risk is the risk that the company is not able or willing to perform the obligations and deliver the goods. When the company no longer produces the goods or provides the service, the off-taker will no longer pay and there is no cash flow to repay the debt. This may paralyze the whole supply chain.

This, however, does not necessarily mean that every facility in the rest of the chain provided by the bank is equally hurt. When a facility just consists of financing the purchase of raw materials, for example, the only effect is that no raw materials will be transferred and thus that the facility is not used. The only loss for the bank is a loss of business in this case and not a loss resulting from a default of the client.

Country risk

The supply chain approach extends the reach of the financing banks to new markets. The bank, under the supply chain structure, will have to acquire extra country risk. Any changes in the business environment of the borrower's country can seriously affect its operating profits and the value of its assets. These could be changes in currency controls, regulatory changes, or geopolitical factors.

Any changes could affect the value of the goods (receivables) as well as the liquidity of the goods. It may become almost impossible to get the goods or funds involved out of the country, for example.

Financing unprocessed goods

When financing different stages of the supply chain, there are a lot of unprocessed or partly processed goods involved. The collateral is therefore subject to fluctuation (also within the hands of the same client) and not always easy to value. In this case, it is essential to be able to monitor the stored goods at any time to be able to follow any developments.

Supply chain finance application: a case of supply chain finance for copper

To illustrate SCF for a commodity bank, an example is chosen to see how the supply chain leads to the production of a certain end product in which copper is an important component.

The activities in this supply chain range from extracting the copper from the El Chino Mine in Mexico to the use of refined copper in the production of final goods.

Figure 3.10: Supply chain copper production process

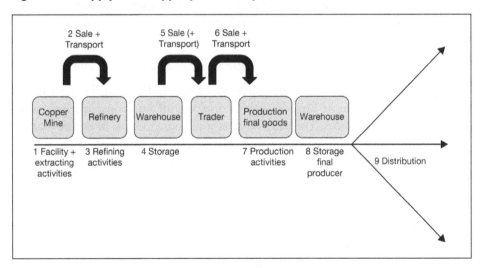

A sample of possible financial products that may be used to finance the different activities within the supply chain will be discussed very briefly, as most of these products are treated separately in other chapters. The discussion on SCF here is divided into several phases:

Stage 1: A Mexican mining company extracts scrap copper from the El Chino Mine chain contract signed for the supplier to deliver copper as raw material in a pre-agreed period of time.

- During this period, a commodity finance bank could provide pre-export finance in the form of financing the extracting activities, including the purchase of equipment, recruiting skilled or non-skilled labor where the extracting activities can take place, etc. The financing facility is based on the expected amount of scrap copper to be extracted over a certain period and any existing sales contracts that can be presented to the bank. To ensure repayment, the bank may use the receivables created by the sales.

Stage 2: The scrap copper is sold and transported to the USA for refinement.

- The bank could provide finance to fund the refinement activities based on the expected amount of refined copper and any existing sales contracts that can be presented to the bank.

- The bank could provide finance to the refining company in the form of financing purchases of raw materials, labor costs and overhead costs. Transport may be financed backed by a BL, air waybill, truck receipt, etc., as security for the bank. Receivables financing may be provided to the seller in this deal, by financing the invoices up to the time of payment.

Stage 3: Copper is refined in the USA.

- End products are produced using the copper as a component. The copper is stored in a warehouse. End products are distributed and sold to the final customer(s). All post-finance products can be offered.

Stage 4: The refined copper is stored in a warehouse until the party is sold to a trader.

- The bank could provide a form of inventory finance. The refined copper that is stored in warehouses is financed against a pledge of warehouse receipts issued by warehouse operators. The bank receives warehouse receipts to ensure that the goods are available to the bank in case of default by the borrower.

Stage 5: The refined copper is possibly transported and sold to a trader (Figure 3.11).

- For the process so far, the bank could also provide a tolling facility. This structure involves a range of companies in the supply chain. Such a tolling facility finances the raw materials for the initial supplier and the transport to the refinery. The facility is secured by the receivables that are created from export to the final user. So the bank actually controls the purpose of the loan.

Figure 3.11: Tolling facility

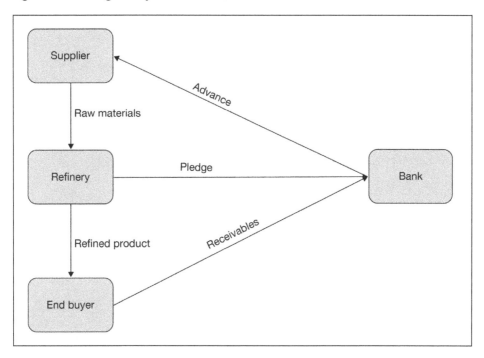

The above solutions not only provide an example of the possible financial products, but also show how the bank may be involved in the whole process throughout the supply chain.

In times of high uncertainty with regard to the financial performance of parties in the global trading environment and their counterparties, SCF may be very useful to institutions, especially those big and ambitious commodity banks, which provide financing to these parties.

As discussed in this chapter, SCF may provide banks with a better insight in the timing of trade flows and possible risks throughout the supply chain. This may create financing opportunities for the bank as well as for potential clients.

Especially during the time when world trade is slowing and demand for commodities has decreased significantly, banks may want to obtain more business from their existing client map to extend their service further up as well as down the supply chain.

Nevertheless, as noted before, a bank needs to be of significant size to successfully provide financing throughout the supply chain – it not only serves a large range of customers, but also a range of customers with different financial needs. This is not a possibility for smaller banks.

CHAPTER 4

Country Risk and Bank Risk and Letters of Credit in Commodity Finance

Country risk and bank risk

Country risk and bank risk are essential in commodity finance. Companies can go bankrupt. If a bank lends to a company, the lending bank takes company risk – the risk of non-payment from the company. If a loan is lent to a bank, the risk is of non-payment by the bank.

Similarly, lending to a country may face non-payment of that sovereignty country, either due to the country's foreign exchange capacity or its willingness to pay. This is called country risk.

To many, bank risk is concrete whereas country risk is remote or more macro. Country risk is more obvious in a country's foreign debt obligation. It is, in fact, the risk of loss to a cross-border exposure or position caused by events that can be outside the scope of control of a single debtor. The concept of country risk evaluates both the capacity and willingness to pay or repay.

Under what situation can a country become insolvent? For domestic currency, the central bank of the country is supposed to produce and control the issuance of the currency to honor the domestic debt, although over-printing will have inflation, as we know. Nevertheless, for foreign currencies, a country may have difficulties in honoring its foreign currency obligation when there is a shortage of such hard currencies. Default of foreign debts may also be linked to a change of regime. The new government does not want to honor the payment obligation of the previous government.

For most emerging market countries, their currencies are not freely convertible. Shortage of hard currencies can make their international payment obligation difficult or not possible. They may have to ask for permission of payment delay, rescheduling of the payment or a total waive of the payment.

By its nature, commodity finance is very much emerging-market oriented, as many emerging market countries are exporting soft, hard commodities or crude oil to get hard currency for their economic development. Commodities are often produced in countries, or associated with countries, which have high 'political' and 'economic' risks. The USA is perhaps the only exception as it both imports and exports commodities.

The discussion on commodity finance is thus often associated with the concept of country risk. After all, commodity finance banks set a 'country limit' to emerging markets as a kind of 'cap' to limit the maximum exposure to a specific country.

There are two categories of lending to commodity producers in emerging markets: either a short-term transactional finance or longer term structured ones such as a kind of pre-export finance (for example, import of equipment for commodity production) or a kind of project finance (for example, in the case of the development of mines and/or minerals) which, obviously, involves country risk. Either short-term commodity finance or long-term ones may have country risk involved. Payments due being blocked by government foreign exchange control, or confiscation of joint ventures assets are all good examples.

Many commodity finance cases indicate that country risk has a concrete impact on commodity trading. In general, an instable economic, political, legal and/or social situation may disturb the expected flow of goods based on which banks provide their finance. Examples of country risk include: the risk that a government ban will prohibit goods to be exported; the risk that export tariffs deteriorate the collateral value or make the goods less saleable after export; the risk that commercial conflict is not properly and fairly settled due to loopholes in the local legal system; and the risk that sudden intervention from the government disrupts the established contractual obligation.

Country risk consideration is critical for commodity finance in LC confirmation and discounting, pre-export finance, warehouse finance either OBF or lending-based finance, and project finance as we have seen.

Lending to commodity traders also involves bank risk if the traders are located in a developed country but have import exposure from emerging markets.

The relevance of bank risk for emerging markets to commodity finance lies in the fact that, in commodity finance, the commodity traders are eager to let someone take over risks related to their export/import business, especially the bank and country risk.

Commodity trading still relies very much on the bank credit products as LCs, guarantee and so on, even though we do see an increasing volume of open account activity in this sector too.

Some developed countries have export-import banks and export insurance agencies specialized in this kind of business, especially for long-term deals, whereas commercial banks are doing more for short-term business.

Why are banks willing to take over the payment risk – involving both bank risk and country risk – for so-called 'difficult countries'? This is because trade finance is to finance trade flow by controlling, one way or another, the proceeds under the flow of goods. It is usually collateralized finance – there is a flow of goods along with the payment of money.

If there is anything unique about commodity finance vis-à-via trade finance, it is the liquidity of commodities in the market. Commodities, especially those listed on the commodity exchanges, offer a very transparent price system and thus provide very liquid trading opportunities. Moreover, if a commodity is considered to be the key or strategic export of the country, it may receive favorable treatment for payment from the government in respect of foreign exchange availability and political risk, during a crisis situation.

This offers a great chance for lenders to use the underlying commodity to liquidate its lending position in case of need. Against such a background, commodity finance banks look more into the legal link to the proceeds of the trade, instead of only focusing on traditional financial analysis of the borrower's financial strength.

The concern for commodity finance banks may shift to the performance of the borrower vis-à-via the commodity. That results in the lender's interest in the potential capacity of the borrower to export, as this capacity itself represents the future repayment capacity. Such a rationale makes commodity finance possible for many 'difficult' countries. And the analysis and monitoring on country risk is a must for commodity banks.

The concept of country risk is a long-standing one. The challenge nowadays is that, while the risk of political turbulence can be foreseen, the unfolding scenario of a political crisis is generally unpredictable. Under the broad globalization background, the next crisis is unlikely to be contained to one single country and will therefore require a strong degree of international coordination.

For country risk, short term and long term will make a difference. In the short term, country risk is more predictable for quick turnover transactional finance, since the probability/chance of being caught in event risk will be less, other things being equal. In the long-tenor commodity deals, country risk is handled by other monitoring/mitigation means. Especially in the case of the import of equipment from developed countries, export credit agency (ECA) cover is used. ECA cover refers to the utilization of the export finance agency's facility to cover part of the equipment buyer's payment risk.

The uncertainty over financing commodity exported from emerging markets presents a challenge to many banks. Sorting out what in the recent decade is cyclical and what is structural in emerging markets' banks and countries is a most complex question on which a lot of bank finance – through the evolution of risk-adjusted return – depends.

For bank risk, the often discussed instrument is an LC. Under an LC, payment of the commodity buyer is based on the strength of the LC issuing bank, because the payment undertaking has shifted from the buyer to the LC issuing bank. Nowadays shipment for US$60–100 m/m of commodity value is common. The classic LC business for these high-value commodity traders is also the focus of many commodity finance banks.

Confirming and discounting receivables under export LCs issued by banks becomes core business for commodity finance banks. Hence, both bank and country risk should be an indispensable subject on the agenda of commodity finance. This chapter is thus devoted to this special subject.

Practical issues for country risk in a commodity finance bank

In theory, country risk is the probability of non-payment/delayed payment for a country. More precisely, it refers to the willingness or ability for a sovereign to honor its external debt. In daily practice, country risk concept goes beyond that.

There is plenty of established literature and practice for the concept of country risk. Similar to the rating for a corporate, the credit rating for a country is intended to measure the overall repayment capacity for a sovereign debt. The credit rating will help facilitate the issuance of sovereign debts in the capital markets. It also determines the cost of the debt issuance.

To a commodity finance bank, the study and credit rating of bank and country risk will help to evaluate a maximum credit exposure to a country.

In a domestic context, when a company is unable or unwilling to repay a loan, a bank as a claim holder may get access to legal action using bankruptcy courts to recoup at least a portion of its original lending. By comparison, a foreign company may be unable to repay the debt, due to the fact that the authorities of the country prohibit payments or limit the payment because of foreign currency shortages or political turmoil. Sovereign borrowers, that is, the government itself, may face insolvency in terms of foreign currency due to the macro-economy difficulties in the country. These events will have an impact on the balance sheet of a commodity bank which has cross-border lending.

For such a rationale, banks usually evaluate the sovereign counterparties, that is, the countries they are doing business with, just like they evaluate other obligors for lending. They set a limit to their total lending exposure to a country.

For banks one measure which is used to manage the lending risk is to set a limit for a borrower. This is the same for a country. Sovereign risk rating is used as a reference for decision making on country exposure and monitoring it thereafter.

We know that banks may face a short-term shortage of funding (liquidity problem) or long-term disability to honor payment (insolvency). Similarly, a country may face both liquidity and insolvency risks, that is, shortage of foreign currencies to honor the debt immediately due, or totally unable to pay (default) its foreign currency debts. Hence, country liquidity risk means the extent to which countries are exposed to the risk of sudden and prolonged disruption for external finance.

In a way, vulnerability to a prolonged shortage of funds is what distinguishes emerging market economies from mature economies, although this macro-economic picture changes a lot after the 2008 financial turmoil. The developed countries may experience imbalances but are extremely unlikely to face disruptions in external finance.[15] The key lesson learned from the 1990s is that fixed exchange rate policy, autonomous monetary policy and free capital flows cannot co-exist for long.

Commodity finance banks dealing a lot with various forms of financial products typically set maximum total exposure allowed for a particular country, so that their potential losses will be limited.

The setting of a country limit is part of the management of country risk. It indicates the maximum exposure the bank is willing to hold for that specific country.

Setting a country limit is an important but a complicated task. Understandably, decision errors may occur when the rating system predicts that a country will get into problems whereas in fact it does not, or the rating system predicts that a country will stay clear of problems whereas in fact it ends up in trouble. These will lead to potential loss of earnings or loss of business opportunities for banks. Commodity banks must have country risk professionals to set the country limit under which they have their exposure to financing commodity trade.

Country limits are decided by a country limit committee in a commodity finance bank. These limits are established on several considerations as follows.

Assessment of the country risk

The assessment on the country risk is often based on both internal and external country risk rating, economic and political development, market information and so on. This is the basis for country limit decision.

Banks rely on a country risk committee where commercial and credit professionals for the country sit down with country risk analysts and senior management in order to reach a consensus towards the country risk.

Countries are divided into categories according to their internal and external credit rating and other related information. The discussion on country limit is based on this assessment of the risk.

According to the category of the country for its creditworthiness, a 'cap' which is called maximum country risk (MCR) acceptable to credit is given. To have a limit above this 'cap' needs more arguments and discussion. Sometimes it may

---

15 Moody's Research, May 2007, Moody's International Policy Perspectives: 'The Asian Crisis ten years later: what we know, what we think we know and what we do not know'.

need top management's 'strategic decision'. This extra country limit room may be given, but there are certain conditions, such as restriction on tenor, product, counterparts and so on.

A country risk discussion is not only a discussion on the amount of total exposure, but also the country risk strategy and conditionality for country limit.

Therefore country limit, when established, may further be divided into short term or long term. Conditions like maximum tenor allowed, specific products to be booked under the limit will be mentioned.

Some banks divide the country limit into 'commercial limit' and 'financial limit'. 'Commercial limit' is used for trade finance deals such as confirming LCs and so on. 'Financial limit' refers to exposure to other banks under the financial strength of the counterpart such as money market limit, financial guarantee and so on.

The bank's strategy towards that country

Even if the consensus towards country risk turns out to be non-optimistic to countries with low country risk credit rating, banks may still consider establishing a limit due to strategic considerations.

Strategic considerations may come from a bank's specific position towards that country, such as its historical relationship with the country (ex-colonies and so on), existence of core clients in that market, intention for expansion and existence of strategic alliance, a subsidiary or branch, etc. Under these circumstances, banks are willing to take the difficult risk merely because country limit available is a must to realise the bank's strategy.

Commercial motivation

In some cases, when the country is not on the strategic priority list, banks may also wish to establish a limit to acquire this part of the market if there are business opportunities together with an understanding of business opportunities. But overall, the return on the potential exposure should be attractive enough. This overall commercial motivation may overrule some of the standard decision criteria. When the East European countries opened up, many banks, due to their geographical and historical links, established large country limits for these countries as huge business potential was estimated. This naturally is also part of the strategy consideration.

The best experts must have enough risk awareness and sufficient country experience. In the meantime, they must have sharp commercial sense and product knowledge. A meeting of a country risk committee may take a long time to make a decision, but the discussion itself helps each of its members in one way or another.

The balance between the commercial and the credit discipline is important. If a commodity finance bank biases too much to the credit or to the commercial, the consequence may therefore be either loss of business opportunities (too strict from the credit) or loss of money (too aggressive from the commercial managers).

Once a limit is set, all the business lines within the bank will have to make sure that their exposure will not exceed the approved country limit.

A rational and scientific assessment of country risk is no easy job and the country credit rating system has its fundamental limitations despite their best efforts. In fact, any risk analytical techniques "use historical benchmarks and historical time series which cannot adequately capture risk when they go beyond these parameters"[16]

A consensus on the assessment is difficult, let alone the decisions for a commodity finance bank on its position vis-à-vis the country.

The success of a commodity bank's country limit credit committee lies in the wisdom of the coordinator (chairman) who must be able to bring together as many different, often conflicting, viewpoints as possible, and take the best of each by balancing the credit consideration and the commercial motivation. The chairman may not necessarily be the country expert but he must utilize the best experts to assist.

Admittedly, to evaluate a country risk and then set a limit to it is not easy. Neither the risks nor the returns are clearly definable. But to register the exposure to a country is, sometimes, an even more challenging task in many commodity banks.

It is not totally surprising that, when and if a crisis does occur, a commodity bank may face different internal figures on exposure to the country in crisis. After all, in practice, the question which (lending) credit risk belongs to which country risk category can present some complications.

One example is regarding off balance sheet items (OBIs). Derivatives are OBIs. The principle is that all activities that contain a direct or indirect credit risk that can be localized in the country concerned are eligible for admittance to the calculation of country risk. Derivatives are off-balance items whose credit equivalent is eligible for admittance to the gross base of calculation. But whether a gross amount or a proportion of it should be registered is the question.

Another example may be exposure to an OECD country's bank branch located in an emerging market. How to register the bank's lending to HSBC in Malaysia, for example, may invite some discussion if there is no clear-cut guideline within the bank.

Various commodity deals need coverage from different sources. Covers in the form of guarantees, insurance policies and other securities can decrease the country risk in a certain risk country, but they also can increase the country risk in another risk country.

---

16 Henry Kaufman, president of Henry Kaufman & Company Inc. *The Future of Banking*, p.163.

In some banks, the bank's investments (to acquire a local bank) and/or equity participation (to purchase part of the shares of a local bank) in another country fall outside the country risk registration. These kinds of investments will often be done out of strategic considerations.

Furthermore, it is necessary to do the country risk reporting on a consolidated base, as a result of which the foreign claims of a foreign office, insofar as these are non-local currency, are already enclosed in the gross liabilities. The balance of claims and outstanding debts with a foreign office remains a part of the gross liabilities, because there is a transfer risk involved.

Besides pure country risk as defined above, there are other risks that relate to a country and need to be registered, controlled and monitored. In banking practice, these risks will be further known as country bound risks.

Initially, the default value for the country performance risk and the country transfer risk should be the country of residence from the borrower. This is because in most cases the country of residence is also the country from which payments will take place (transfer risk) and from which delivery has to be made (performance risk). Sometimes the delivery of the repayment may have to be made from countries other than the country of residence. Several country risks have to be registered on a percentage basis. Typical examples are shipping finance or aircraft finance.

In some banks, a maximum of three countries can be mentioned in terms of percentage of their share in the performance risk. The total sum of these percentages has to be one hundred.

Under the country risk concept, transfer risk particularly refers to a case where the obligor of the debtor can pay but the local government blocks the payment due to shortage of hard currencies. In calculating the transfer risk, the ability to repay a credit facility can depend on more or different countries than the country of residence. This is possible if there is an economical dependence on other countries.

It is very important to precisely quantify the risks and to properly register the risks, especially in the case of emerging market countries. This explains why in many banks the risk-weighing method is introduced, to avoid over-reporting of country risk.

The purpose of risk weighing is to give a realistic and actual picture of country exposure. Some of the nominal exposure may be over-reported on its own. This is due to the fact that the exposure of products booked under country limit may indicate a different degree of risk to the bank.

Money market exposure, for example, is calculated as 100% exposure. Failure of the borrower will lead to the full amount of loss to the bank. Trade finance exposure however may offer some chance of recovery if the issuing bank goes bankrupt. A sight LC may give an even bigger chance as the goods under an LC may be available as collateral before the title documents are released.

The degree of risk for derivative products and the repurchase agreement transactions may also vary. A bank may have real risk if a derivative counterparty fails to fulfil the margin calls, or collateral under repurchase is going far beyond its market value which was estimated earlier.

For a small bank whose equity base will not allow a huge country limit, it is essential to have a realistic registration of country exposure. Risk weighing will enable the bank to prevent overestimation or underestimation of its exposure to a difficult country. Overestimation (too big an exposure registration) may lead to less capacity for good business, whereas underestimation may lead to a nasty surprise when the country in question suffers a serious crisis.

Bank risk in commodity finance

In commodity finance, lending to commodity traders or commodity producers involves country risk. Under many circumstances, it also involves bank risk. An LC is the example which we have used for extensive discussion.

Under the LC the payment risk of the buyer is converted into that of the issuing bank. Other examples are bank guarantees or standby LCs, corporate drafts avalised by a bank and so on.

Unless the government blocks the payment, a bank must effect payment under an LC with complied documents. This is an advantage of secured payment under an LC.

Another advantage is that an LC is UCP 600 regulated. This provides certainty of venue in case of dispute for payment, as it is a conditional undertaking of the bank which issues the LC. Of course, if the issuing bank goes bankrupt, the payment undertaking disappears.

For a commodity finance bank, the credit status of the issuing bank is well followed by giving bank credit rating and a bank limit thereafter. The conditions for a bank to pay are specified under the LC.

Commodity clients in general intend to reduce payment risk on their counterparts through reliable third parties such as banks. LCs are thus used widely in the commodity industry as this is the fast and straightforward debt-clearing instrument, covered by uniform common practice rules (UCP).

Given a large turnover of volume of commodity finance, commodity banks often provide funding by 'discounting' the LC and advancing the proceeds to its client – a product we discussed. Such a kind of funding is based on an undertaking of payment from a bank – the LC issuing bank, rather than that of its client – the applicant of the LC.

This concept of shifting a corporate payment risk into a bank risk can be justified by many common-sense assumptions.

First, people tend to trust bank risk more than corporate risk, despite the fact that this point has being challenged recently. The argument goes that banks are established with strict control and scrutiny from the central bank, the regulator. This is necessary because banks are supposed to handle funds from the depositors. They are not supposed to risk the money taken from the public.

Second, banks are established with a higher threshold of required capital as minimum equity than that for companies, a threshold that not many can meet. Although a bank is a corporate itself, the threshold of establishment of a bank is much higher than that of a corporate.

In many countries, the minimum capital to be invested for a bank is a requirement which may block many who intend to venture into this territory. This capital adequacy request makes equity available as a cushion to offset the risk (loan) a bank is taking. Accordingly, the threshold itself helps to exclude those less solid players and/or less serious players.

Third, banks are under regular check by the central bank, the so-called 'bank of banks'. The central bank as a regulator will issue guidance for banking business. In the meantime, the probability of bankruptcy of a bank is much lower than that of a corporate, if ever a bank is allowed to go bust. Moreover, the central bank will also have rescue measures or other private deposit insurance programs in place, so as to ensure the confidence of the public towards the banking system. That explains why we see far less bank bankruptcy cases than company bankruptcy cases in almost all countries.

The consensus is that banks are more vital to the national economy than corporates. This fact is further evidenced by the banking crisis that occurred in developing as well as developed countries, such as Japan, Scandinavia and even the USA itself (the savings and loans crisis).

The probability for a central bank to bail out a bank in difficulty is higher than to bail out a corporate, because the economic and social costs of a bailout are almost in all cases lower than the repercussion of the bankruptcy of a large bank. A full default of a bank may trigger bank runs, upon rumors in the market. Such bank runs will threaten the confidence in the banking system itself.

Fourth, the banking sector as an industry has already long been established. There are rules and regulations for common practice attached to this industry, such as UCP 600 and so on. UCP 500, which is the base of the present UCP 600, was established first in 1933. These rules and regulations are widely accepted and have withstood all tests of crises and defaults.

With the above in mind, people very often prefer to accept bank risk when doing business in commodity finance, especially when business is linked to emerging markets. Hence, an LC as an instrument is preferred and widely used.

Whenever possible, commodity traders will have a bank involved in mitigating the payment risk from their buyers by doing the confirmation and discounting. Consequently, to commodity finance banks, confirmation and discounting LCs issued by their acceptable foreign correspondents is also an attractive source of earnings, especially for those which are specialised in this part of business. As this is a welcomed product both to commodity traders and their banks, it becomes popular business in commodity finance. Therefore, apart from direct lending to commodity producers and traders, banks are offering to companies bank risk instruments such as an LC, a standby LC, bank guarantees, trade finance facilities and so on.

We understand that banks are established to handle public savings. The trust in the banking system is the lifeline for a banking system to work. Central banks are, therefore, making their best effort to keep such a trust in place, by setting rules and regulations, monitoring the performance and rescuing some of them when necessary. Accordingly, a commodity finance bank often takes bank risk as a counterparty coverage to finance. As this is relatively easier and straightforward, LC business becomes a relationship starting point between a commodity finance bank and a commodity trader, that is, commodity banks provide finance to clients but their repayment of the funding is from a bank counterparty. Consequently, commodity finance banks have trade-related bank exposure – the exposure on banks that originate from the payment stream that is associated with the trade of goods or the performance of services.

LCs and bank guarantees are *the* typical instruments for bank risk. To solve the trust issues between supplier and off-taker, the house banks of both parties facilitate the payment stream. The large size of commodity finance deals makes a bank's role on issuing an LC or discount LCs critical. Hence, to take on bank exposure in case the bank guarantees to its customer (the supplier) payment from the bank of the off-taker on a 'without recourse' basis becomes routine in commodity banks.

Instruments that swap corporate risk into bank risk can take several forms, the most common being the confirmation of a trade LC issued by the importer's bank. Alternatively, the importer's bank can have issued a standby LC, guarantee or performance bond in order to back their client for credit enhancement purposes. A commodity bank can counter-guarantee this commitment in favor of its customer and as such take over the credit risk on the bank. These products were discussed earlier.

When a commodity bank pays to its client under an LC and then gets reimbursed some time later, the commodity bank only takes on bank exposure at the request of its customer. The bank takes on this exposure to facilitate the (trade) transaction. In principle, *this* exposure is not a part of the ongoing direct financing of the issuing bank – the obligor of the commodity deal. Such a deal can be interpreted as the commodity finance bank financing its client but taking bank payment as a collateral.

The Basel Committee lists explicitly that, 'Import and Export letters of credit and similar transactions could be accounted for at their actual remaining maturity'.[17]

Practical issues for bank risk in commodity finance

Credit limits are established for a correspondent bank in commodity banks. This is bank limit. The establishment of a bank limit is based on bank risk assessment, the strategy of the bank towards that specific correspondent bank and commercial motivation, that is, risk-return estimation from market information. The department of financial institutions in the bank is often involved in setting the bank limits in cooperation with credit colleagues.

In serving the needs of clients, a couple of practical issues linked to bank limit may, however, emerge in this procedure:

Banks without external credit rating

Banks have their external rating agencies such as S&P, Fitch and Moody's. But it is very likely that a commodity finance client presents the need of confirming a small or new bank. It is usually difficult to get bank limit approval for those (new) names without external rating. Nevertheless, if a client is the 'core client' which desperately needs a bank to take over the payment risk from such a new or small bank, potential of such a capacity, if available, will make a commodity bank a real 'one-stop service centre'. It will differentiate the bank from other competitors.

It is understandable that commodity finance clients may rely on their home banks to discount LCs from banks without external ratings, because they do not know these banks.

On the other hand, such a newly established bank has limited correspondents, and will value your initiative in helping them. However, if the credit committee within the bank is not in a position to approve a limit, it is rather awkward to develop a relationship. What then are the possible solutions?

If an unrated bank is noticed as interesting to a bank's client, the bank can well follow the development of this unrated bank so as to establish a credit limit in the future. There are ways to evaluate a bank. We have to bear in mind that the development of any bank has its lifecycle and the initial contact is often as interesting as the beginning part. The bank can study the local media for that bank. It can also check the attitude

---

17 Paragraph 322 of 'International convergence of capital measurement and capital standards' from the Basel Committee of Banking Supervision.

of the regulator towards this bank by researching the management and shareholders' backgrounds and the competitive advantages of the bank, and by listening to the murmuring of the market for this bank – all these measures will enable a bank to formulate a strategic view on this unrated bank.

If an unrated bank, with the above-mentioned data, turns out to be potentially interesting, it is the task of the department of financial institutions to persuade the credit department for a line. If the credit department insists on a credit rating, it is possible that a rating company does the rating on a fee basis.

If a limit is not possible anyway, exotic solutions are considered such as confirmation (or issuance of irrevocable reimbursement undertaking) by another bigger or better known bank, insurance cover, cash cover, or, discount with recourse to the client.

Limit size and business need

Banks need a credit limit to do confirmation and discounting LCs issued by the counterparty, as the commodity finance bank advances the proceeds to their clients based on the payment undertaking of the issuing bank.

Commodity deals are often large in size. Depending on the commodity price, the average amount of commodity per LC varies. If the iron ore shipment is shipped by Capsize vessel, the vessel can load iron ore up to 150,000 mt; or by Panamax, the vessel can load up to 60,000 to 70,000 mt. If the current market price is US$180 mt, the LC amount for Capsize LC is US$27 mln (+/- 10%) and Panamax LC is US$10.8 m/m to US$12.6 m/m (+/- 10%).

Fuel oil is shipped by 20,000–30,000 mt oil tanker for inter-Asia trade. But if a trader is buying from the Middle East to China they use tanker up to 100,000 mt. If the market price is say, US$810 mt (7.3 barrels –> mt), the normal LC amount for fuel oil is US$16.2 m/m–24.3m/m (+/- 5%) while a large ticket is up to US$81 m/m.

When the soybean price is at the level of US$300 to US$400 mt and usually shipped by Panamax vessel, LC amount ends up around US$30 m/m or above.

With deals of such a size, bank credit limits should be substantial. A bank cannot work with a US$1 m/m to US$2 m/m credit limit if the bank decides to do commodity finance.

Bank limit utilization and the speed of credit approval

Apart from the amount of bank limit, the speed of approval for a credit limit, or temporary increase of a limit, is critical in commodity finance.

As the size of commodity deals is usually large, it is not unusual that a solution is needed for taking over the bank risk – either by asking for a special limit increase – temporary or permanent – or by selling the bank risk in the secondary market.

When an approval is needed, the speed of approval is important as commodity finance is often on a transactional basis. The client simply needs a 'yes' or 'no' as soon as possible. If it is a 'yes', the client is happy. If it is a 'no', they have to move on to find a solution with other banks.

For approving a bank limit, a credit department needs a set of information on the target bank, including a series of financials, a business plan and the management background of the bank. Some of them may not be readily available or not available in English.

It can happen, however, that an important client of the bank may need a deal to be approved (for example, confirming an LC issued by an unknown bank) but the bank limit is not yet in place.

To have certain 'short-cut' procedures established in a commodity bank is necessary either for the ad hoc approval of a bank limit, or for a temporary excess to accommodate one deal.

Delaying approval may end up with a loss of business opportunities, as many commodity traders have several banks – often competitors to each other – to serve them. If one bank is slow, the deal will simply be placed with a competitor. If this happens repeatedly, the client will lose interest in staying with the bank.

This 'short-cut' of approval is especially important for commercial reasons. In some cases, competent people should be authorized to approve a deal on an ad hoc basis with a limited amount. Of course, this quick approval should not be beyond credit discipline.

Secondly, as well as the approval to 'stretch' capacity to absorb bank risk, another key point is a commodity bank's ability to distribute deals into the secondary market. This is called risk distribution.

One of the spin-off benefits for risk distribution is to see how other banks evaluate a certain bank and the market reaction. It is very interesting to notice the price change in the secondary market when news is announced concerning some banks. Therefore, price information on the bank is the vote from the market for that bank's risk.

Letters of credit in commodity finance

Given the importance of letters of credit in commodity finance, we will look at this in more detail, not only as payment undertaking but also as a financing instrument.

Letters of credit as a payment undertaking

Fundamentals

Letters of credit are intensively used in commodity trading, particularly in emerging market countries, where a large volume of import takes place.

When companies are doing business for the first time in commodity business, an LC is an attractive trade finance method for payment settlement. The bottom line is that the beneficiary, that is, the seller in the transaction, wants to have an assurance from a bank known to them, one they trust, one in their own country, that they will be paid under the LC.

An LC provides such a security of payment, with bank credit to replace the buyer's credit. When the LC arrives and the seller is notified of it, they can check the cost of the advising bank (normally the chosen bank of the seller or trader) asking a bank to add their confirmation to the LC. This usually gives the trader the vital option of getting the confirming bank to vet the documents and accept them before advising the opening bank, which eliminates the risk of documents being sent on a collection basis.

Although an LC is a long-existing settlement for commodity trade, very often some basic concepts under LCs are misunderstood. For example, the difference of the maximum duration of an LC for commodity versus the tenor of the LC is often neglected.

An LC often defines a document presentation period till the LC expires. This is the period when the confirming bank is supposed to cover the risk. Accordingly, this is also the period when the LC beneficiary must pay the confirming bank the fee of confirmation. This is because the commodity bank has committed its capacity to take over the payment risk.

As a matter of fact, the maximum duration of trade cycle varies. For iron ore shipment from Brazil to China, the shipment journey is around 45 days. Therefore, the LC will state shipment latest date 'approx 2 months' upon LC issuance with a presentation period of around 21–30 days, maximum LC duration may be up to three months. And shipment from Brazil is from a major producer such as CVRD, the number one iron ore producer in the world, or CSN, also a major one. If shipment is from Australia or India, the LC cycle can fit the general rule (LC tenor + 6 weeks) as the shipment date is around one month with the presentation period around 14 days.

For a steel product LC, the shipment date is usually two months after LC issuance with presentation period around 14–21 days. The two-month shipment date is for the steel mill to plan/schedule production.

The tenor and presentation period are two different concepts and thus have different risk implications, different price structures and purposes.

The tenor is a pre-agreed repayment term where funding is provided. The presentation period is a committed period for taking the risk but real risk occurs only after documents are presented. The risk implication is reflected on price: the price for tenor is confirmation plus discount premium, whereas the price for the presentation period is confirmation charges only. No presentation, no funding. This is for preparation of goods under sales contract.

A confirming bank must understand this fundamental principle to judge if the LC is for facilitating the trade or for extra financing. And to disturb this by imposing a restriction for the confirmation period is frustrating for the client.

Under a hard commodity contract, two to three months for the presentation period is normal. Under a capital goods contract for build-operate-transfer (BOT) projects, part of the presentation period for up to one year is also not unusual. But for oil transactions, a 360-day LC is likely to be a financing LC.

As such, the risk focus is more to 'tenor' instead of 'presentation period'. Only under the circumstances of a crisis are banks nervous so that limitation is given to an 'all-in' period, that is, tenor plus presentation period.

There are special forms of LCs used in commodity finance and some types of these LCs are linked to bank risk. An LC, an instrument for trade finance, is further used in commodity finance for financing purposes as well. We start with a straightforward LC.

Straightforward letter of credit confirmation/discounting

In commodity finance, the background for the confirmation of an LC is that the seller may not be too familiar with the issuing bank of the LC. The seller is neither in a position nor interested in evaluating the creditworthiness of the issuing bank, but intends to have security of payment. The concern from the seller may also come from a country-risk perspective: foreign exchange control, financial crisis, political turbulence and so on.

With such a background, a commodity bank can function as an advising bank, a confirming bank and a discounting bank.

An advising bank, usually located in the country of the seller, may 'confirm' an LC. This is known as 'confirmation of letter of credit', or 'commitment to negotiation (CTN)' as some may call it. As commodity finance volume is easily a couple of million, to secure a payment as such will be a priority of the seller.

Figure 4.1: Beneficiary-paid finance of usance LC (confirming, negotiating and discounting)

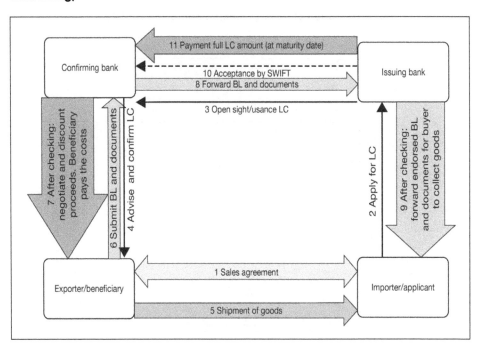

The task of confirmation of an LC is not exclusively reserved for the first advising bank. Sometimes another bank – as the second advising bank – may play this role as well.

Many commodity trading companies have a policy for 'global confirmation', that is, in general they confirm all the LCs received by their in-house bank. This will cover all the payment risk of the issuing bank plus country risk on the LC issuing banks.

Once an LC is confirmed by a bank, the payment risk of the issuing bank is to be covered by the bank which adds its confirmation. Under this confirmation concept, the confirming bank is supposed to take over the payment risk from the issuing bank and the country where the bank is located. The seller is often paid 'without recourse'.

Silent confirmation

Figure 4.2: Silent confirmation of an LC ('commitment to negotiate')

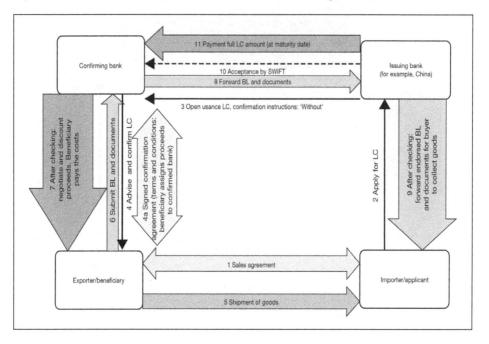

Further to straightforward LC confirmation, there is 'silent confirmation'. Silent confirmation occurs when, in some countries at least, some issuing banks do not like their LCs to be 'openly confirmed' by a foreign bank. They regard this as 'no confidence' in their payment undertaking. In the confirmation instruction of an LC, they explicitly indicate: 'without'.

Despite the unwillingness from the issuing bank for the confirmation, sellers, however, will have these LCs confirmed anyway – the seller intends to have the payment fully covered. This is a service, offered by a commodity bank, which is called 'silent confirmation'. It is a 'without recourse finance' provided by the confirming bank to the beneficiary.

Until UCP 500, the confirming bank was not officially in the legal framework of an LC when it adds its 'silent confirmation', that is, the undertaking of payment of the LC is without the instruction/permission of the issuing bank.

The silent confirmation arrangement between the confirming bank and its client (the beneficiary of the LC) was regarded as a separate arrangement between the beneficiary (the seller) and the confirming bank.

While the undertaking of payment of the confirming bank is on a without recourse basis, the bank which added its silent confirmation may not acquire the same right and protection of a bank which adds open confirmation, if the confirming bank is the nominated bank. Such a right and protection are now explicitly authorized by the issuing bank under the framework of UCP 600. It will allow the confirming bank to get reimbursement from the issuing bank after the confirming bank's effecting payment to the beneficiary.

The risk of silent confirmation lies in the fact that the confirming bank adding such a confirmation commits itself to the beneficiary with the recovery from the issuing bank uncertain. As such, many commodity banks make special arrangement with the beneficiary of the LC to have its right assigned to the confirming bank in case of argument with the issuing bank.

As silent confirmation is often regarded as a separate financing arrangement between the beneficiary of the LC and the financing bank, the financing bank does not appear in the legal framework of the transaction vis-à-vis the issuing bank and is supposed not to be protected if the LC issuing bank declines the payment by alleged discrepancy.

Under a UCP 500 situation, banks tended to solve the problem by adopting a restrictive policy, such as a letter of assignment from the beneficiary etc. With UCP 600 in place, where the negotiating bank's position is reinforced provided that it is a nominated bank, the position of the confirming bank is defined more clearly, although UCP 600 itself does not delete this risk entirely in the daily business.

Letters of credit as an instrument for financing

Although an LC is, originally at least, for facilitating trade flow between the buyer and the seller, it is developed so much that it is also used as an instrument for financing. This intention of financing is more outright in commodity finance where large volumes are involved.

The motivation of financing can be varied, such as the liquidity needs of the buyer, the gap of domestic interest rate versus that of abroad, or to delay payment for speculation of foreign exchange appreciation.

A usance LC, confirmation cost of which is usually paid by the beneficiary but may be paid by the applicant as well, is a common instrument to provide funding under the payment undertaking from the issuing bank: the issuing bank is allowed to pay after a pre-agreed period.

For open confirmation of an LC, the structure of finance under the LC is well recognized – a simple assignment of the proceeds of the LC from the beneficiary of the LC to an assignee. The issuing/paying bank is notified of the assignment (making this a legal assignment), and is therefore obliged to make payment of the proceeds per the assignment to the assignee (that is, the confirming bank). The assignee is able to sue in its own name if the LC is not paid, though under the proposed documentation, the confirming bank has the right to demand the beneficiary to do so. In certain enumerated circumstances, the confirming bank will have recourse to the beneficiary of the LC.

Limited recourse is often linked to some special situations, but cannot be applied to disputes between the issuing bank and the confirming bank over document compliance. Usually the issuing bank has already accepted the documents and has therefore committed to pay the LC amount upon maturity, and the risk of non-conforming documents is removed.

Limited recourse is necessary due to other reasons, one of which is 'fraud in trade'. This is beyond the control of banks. What remains (under a documentary credit situation) are the risks of discovery of fraud (in the documents) and a stop payment (legal injunction) request from the applicant (for disputes over the goods, not the documents); however, both circumstances have been dealt with specifically in the documentation, and will trigger recourse to the beneficiary. These would have been the same rights accorded under a negotiation of the LC.

Under a 'back-to-back' structure, if the master LC at usance is up to 90 days, the maximum LC cycle can be up to 180 days (that is, LC tenor 90 days plus 'shipment and presentation' dates for another 90 days). An LC payment cost can be paid by the confirming bank to the beneficiary from this basic infrastructure, as we have already seen.

When letters of credit are used for financing purposes, confirmation and the discounting cost of a usance LC can be paid by the applicant, the beneficiary or by the issuing bank, depending on who needs the financing.

Structured LCs, which we will discuss below, are explicitly used for top commodity traders to win extra income using LC forms to match their trade flows. The tenor and cost of such financing is dependent on the (borrowing) cost abroad and at home.

Whether the cost of confirmation and discounting is paid by the beneficiary, the applicant or the issuing bank, it points to one fact that an LC is used beyond the original purpose of mere trade finance. These LCs are 'invented', exclusively and explicitly, for financing purposes under an LC. Some banks call them 'disguised' trade finance products.

Structured (synthetic) letters of credit

A structured LC is quite an innovative product which originated from major commodity companies spotting the chance to reap profits from large commodity trade volumes. It can be regarded as a derivative of commodity finance.

Structured LCs and synthetic LCs are in fact different, although they are roughly referred to as structured LCs.

1. Structured LCs: The goods are imported into the country of the issuing bank but trade flow is between two related parties often in one group.

2. Synthetic LCs: The goods are imported to another country other than where the issuing bank is domiciled.

Figure 4.3: Structured intra-group LC (real trade flow, but using an LC as a financing vehicle)

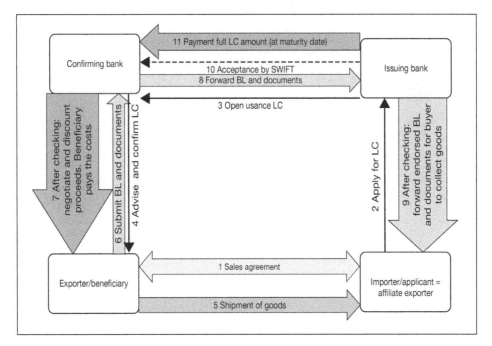

Figure 4.4: Structured synthetic LC (LC used as a financing vehicle, but does not reflect the underlying trade flow)

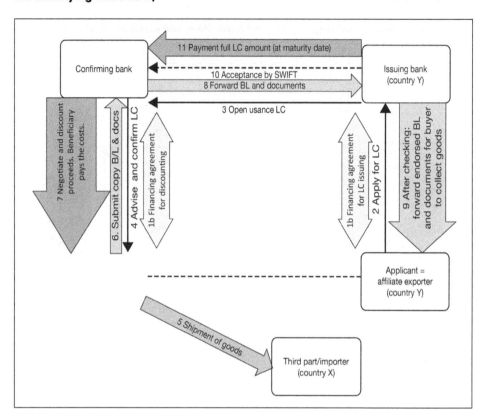

What motivates traders to have structured LCs or synthetic LCs? LCs are documentary credit and finance is based on documents.

Under UCP rules, banks deal with documents, not with goods, services or performance to which the documents may relate. Therefore, the issuing bank is irrevocably bound to honor the credit as at the time it is issued. In this respect, the trade relationship is there by its very nature.

This motivates commodity traders to 'structure' their large commodity trade flows against the concept that banks are dealing with documents and that once documents under the LC are in order, the issuing bank should honor its obligation.

The challenge to structured LCs is that, in general, the definition of trade finance should read the actual trade flow with the attached documents. But in a structured LC the actual trade flow is separated from the document flow.

Although this flow is still governed by UCP 600 for the county where the issuing bank is situated, there is no real trade flow of goods to that country under 'synthetic' LCs. This makes it different from 'normal LCs'.

Besides that, the structure is meant to fund banks at either attractive rates or to fund banks that cannot attract funds in foreign currency. Structured LCs are, therefore, more of a financing instrument rather than facilitating the underlying trade.

In discussing a structured LC, there is no denying the financing nature of the deal. As the flow of the goods is separated, the major worry on structured LCs or intra-group financing is fraud – fraudulent documents with no commodities.

The chance of fraud is less, of course, if the trading company involved in structured LC is a top-rated company. The company is unlikely to risk their reputation.

Another risk worry is that such a structured deal may not be regarded as a genuine trade finance by the regulator of the country where the LC is issued, and therefore there is no protection/priority for government payment under a moratorium period. This risk is mostly mitigated if the issuing bank's credit worthiness is so strong that its default is remote.

Letter of credit refinance

Apart from the fact that a special structure can be created to get funding under an LC, exiting LCs can be extended to get extra funding possibilities.

A sight LC, for example, can be on purpose extended to usance by allowing the buyer to pay at a pre-agreed period (the usance tenor). At the surface, such an LC is nothing different from plain usance LC. But under a direct applicant paid LC, the applicant, via their bank, searches for a cheap funding arrangement upfront and the negotiation bank agrees beforehand to discount at a pre-arranged rate. This is sometimes called usance LC pay at sight (UPAS).

It may also happen that the usance part of LC is totally outsourced to some designated banks. Despite the usance tenor, the negotiation bank is requested by a swift message from the issuing bank, to pay only at sight to the beneficiary but a third-party bank mentioned in the swift should settle the LC with the negotiation bank. The issuing bank promises to reimburse this financing bank on the maturity date. This is sometimes called LC refinance.

Applicant-paid finance

Figure 4.5: Applicant-paid finance of usance LC (confirming, negotiating and discounting: usance paid at sight – UPAS)

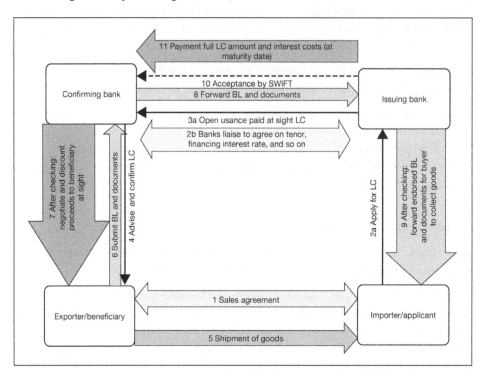

The issuing bank makes a prior arrangement (price, tenor and so on) with a correspondent bank to refinance their usance LC, which is payable to the beneficiary at sight basis. The correspondent bank is the nominated bank and often, but not necessarily, the advising/negotiation bank.

Such an LC is not so much different from a normal usance LC. Rather, the financing request (and price) is initiated by the issuing bank instead of the beneficiary. The finance is provided to the applicant under the payment undertaking of the issuing bank.

The following requesting letter from the issuing bank on behalf of the applicant can best explain the situation:

Example 4.1

We, xxx (Applicant) have entered into an agreement with the following Supplier (Beneficiary) based at (Country) for purchase of (Commodity xxx). In this regard, we shall establish an LC the salient features of which are as follows:

LC opening bank:	XXX Bank
LC amount:	US$ xxx Mn (+/-10%)
Tenor of LC:	180 days/360 days usance from the date of BL
Beneficiary:	xxx Company address:
Applicant:	xxx Company address:
LC opening date:	xxx
Description of goods:	xxx
Country of origin of goods:	xxx
LC confirmation:	May add (Charges to account of beneficiary)
LC financing/discounting:	Required (Charges to applicant's account)

The transaction needs to be in such a way that the beneficiary needs to be paid at sight, upon the presentation of credit compliant documents. The discounting interest from the date of negotiation till the maturity date is to our account. The principal amount along with the usance interest shall be paid by the issuing bank to the negotiating bank at the maturity (180 days from BL date).

XXX shall send the LC (SWIFT) to your bank and you shall send the same to their advising bank to further advise the beneficiary. Once the goods are shipped, the beneficiary presents the documents through the advising bank to you for negotiation/discounting. You shall fund the beneficiary's account (subject to documents being credit compliant) with the advising bank and inform the value of goods and interest to the issuing bank to be payable on due date.

In this regard, please advise on the feasibility of such a transaction with your bank and accordingly advise us of your best competitive applicable LIBOR-linked quotes for discounting the LC.

Also attached herewith the draft LC. Waiting for your comments.

Obviously, applicant-paid finance needs a pre-agreement. Very often in the text of LC, the additional condition is clearly defined, especially that the acceptance and discounting charges are for the account of the applicant and the quotation of discounting interest rate (Libor + xx%).

The rate requested is indicated in 'Libor + xxx bp' instead of 'COF + xx bp'. This is because Libor is the one international uniform benchmark for inter-bank borrowing.

Post finance

Figure 4.6: Post-financing of an LC (extension of credit under UCP 600)

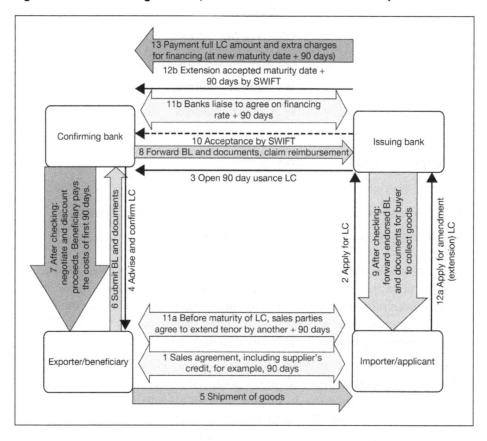

LC refinancing may include also sight or usance LC deals which were settled over, but the issuing bank requests an extra period for financing them (or their clients).

Post financing of an LC is a form of refinancing the issuing bank. The confirming bank has paid the beneficiary at sight basis (as instructed in the LC) but the issuing bank is allowed to 'reimburse' the paying bank after a certain period, i.e. the issuing bank is being post-financed. The issuing bank is obliged to pay on the maturity date of that period the face value of the documents increased by interest from the confirming bank's payment to the beneficiary until the maturity date.

Very often, such a request comes from the LC issuing bank for the bank itself or on behalf of its client:

Example 4.2

RE: OUR LC REF: xxxxxxx FOR US$ xxxxxxxx

IN FAVOR OF ISSUED TO YOUR BANK ON xxxxxxxx

APPLICANT: xxxxxxxx

BENEFICIARY: xxxxxxxxx

We kindly request you to cancel our reimbursement authorisation in field 78 and in field 53a on our above referenced LC, and take B/M paragraph into consideration instead.

Further to our agreement with Mr Xxxxxx at your department, please note that we hereby request you to re-finance the a/m letter of credit for a period of 180 days from the date of your payment to the beneficiary for the value of the documents strictly complying with the LC terms.

We confirm that we will pay the principal amount plus the interest to be calculated at the rate of Libor for the corresponding period plus a margin of xxxx percent per annum at maturity together with the principal amount according to your instructions.

Please inform us of the exact principal amount, interest rate, interest amount and the maturity date by authenticated SWIFT message three working days prior to your payment to the beneficiary.

Accordingly, if such a request is in the interest of the commodity bank, the bank should send a message, see the following:

Example 4.3

Re. your post financing request under your LC

Ref. No.xxxxxxx.

We will finance you for US$ xxxxxxxxxx with value date xxxxxxxxx at 6 months Libor plus xxxxxx percent.

Please note that the interest rate for the period between xxxx and xxxxx has been fixed as follows:

Libor rate 6M: xxx PCT

Spread: xxxPCT

All-in rate: xxxxPCT

Therefore, we kindly request you to transfer US$ Xxxxxxxx being US$ xxxxx principal amount plus US$xxxxxx interest amount to our account no. Xxxxxxx with xxxxxxxx Bank New York, USA. (CHASUS33) with value date xxxxxx quoting our ref xxxxxx.

Under a post-financing structure, we are dealing with the discounting of an LC that is not negotiable. This means that any discounting a commodity bank does may fall outside the UCP rules and the laws governing documentary credit.

LC refinancing may move further to finance LC issued to other banks. As mentioned above, some banks outsource the funding needs with their correspondent banks. The bank is becoming a reimbursement bank.

In such cases, the bank is financing *de facto* the issuing bank which will use the funding for trade finance as it is supposed to be. In some countries, credit is extended for imports of goods by overseas banks using letter of undertaking (LUT) or letter of comfort (LOC), subject to certain terms and conditions when the LC is settled.

Bank risk for emerging market banks: payment dispute and delay

Although outright default of a bank is rare, it is is not unusual for payment to be delayed with emerging market banks under an LC. Such delays can be explained by various reasons.

Liquidity is one of the obvious explanations, as many emerging market banks may fail to manage their assets and liabilities very well.

Although they know they should pay on the due date, they may have a last-minute problem. This last-minute problem can be linked to price movement of the commodity, foreign exchange regulations of the country, or simply, the bank intends to put their client (applicant) under pressure by not paying. The last situation happens very often for banks with weak credit risk management skills concerning their applicant.

A more complex case can be that the payment obligation is uncertain. This happens typically under an LC when a 'discrepancy' is found. Under such circumstances, the issuing bank's LC payment undertaking is at stake.

In a volatile financial climate, banks and lawyers will pounce on any error in your documentation. You have to get it right, otherwise you risk paying a high price.

'Discrepancy argument' can, in fact, be a disguised as 'commercial conflict'. By prolonging the payment undertaking or by making that questionable, the buyer intends to start to renegotiate the price using the alleged discrepancy. It can also be that the buyer wants to buy time to check the quality or speculate on the price movement for the underlying commodity.

Despite the fact that banks are only dealing with documents rather than goods, banks are often victims of commercial conflict between the buyer and the seller, or rather, in the context of an LC, the applicant and the beneficiary.

For the LC business of a commodity bank, such delays are more difficult to handle than those straightforward non-payments under obligation. 'Discrepancy arguments' may lead to complicated procedures.

It is recognized that the essence of the LC is that it allows the drawing of funds on the presentation of 'conforming' documents, that is, documents conforming to the conditions stipulated in the LC. The trouble is, there are invariably typographical errors, miss-spelt words or names, or misplaced colons or commas within the presented documents. The LC issuing bank, who is supposed to pay, will jump on these errors and advise the trader that the documents do not conform to the LC.

The utmost care in preparing documents and timely action are vital. That explains why a qualified/prudent trade service department is a must for a commodity bank – a subject we will deal with in Chapter 6.

It used to be that, in some cases, these errors could be corrected and the documents re-presented as conforming. But nowadays it is not as easy as that. In the current climate, the paying bank will insist on sending these documents on a 'collection basis'. This does not detract from the status of ownership of the goods, but it does place the trader in an undesirable position.

Under such a circumstance, the documents go to the buyer's opening bank, and this bank asks the buyer if they will accept them. Should the market level or situation have changed during the two months or so since the LC has been operative, the buyer (in many cases) will try to use the excuse of non-conforming documents to either reduce the contractual price or, worse still, to refuse the cargo.

The tough overall financial situation will be with us for a long time to come, so it is vital that all terms and conditions under an LC are vetted properly and then double-checked.

Moreover, for commodity traders, confirmation of an LC from his in-house bank is not always guaranteed. Despite the efforts from both the beneficiary and the confirming bank, it will not prevent the bank from sometimes refusing to add its confirmation to another decent bank, purely because its own credit line for that bank is fully utilized. Then all kinds of delays or non-payments will be left to the trading companies to handle themselves.

To ensure that LCs they received from their counterparties are duly confirmed, many of the commodity traders are banking with several names to ensure the request of confirmation may be honored by at least one of these banks. Some commodity traders, especially those top ones, even offer the confirmation business to a couple of banks to let these banks compete with each other. By doing this, they intend to get the lowest confirmation fee.

It is worth mentioning that as far as LCs are concerned, the parties may all think that trading contracts were exchanged and that the terms of these contracts are binding. They normally are, but when such terms, names, types of product, names of ship, and so on, are used within the LC, the LC is the crucial document and rules the negotiation. Even if you are sure the discrepancy is due to commercial conflict, you have to deal with such discrepancy arguments first.

Facing such challenges of non-payment under discrepancy arguments, the confirming bank can choose from several options. One is to go for an International Chamber of Commerce (ICC) opinion.

The ICC is supposed to be the organization which may give judgment on the validity of the alleged discrepancy. ICC arbitrage is another solution provided that both parties agree to the judgment of the ICC arbitrage committee. Court is the last resort.

Under certain circumstances, when discrepancy is unfortunately valid, the beneficiary's bank may have to give in by accepting a reduction of payment. This is not uncommon in bank risk business for commodity finance banks.

Fundamentally, we can realize that the delay/decline of payment under the excuse of alleged discrepancy lies in the fact that there is commercial conflict between the buyer and seller. Problem prevention in the daily operation is thus critical.

The following question list is for factors which may hint at the potential discrepancies under an LC:

- Is the commodity price underlying the LC going up or down?

  - The problem often comes when the commodity price is going down, so that the buyer intends to re-negotiate the contract price, or simply get rid of the LC.

- Is the applicant the end-user or a trader?

  - Traders (intermediaries) tend to make a problem if they are stuck because of their end buyer.

- Do the applicant and beneficiary have a good and long-lasting relationship with each other?

  - If yes, any problem among them tends to have an easier solution as they want to maintain this long-term relationship for long-term gains.

Other particular points of interest for commodity finance documents for metal, agricultural products and energy deals include:

- quality documents (SGS) for hard commodities

- healthy regulation documents for soft commodity

- improper release of letters of indemnity (LOI) for oil deals etc.

As commodity price and commodity quality are often problem sources, it is recommended that relationship managers of the client (the beneficiary or the seller) communicate with trade service department if there is sharp movement of the commodity price, and a change of local regulation for import and export. Prevention of trade service loss is thus team cooperation.

If a problem still occurs despite all the above efforts, a commodity bank must take great care to rescue its position:

- Check the status of discrepancy first from the expert opinion in the bank to decide the banks' position and status to negotiate solutions with the LC issuing bank.

- If a strong position is confirmed, the negotiating bank will follow: ICC opinion > ICC arbitrage > legal action, depending on the counterparty's attitude.

Legal action is the last resort in all cases. This is because it takes time, costs money, threatens the relationship and most of all, the result is unpredictable.

In concluding our discussion on bank risk, we admit that non-payment under an LC is a terrible worry for all traders. This is because an LC and the rules and regulations around it are supposed to secure the payment. It blasts the original calculation for the cargo to pieces because, instead of the original 1.5% all-in margin for the LC costs, for example, traders are now faced with non-confirmation or with an extra 2–3% premium to confirm the LC for the cargo that is due to be shipped.

The agony of this moment is that the trader has no other choice but to ship the cargo as the mill has it all available at the port and wants to be paid. This ship is chartered or liner terms are booked, and the trader faces dead freight if it does not ship. So the trader has to ship to the destination at extra costs or without confirming the credit, but must make sure that everybody in the company is aware of the terrible risks and consequences should the presentation fail to be made cleanly.

There are many ways for traders and their commodity banks to reduce the risk, as we have discussed extensively in this chapter, but the most important ones should be 'know your client' and 'know the commodity market'.

CHAPTER 5

Commodity Finance and Risk Management

Multiple risks and risk analysis in commodity finance

Commodity finance and its multiple risks[18]

In previous chapters, we have discussed some of the ways of managing and mitigating the risk in commodity finance. For example, we have had systematic discussion on managing bank and country risk. In this chapter, we will start with the basics of risks in commodity finance. We will then establish a systematic examination of risk mitigation approaches and instruments.

As the purpose of commodity finance is to finance commodity producers and traders, we will, first of all, see what the unique aspects in evaluating commodity trading companies are. We will then examine how credit risk is allocated and reallocated using the supply chain approach.

In risk discussion, 'collateral' is highlighted. We understand the importance of collateral under commodity finance especially collateral for those thinly capitalized traders. Hence, the second approach to be discussed is the evaluation of collateral and the management of collateral. Third, we will discuss some of the instruments used – not exclusively but very often –– in commodity finance, such as forfaiting for bank risk, political insurance for commercial and commodity delivery risk and other instruments. Last but not least, as fraud is often a threat to commodity finance, this subject will be dealt with in detail.

Before an in-depth analysis of risk management, the understanding of advantages and disadvantages in commodity finance is the priority.

As far as credit risk is concerned, one of the advantages is that the underlying assets (commodities, especially those listed on commodity exchanges) are, mostly if not all, easily marketable; reference prices are transparent and hedging of price risk is often

---

18 Eelco in his comments mentioned that market risk falls out in a number of categories (flat price risk, time spread risk and basis risk) and that 'counterparty default risk' whether under a forward contract or a LC (discrepancies), is a 'wrong-way risk', i.e. the likelihood of occurrence increases with the magnitude of impact.

possible. Assets as such are often of good credit quality or else financing risk can be insured or likely to be converted into a bank risk via an LC or letter of guarantee.

As the commodity trade turnover is quick, the financing tenor, that is, asset conversion period, is usually short or very short. This is obviously another advantage from the perspective of a bank which provides financing. Relatively short tenor of credit facilities gives comfort and flexibility to banks which provide finance.

A typical disadvantage, however, is that, many trading companies for commodities are unrated companies and vulnerable to changing volume and changing commodity price. They are in general highly leveraged, relying on banks to finance their trade flow.

Another disadvantage is that trade flow of commodities, involving a vast amount of money, is linked to emerging markets where country risk is something that has to be factored into the consideration in all financing mechanism and products, as commodity finance involves risks more than credit risk alone.

Credit risk apart, commodity finance bears market risk, foreign exchange risk, operational risk, legal risk, compliance risk, reputation risk (environmental issues) and so on. Commodity trading companies, as well as the banks that are financing them, have to work with multiple counterparties and have to be aware of the counterparty solvency. They thus face multiple risks.

As the commodity market is changing day and night, the commodity finance business has market risk.

The short-term and long-term supply may change, as might the demand side. Commodity price changes every minute like stocks in the stock exchange. The commodity trading companies and the commodity finance banks need to have a sense of whether their counterparties' trading exposures and finance are in a good condition; otherwise they may be unduly exposed to the risk of non-performance by the counterparty.

Overall, commodity finance has its inherent risk as it usually involves large amount of funds and it also involves emerging markets' uncertainty: typical denominators in commodity finance flows are non-OECD banks and corporates.

Regarding the built-in one dimension of risks for commodity finance deals – the country risk, which is often discussed in commodity finance – the new element in country risk from emerging markets is the 'policy risk', that is, uncertainty of regulatory environment and government policy, either linked to subsidies of agricultural products, or linked to trade barriers such as import quotas.

Whereas legal contracts are used as protection of the interest of the company, shifting laws and regulations render them void. For import and export of commodities, governments may have implicit or explicit shift of regulations. That has an impact on the transactions negotiated and agreed.

Given the large amounts for commodity transactions, logistics also plays a significant role in commodity trading. Some risks in transportation can have an impact on the deal itself, such as commodities being susceptible to damage, risk of freight rate changes which erode the total profitability of the deal, changes in storage and handling costs and so on. All these may lead to disputes. As we know, a dispute in commodity finance needs a prompt solution. Otherwise demurrage fee will make the dispute more complicated.

To the lending bank, the obligors of trade finance facilities are often commodity trading companies, some of which have limited trading records to allow a sound judgment on their capacity, or they operate in countries with high country risk and limited market risk management processes. They are exposed to operational risk – volatilities of assets and markets – and are often unable to repay loans from their own purse other than the commodity being liquidated, as they are highly geared to bank finance. In crisis situations, banks can scarcely find ways to enforce their rights for credit recovery.

For discussion purposes, we will focus on some risks often seen in commodity finance:

Commodity price risk

As most commodities are listed in a commodity exchange, price is transparent and fluctuates according to supply and demand. During the transaction period, clients of a commodity finance bank may face this kind of price risk, unless they hedge the price via the futures market, which costs money.

Product risk

Commodities as products can be destroyed, damaged or turn bad during the storage period and in the transportation period.

Operational risk

Handling documents and securing collateral in trade and commodity finance could induce higher than average operational risk. This operational risk is more in commodity finance partially due to the fact that the transaction amount is huge, and partially because of the seasonal demand for commodities. Any mistake in documentation and in quantity/quality measurement may lead to losses. Operational risk was disregarded in BIS I but will have major impact on total capital requirements in BIS III.

Country risk

Many commodities are produced in emerging market countries. Emerging markets are supposed to be high-risk countries facing political and economical instability, short of foreign currencies, strict capital outflow restrictions etc. These countries are often non-transparent markets with unstable regimes in politically and socially unstable countries. Traders there are exposed to different forms of counterparty country risk.

Fraud risk

As commodity finance is often using commodity as collateral, banks are often providing finance on title documents. These documents (BL/warehouse receipts) can be fraudulent and finance provided may end up with a huge loss for the bank. With large amounts of money involved in commodity finance, motivation for fraud is higher.

Reputation risk

Reputation risk for lending banks can be described as the risk that the bank's reputation is damaged by one or more events that occur during the procedure of offering and executing banking finance facilities. The risk can be linked to the above-mentioned events, or individual behavior that challenges the integrity of the bank (that is, the risk of the integrity of the commodity bank or the financial system) being affected by the improper, unethical conduct of the organization, its employees or management, if such a conduct is in contravention of legislation and regulation and the standards set by society or by the institution itself. Financing those trading companies for commodities, the production of which will pollute the environment, is one typical example.

Legal risk

Legal risk can be described as the risk of invalid legal right (assignment, pledge and so on) due to the jurisdiction difference. Hence, the existing legal agreement becomes invalid, illegal, or unenforceable (or the security rights created are ineffective). It may also refer to improper legal advice which turns out to be misleading. Legal risk often emerges only when loopholes/deficiencies in the legal agreement are found by the counterparty in case of dispute.

Compliance risk

Compliance risk can be described as the risk for potential loss/penalty due to negligence of compliance rules and regulations, including a money laundering event. Financing trade flows linked to regions which are on the sanction list is such an example, and another is facilitating cash flow in the name of commodity finance but for money laundering purposes. This kind of compliance risk has attracted increasing attention for many commodity banks.

Risks will lead to delay and defaults. The last part of the chapter will discuss the exit of commodity finance: handling defaults and bad debts (see 'Default and bad debts for commodity finance').

Financing commodity trading companies: multiple risk management

Most borrowers in commodity finance are trading companies. To lend to them, a commodity bank must evaluate multiple risks of a commodity trading company to whom the bank offers credit facility.

The following questions come into the picture when analyzing risk:

- Key trade flows of the clients: What are the kind of commodities, single or multi commodities, origin and off-taker countries? What are the main suppliers and off-takers, the key payment terms, Inco terms and transaction size, and tenor?

- Market position, commodity sector and market outlook: What kind of market position this company has, its market share and the forecast of market development for that commodity in which the company is involved.

- Key business risks and mitigants: How the client hedges the commodity price risk, counterparty default risk, country risk and so on.

To apply for a credit facility, commodity trading companies usually have to deal with at least the following items:

Company profile

This is a general client information sheet and includes the company's background, the organization chart, the shareholders, merger and acquisition if any, the business model, management team and current events. For commodity finance, management's experience often plays an important role in success. Their professional record (market knowledge and network), positive or negative, can have an impact on business.

Business activities

This refers to a business model and business strategy, the company's position in that part of commodity market, its trading pattern, geographical area coverage, major suppliers and buyers. Market analysis is included which covers commodity price forecast. This will throw light on future business potential and sustainability of the business.

Financial analysis

Traditional financial analysis on balance sheet, income statement and financial ratio analysis should apply to commodity companies. Time series analysis will indicate the trend, and peer group analysis will indicate the market position and whether the performance is below or above the average. The track record, as well as the current facility with other banks, should be examined. Liquidity and cash flow analysis is critical for the repayment ability of the commodity trading companies.

Management of the company and the risk management capacity

The competence of management and its role in managing different risks; whether or not all commodity prices are hedged or not and what is the management guideline is also relevant.

Corporate social responsibility analysis and client integrity

Many of the commodity trading companies may be involved in trading commodities with environmental impact. Corporate social responsibility is a consideration for banks to lend to trading companies, to avoid venturing into reputation danger for the financing bank.

Overall rating and facility recommended

The overall analysis will arrive at an internal rating and then the relevant facility will be recommended for approval.

A commodity finance facility extended to a commodity trader depends on several things: (i) the commodity sector in which the trader is operating; (ii) the financial strength of the borrower; (iii) the historical track record (how experienced the borrower is in this trade); and (iv) the market standing of the borrower.

Commodity sector in which the trader is operating

Soft, hard and energy commodities do have their own individual characteristics as previously explained. The amount to be financed, the tenor and the terms and conditions will thus vary.

Soft commodity traders very often have cyclical cash flows. Energy traders need short but large amounts of credit facility, whereas metal clients may be exposed to more price risk as the price of non-listed hard commodities (for example, steel, scrap and so on) is less transparent. Moreover, fast-growing economies may have a bigger need for energy whereas fast development of infrastructure of the economy may need more steel, copper, aluminum and so on.

Energy deals tend to have a quicker turnover and shipment. Agricultural products are often subject to natural conditions such as weather.

The trading of agricultural products is very often linked to government support policy. Hence, even though some countries are on the sanction list, important export of agricultural products will still be allowed for basic food. The price of such agricultural products can be subsidized. The increase and decrease of a subsidiary to agricultural products can have an impact on contracted profits.

The financial strength of the borrower

For the financial strength of the borrower, we look at profitability, liquidity and solvency as we analyze any companies. But for commodity companies, some unique points are worthy of our attention.

To evaluate the financial strength of any company, the first is the company's own equity – not the registered equity alone. Commodity trading companies are no exception. Other issues linked to equity are shareholder's position, his willingness to guarantee, and willingness to inject more capital in case of need.

In some cases, if the trading company is a subsidiary of a group, the strength of the mother company is relevant. A letter of comfort may also help to reinforce the situation of the subsidiary. At least it creates the awareness in the group about what the subsidiary is doing.

The profitability of the company is important in all cases as it is the capacity of the company to repay the facility. To evaluate the profitability of a commodity company it is important to take the industry as a whole. Industry conditions often dictate a trading firm's actions and its profitability.

During difficult trading environments, it is not uncommon for trading firms to break-even or even to book a small loss. A substantial profit during difficult trading periods may often indicate that large speculative positions were taken. Consistency in relation to market conditions and competitors is the measurement of profitability that a bank should rely on. Illogical reactions to a trading company's loss can quickly destroy a profitable relationship that took years to build.

For profitability, we usually look at gross margin and net margin development (both in percentage and absolute terms, for example margin per metric tons). For a single commodity trader, we try to perform peer group analysis about the margin development trend. However, there are differences between an independent trader and the trading arm of a commodity producing group.

The two key ratios which we look at are net working capital (current assets -/- current liabilities) and current ratio (current assets/current liabilities). This matches the trading and funding nature of a trader.

We all know many commodity traders are highly leveraged. If they have US$100 million short-term debt, but US$120 million commodity which they can sell easily within a couple of days, any bank will feel comfortable to finance. That is why we look how quick a trader can turn its assets to cover its liabilities.

If applicable, we should use the adjusted net working capital and current ratio, since not all the 'current' assets are liquid assets such as intercompany receivables/payables, tax receivables and prepayments. In these cases, we will make adjustments. Not only to assess the liquidity of its assets, but also the quality of its assets (receivable quality: receivables covered by LC, credit insurance or open accounts; and inventory quality: whether the price risk is hedged). Furthermore, it is important to ask whether the trader has sufficient bank lines to support its business and pay margin calls.

For solvency, it is also important to link to the business profile of a trader. If it is a trader with a low-risk facility (for example, only a back-to-back facility), we may consider that low solvency is acceptable. If the trader does take position and hold stocks in trading, the trading company is more exposed to market risks.

When a bank wants to see a higher level of solvency, the important question is to ask whether the solvency level is sufficient to cover its risks (for example, if commodity price drops by 20%, what is the impact of its solvency position)?

The gearing ratio (debt/net worth) for commodity trading companies is to be examined for risk evaluation. Leverage is measured by total bank limits (plus any other *pari passu* debt divided by tangible net worth plus subordinated debt).

Liabilities should only be included in the analysis of leverage if they are *pari passu* with bank debt. A general rule of thumb is to keep potential bank debt leverage at 10 to 1 or less. For some agricultural traders, we see the financial covenant level set at five or six times. It is dependent on the business profile.

Many commodity companies do have inventory or warehouse warrants. As inventory is used for collateral purposes, the evaluation of inventory is crucial in bank finance extended to commodity finance companies. In this field, a mark-to-market approach is used. Sometimes a more conservative 'lower of cost' approach is used. A mark-to-market approach presents the 'then' market price of inventory and accounts for unrealized gains and losses on their income statement.

Cash flow definitely plays a role in evaluating the financial strength of a trading company. It not only reflects the financial capacity but also its record in the industry. A mature trading company should have a stable upstream and downstream cash flow relationship. Consequently, the cash flow of its own is stable. A sudden and big disruption of cash flow may give the signal that some problems are occurring in the supply chain.

Historical track record and market standing of the borrower

The historical track record of the commodity trading company is relevant in evaluating a commodity trading company. Commodity trade is a kind of niche business, so a trading company may choose to be a conglomerate ('doing all') player or a niche player ('specialized in some'). Another alternative is, some commodity companies simply move into new markets along their business line, finally with success or failure.

Generally, if a trader shows volatile results, it could mean that it has less proper risk management or many speculation activities. For a trader who simply plays the role of go-between, cash flow is relevant but not critical, since it could be very volatile due to price and volume movement. Instead of cash flow, we focus more on the liquidity of the underlying commodities.

Different commodity finance facilities offered to a client may have different risk implications. Usually for risk appetite evolution purposes, commodity finance banks tend to start with transactional deals. This includes facilities for issuing LCs for purchase, back-to-back, front-to-back, standby LCs, freight finance, countersigning of LOIs and issuance of guarantees. These are self-liquidating deals with incoming proceeds to cover the exposure of the facility so that the next deal can start.

Once a track record of transactions is established, the commodity finance bank will move on to secured facilities such as full set bills of lading (BLs) to order and blank endorsed, or to the order of the financing bank, goods pledged to the financing bank according to local law, or goods stored to the order of the financing bank with legal opinion on assignment and enforceability and properly assigned receivables, sometimes including notification to and acknowledgement by the debtor. Third-party coverage such as the export credit agency (ECA) or Exim bank covered export finance is also under this secured facility category.

The most relaxed facilities are clean facilities with little restriction to use the funds under the facility. Customers can utilize the facility for any purpose as agreed in the facility terms and conditions. Such facilities are usually offered to investment-grade companies based on their balance sheet situation. There is no security documentation in place, nor are they necessarily daily monitored by the financing bank.

Risk management in commodity finance: the supply chain approach

Commodities move as they are being bought, held, converted and sold onwards along a supply chain. A strong tendency emerging in commodity finance is the development of a supply chain approach.

Trading companies, especially those top players, are coming into a rounded chain involvement in trading, logistics, infrastructure assets and so on. With the supply chain lengthening as a result of globalization and outsourcing of multinationals, companies in the chain are also experiencing needs of financing.

For commodity finance banks, to look into this supply chain to finance upstream and downstream players is a way to access more business opportunities. This is a commercial motivation. In the meantime, this will also enable commodity finance banks to get a broader view of related risk and mitigate relevant risks as such. Not only is this upstream integration and downstream integration good expansion for business but also an approach to mitigate the transaction risk – a focused topic for this chapter.

Examples abound where commodity finance banks suffer from losses due to the fact that one of the players in the supply chain fails to fulfill his/her obligation, which leads to the failure of the whole supply chain.

In essence, SCF intends to offer solutions for financing goods as they move from origin to destination. The credit worthiness of the supply chain as a whole is examined and finance is offered to the parties in the chain based on a holistic calculation and risk is mitigated as well along the SCF.

We have mentioned some supply chain examples in previous chapters. The following example is used here to illustrate in more detail the supply chain stages for one commodity: palm oil.

As we can see, from 'before cultivation' until 'after consumption', many corporates are involved. A bank may choose to finance any one of them or all of them.

When a commodity finance bank decides to finance one of them, the risk evaluation may spread further to its upstream or downstream counterparty. Sometimes one of the supply chain companies may not be qualified as a counterparty, but by using the supply chain approach, an impossible borrower will become a possible borrower.

Figure 5.1: Supply chain framework for palm oil

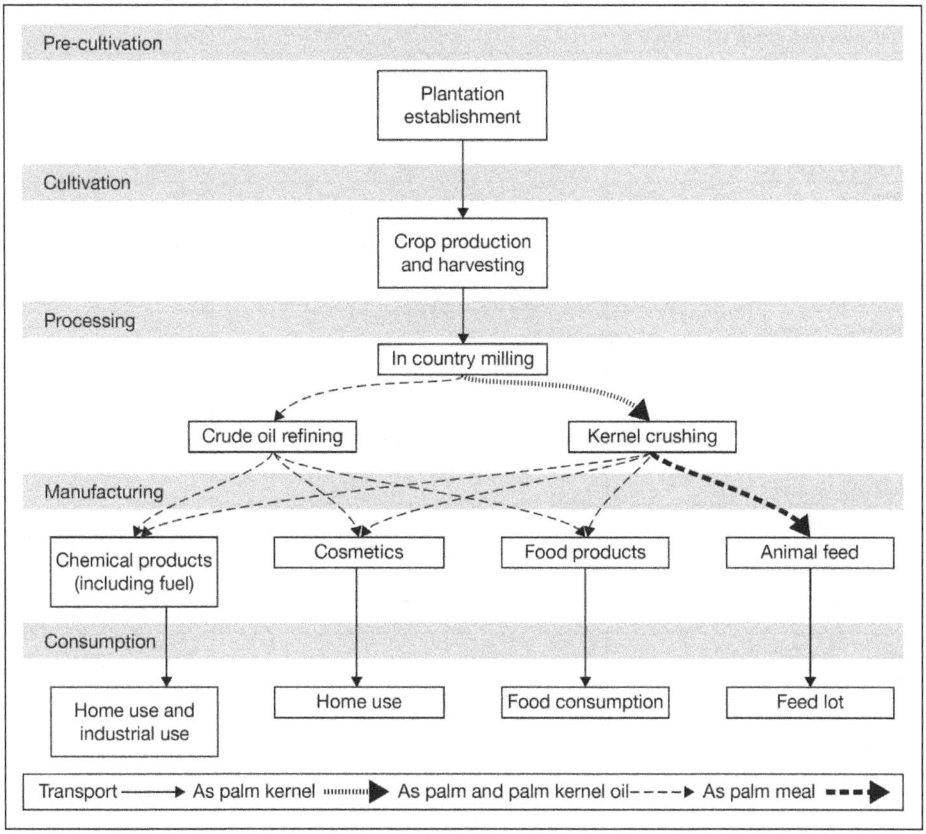

Source: Example taken from IISD/Scot Wilson GCSA analysis project for DEFRA and from WWF 'From seed to frying pan: the Malaysian oil palm sector'.

Risk mitigation via a supply chain is not new. The most typical example is the back-to-back structure in commodity finance, which is usually used for a trading company which has just started its record with the commodity finance bank.

Back-to-back or front-to-back facilities are popular products for many commodity finance banks. The financing bank, by closely monitoring the upstream and downstream commodity flow, mitigates the borrower's credit risk by linking upstream and downstream in the supply chain.

Commodity finance banks have strict internal rules and regulations to examine the deals with matching LCs for both upstream and downstream, from the buyer to the trader and then to the end-supplier. The table below lists the technical details that a bank should check in these deals.

Table 5.1: Back-to-back terms for commodity clients

Borrower under back to back facility			Date	
MLC:		BBLC:		
Buyer: applicant of master LC		Supplier: beneficiary of the baby LC		
Buyers:		Supplier:		
Terms and conditions	*Master LC*	*Baby LC*	*Mismatch*	
Amount				
Delivery term				
Expiry date				
Tenor				
Latest shipment date				
Shipment route	To	To		
Presentation with (days)	Days	Days		
Partial shipment				
Transhipment				
Full set title documents				
BL consign to:				
Marked freight				
Notify party				
Insurance to be covered by:				
Negotiation restricted to:				
TT reimbursement				
Sanctions clauses				
Delivery term				
Other discrepancies:				
Solution/recommendation:				

Source: Author.

In essence, traditional structured pre-export commodity finance as explained in Chapter 3 is a good example of upstream and/or downstream mitigation of risks in commodity finance by linking the processor, the supplier, the trader and the end-user together.

To start with, it extends to externalize the credit risk and to commoditize the transaction by detaching the trade supply chain flow from the borrower's financial strength. This kind of structure is also suitable for financing entities without any track record, as it largely leverages on the strength of the underlying commodity by using it as primary collateral.

Similarly, in the Ghana Cocoa Board case[19], the supplier alone may not be qualified as a borrower for country risk and its financial strength, especially the hard currency position. Commodity banks look beyond the supplier further into the upstream – their buyers, the buyer's bank – and downstream to control the cash flow into the

---

19 Details of the Ghana Cocoa Board case will be discussed in Chapter 8.

sub-suppliers of the supplier. Lending to the supplier is thus controlled to ensure that the supplier pays his sub-suppliers (of raw materials, machines and so on).

The structured commodity finance arrangements are based on closed-end, self-liquidating commercial transactions with procures in the market. The rationale behind the structured commodity finance is that, in many emerging markets, cross-border performance-related finance is sometimes an issue. The underlying question is how to get paid by liquidation of a flow of commodities exported by an emerging market country.

By structuring the deal along the supply chain, lenders can reduce a number of risks inherent in commodity finance. Credit risk on the borrower, who eventually exports goods, may be mitigated by recourse to the buyer, the off-taker, via assignment of export receivables, while currency, transfer or devaluation risk may be alleviated by receivables paid in to an offshore collection account. The risk on whether the exporter may deliver (performance risk) is mitigated by the refund guarantee of a (local) bank.

Hence, structured commodity finance seeks to secure repayment of bank lending by channeling funds from pre-identified sources through a chain of assignments, pledges and other security instruments. By structuring the supply chain trade circle and connecting the parties in this commodity's supply chain trade circle, structured commodity finance is supposed to transform non-acceptable payment into acceptable production and delivery risks.

Under structured commodity finance, the receivables arising under the export contracts for the commodities are assigned to establish a collection account in a suitable offshore location into which purchasers of the commodities are directed to pay the assigned export receivables.

Various credit-enhancement devices in the supply chain can complement the traditional core structure. Examples of credit-enhancement include guarantees (payment or performance guarantee provided by a financial institution or other third party which will give payment or delivery security), insurance cover and commodity price hedges in the case of export contracts on a floating-price basis.

What transactions are most suitable for this kind of structured commodity finance? One very important guideline is that the product should be made available mainly in emerging markets, which are procuring commodities in substantial quantities that clearly exceed domestic needs. In other words, you may identify a so-called 'push-out' factor there.

The reasoning behind it is that export-driven companies in these countries have resilience to shocks (both political and economic) that allow structured lending to capture the cash flow generated by the underlying commodity flow with a higher degree of certainty.

Lending based on assets is the backbone for structured commodity finance. Actual individual structures may be stronger or weaker, but a basic mindset behind them is that emerging market performance risk is better than emerging market payment risk. Therefore, performance risk deals are targeted.

To achieve this, a robust attitude to securing performance must be taken. This is done by ring-funding the current assets, as the only worthwhile part of the balance sheet from the liabilities (especially third-party creditors) and by preferring title to and control over the receivables, the sales contract and, ideally when possible, the inventory (underlying commodity) as well.

Clients who enter into structured commodity finance are those who often do not have an alternative and who intend to borrow large amounts but fail to do so in normal, plain vanilla deals.

This classic structure for commodity finance thus continues to be based on a combination of taking security under the supply chain over the physical commodities. This is done in the form of a local law pledge or similar security interest. Such a structured way is often used for soft (agricultural) commodities as well as mineral and metal industries.

SCF is thus recognized as extending the risk management beyond one single borrower, or one single transaction. An 'unqualified' borrowing party (often an emerging market producer) is made possible to get access to financing by dividing the credit risk among parties in the supply chain. The role each party can play is linked to their title to the goods under the commodity flow.

Figure 5.2 summarizes such a rationale.

Figure 5.2: Supply chain risk mitigation in pre-export finance

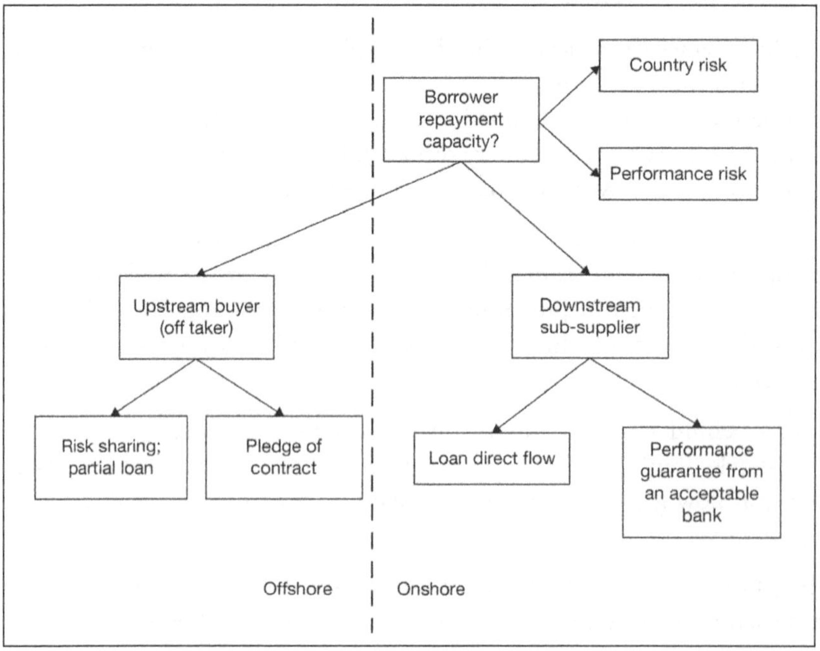

Risk management in commodity finance: the collateral management approach

Principles of collateral management

To some extent, we can say there is no commodity finance without collateral because commodity finance is asset-backed finance.

The understanding, monitoring and controlling of collateral is so critical to commodity finance banks that commodity banks must have a clear and effective procedure in place for collateral management. The structure must give banks clear rights over the collateral (including the possibility to liquidate it in case of default) supported by legal opinion.

Collateral can take various forms such as:

- commodities – produced, or shipped, can be represented by title documents

- accounts – cash balances in collection and operating accounts

- contract rights – receivables and future contracts and so on.

Moreover, the lending bank should have effective control over the exposure to guarantors and collateral-management service providers.

Collateral management is in fact a constant search for details (monitoring requirement) and for protection (control requirement) against often conflicting legal and economic ownership interests.

As a rule of thumb, collateral value used as a benchmark to finance should not be greater than the current market value and should be marked to market frequently. In addition to statistical revaluation, it should be revaluated by professional appraisers as well. Collateral risk depends on the nature of the collateral and the liquidity of the collateral.

Very often physical collateral is represented by title documents. Unless for top-rated commodity trading houses, for the vast bulk of commodity traders, secured lending is made possible if the bank can have possession of negotiable title documents, which represent commodities themselves.

Title documents can be negotiable licenced warehouse receipts, London Metal Exchange (LME) warrants, negotiable bills of lading, etc. Secured lending is possible if the lender is secured by a pool of assets such as inventory and accounts receivable.

All secured borrowers will be on a transitional, collateral pool. It is often the case that the bank's normal criteria for the extension of unsecured credit are not met.

As discussed above, in commodity firms, reference can be made to the inherent volatility, thin capitalization, and esoteric industry risks – all can be the reasons for refusing to lend unsecured.

Security, if properly used, is a device to make possible a loan where otherwise it would have been impossible or unlikely.

The credit risk management objectives have been summarized by three main principles: protection, seniority and control.

Protection

The lending bank's position should be protected in the sense that net realized value of the specific collateral should be sufficient to cover the bank's exposure, recognizing that the face value of the collateral may well have shrunk or will shrink during liquidation.

Seniority

The lending bank's legal right is ranked as top in the case of claim, that is, other creditors, if any, should not enjoy the same right. Proper filing and observance of correct collateral is the first step to ensure seniority. Procedures under the Uniform Commercial Code will help to prevent other creditors from gaining access to the secured assets in the event of liquidation.

Control

Detailed understanding of the customer's trade cycle is necessary to reconcile the tenor of each advance. Upon the borrower's sale of the goods and subsequent receipt of the funds, the bank's advance should be repaid, or collateral subtracted for the overall pool.

If we check any details of legal agreement, in many ways the agreement reflects these risk management concerns. The following is an example of a simple pledge of a bank account agreement.

Example 5.1: Comments on a sample pledge agreement

THIS AGREEMENT AND DEED OF PLEDGE OF BANK ACCOUNT is made on (date) between:

Bank A (the Pledgor); and

Bank B (the Pledgee).

It is agreed as follows:

1. Definitions of terms in this agreement

This part will clarify the legal terms used in the agreement to avoid any misunderstanding or ambiguity.

2. Creation of Right of Pledge and Covenant to Pledge

This part will discuss the right transfer in the agreement and purpose.

3. Authorisation to Collect and Dispose of Account Receivables

Here the pledgee will agree with the Pledgor that the Pledgor is not authorized to dispose of any monies from time to time deposited in the Accounts, until the obligation of the pledgor is fully discharged.

The pledgor's right is under protection.

4. Ranking

By clearly securing the ranking, the 'priority' principle is established, i.e. no other party can claim right.

5. Representations, Warranties and Undertakings

5.1 The Pledgor hereby declares, represents and warrants to the Pledgee that:

(a) it is duly incorporated and validly existing under [law] and it has the corporate power and capacity to enter into and perform its obligations under this Deed of Pledge and the transactions contemplated by this Deed of Pledge;

(b) it has taken all necessary action (including the obtaining of any necessary consents) in order to authorize the entry into, and performance and delivery of, this Deed of Pledge, and the transactions contemplated by this Deed of Pledge;

This is to secure the validity of the deed.

(c) this Deed of Pledge has been duly executed and delivered by it and constitutes its legal, valid and binding obligations, subject to applicable laws relating to creditors' rights generally, public policy and to the availability of specific enforcement;

(d) the entry into and performance of this Deed of Pledge does not and will not conflict with any applicable law or regulation or any applicable official or judicial order, its articles of association, or any agreement or document to which it is a party or which is binding upon it or any of its assets;

This clause will eliminate the legal risk that the right under this pledge is eroded due to difference of jurisdiction and/or other rules and regulations.

(e) no actions or administrative proceedings of or before any court or agency have been started or threatened in writing which if adversely determined are reasonably likely to materially adversely affect its ability to observe or perform its obligations under or pursuant to this Deed of Pledge;

(f) it has the authority to give as security the rights of pledge purported to be created by this Deed of Pledge;

(g) it is proprietor in respect of the Account Receivables pledged pursuant to Clause 2.2; and

(h) the rights of pledge purported to be created by this Deed of Pledge are valid and enforceable rights of pledge, ranking as provided in the first sentence of Clause 4.

5.2 The Pledgor undertakes to the Pledgee that the representations and warranties contained in Clause o shall at all times remain true and correct until all Secured Obligations shall have been finally discharged and there is no possibility of any further Secured Obligation coming into existence.

6. Foreclosure of Receivables

If an Event of Default has occurred and provided that there is a failure in the performance of the Secured Obligations, the Pledgee may foreclose the Receivables in accordance with Sections 3:248 et seq. of the Civil Code for purposes of applying the proceeds to satisfy the Secured Obligations.

7. Application of Proceeds

7.1 Subject to the payment of any claims having priority to the rights of pledge established pursuant to this Deed of Pledge, the Pledgee shall apply all monies received, recovered or realised by it pursuant to this Deed of Pledge, which shall include the proceeds of any conversion of currency (the Proceeds) to settle from time to time the Secured Obligations that are payable at that time in a manner provided for in the [Credit] Agreement, but without prejudice to Section 3:253 of the Civil Code or the right of the Pledgee to recover any shortfall from the Pledgor or any other party or person liable in connection with such shortfall and the Proceeds may, at the sole discretion of the Pledgee and to the extent permitted by applicable law, be credited to any bank account and may be held in such account for as long as the Pledgee shall think fit with interest accruing thereon at such rate, if any, as the Pledgee may deem fit (acting reasonably) pending its application from time to time (as the Pledgee shall be entitled to do at its sole discretion, but subject to any restrictions pursuant to applicable law).

7.2 For the purpose of or pending the discharge of any of the Secured Obligations, the Pledgee may convert any monies received, recovered or realized or subject to application by the Pledgee under this Deed of Pledge (including the proceeds of any previous conversion under this Clause 0) from their existing currency or denomination into the currency or denomination of the Secured Obligations.

8. Remedies

No failure on the part of the Pledgee to exercise, and no delay on its part in exercising, any right or remedy under this Deed of Pledge will operate as a waiver thereof, nor will any single or partial exercise of any right or remedy preclude any other or further exercise thereof or the exercise of any other right or remedy.

9. Set-Off

The Pledgee is authorized to apply or set-off (without prior notice) any credit balance and claim (whether or not then due or payable) to which the Pledgor is at any time entitled on any account at any office of the Pledgee in or towards payment of or against all or any part of the Secured Obligations.

10. Termination

Terms and conditions of termination of the contract is set.

11. Partial Invalidity

12. Evidence of Secured Obligations

A certificate by the Pledgee as to the existence and amount of the Secured Obligations shall be conclusive evidence as against the Pledgor, save to the extent of contrary evidence if any.

13. Variation

No variation or amendment of this Deed of Pledge shall be effective unless it is in writing, duly signed by (or by some person duly authorised by) each of the parties.

This blocks any one way change to alter the agreement terms.

14. Power to Assign

15. Governing Law and Jurisdiction

15.1 This Deed of Pledge and any matter arising between the parties under or in connection with this Deed of Pledge, and any non-contractual obligations arising out of or in relation to this pledge.

15.2 The Pledgor irrevocably agrees for the benefit of the Pledgee that (court name and location) shall have exclusive jurisdiction with respect to any disputes that may arise out of or in connection with this Deed of Pledge, including, without limitation, disputes relating to any non-contractual obligations arising out of or in connection with this Deed of Pledge. Nothing in this Deed of Pledge will limit the right of the Pledgee to take proceedings against the Pledgor in any other court of competent jurisdiction, nor will the taking of proceedings in one or more jurisdictions prevent proceedings being taken in any other jurisdiction, whether concurrently or not.

This part exclusively avoids legal risk of law not applicable/enforceable due to difference of jurisdictions.

Representative of Bank A as Pledgor (sign)

Representative of Bank B as Pledgee (sign)

Collateral control in warehouse finance

In commodity finance, collateral such as inventory stock is used as support to the lending facility provided. Stock finance is short-term finance extended to customers against the security of commodities before shipment and/or sales. This kind of warehouse finance will enable customers to procure the goods in origin and store them under approved warehouse keeper's custody for shipment. Similarly, warehouse finance will also enable the customers to store the goods at the destination under the approved warehouse keeper's custody.

The general rule is that the commodities should be pledged to the bank providing finance. The funding bank should arrange the security documentation on the basis of the location of the goods. Neutral third parties (warehouse keepers, forwarders, specialized collateral management companies, port authorities, etc.) provide surveillance, control and monitoring services. The country in which the goods are stored, the types of goods involved and the storage facility in which the goods are stored will all be taken into consideration for warehouse finance.

Moreover, the legal aspect – that is, the legal documentation of the warehouse finance – is also very crucial to ensure the lending banks' security on the goods as collateral. Especially for emerging markets, the opinion of a professional legal expert familiar with the legal environment on security documentation will ensure the enforceability of the lending bank's right on the collateral in that jurisdiction.

A warehouse may provide a storage function but can also provide services such as packaging, labelling, freight consolidation, etc.

Collateral control starts with the selection of the places in which the collaterals lie. Warehouses that are to be used for collateral management purposes can be divided into several categories:

Field warehouses

Field warehouses are provided by the foreign trading partner or borrower. A field warehouse is a public warehouse established by a bona fide public warehouser on the premises of a business concern for the purpose of acquiring custodianships of commodities owned by that business concern. Field warehouses are different from a 'terminal' or other public warehouses in the sense that the field warehouse exists only for the purpose of receiving deposits of commodities belonging to a single depositor and the warehouse is physically located on the premises of the depositor. Control over access to this enclosed space rests exclusively with the field warehouse man to ensure the control of the goods.

The field warehousing is simple and direct if the lending bank has a reliable field-warehousing man and a solid warehousing arrangement. The lending bank must evaluate the liquidation value of field-warehoused collateral and satisfy him that it is adequately insured and that the borrower has unencumbered title to the goods.

Reliable public warehouses: bonded warehouse or non-bonded warehouse

In many ports there are public warehouse companies and depots that are known to be reliable and properly insured. To deposit collateral in these warehouses is supposed to be a reliable way of collateral management, to secure lending to commodity trading companies.

Some of the warehouses are exclusively for commodity exchanges such as London Metal Exchange, London International Financial Futures and Options Exchange, New York Board of Trade and Chicago Board of Trade. These are good acceptable warehouses for stock finance. Some other warehouses linked to specialized trade associations are also recommended warehouse for stock finance: the Federation of Oils, Seeds, and Fats Association (FOSFA), The Grain and Fed Trade Association (GAFAT), and the Minor Metals Trade Associate (MMTA).

A bonded warehouse is used for the storage of goods before export, that is, before duties and taxes are levied. The commodities stored in the bonded warehouses are only to be released by customs for export.

Goods transferred from a bonded warehouse to a non-bonded warehouse are considered as import and vice versa. Goods imported in a country but still stored in a bonded warehouse are more flexible for re-export. Bonded warehouse finance is to finance cargo stored in bonded warehouses against a pledge of warehouse receipts issued by warehouse operators/collateral managers internationally known, such as C. Steingweg and Cornelder.

Goods in bonded warehouses are stored under customs supervision and may only be removed under certain conditions. This may improve the bank's control over the goods. Moreover, re-export of imported goods stored in a bonded warehouse can be effected without custom clearance.

The majority of the non-bonded stock financing will cover export-ready cargos of metals (such as zinc, lead, and aluminium) at the loading port. Non-bonded warehouses will include port authorities.

Such non-bonded warehouses are operated by state-owned or private companies. These companies will actually offer nothing else other than the lease of warehouse space.

If commodity banks intend to finance such warehouse stocks, the collateral management role is the key. Usually this role is to be entrusted to internationally known warehouses such as C. Steinweg and Cornelder. But more often nowadays, port authority-owned companies or reliable logistics companies with good records are becoming involved in performing this collateral management role.

Considerations on risk management for warehouse finance

Warehouse finance controls collateral in the warehouses. When a commodity bank is doing this kind of business, the following points for risk management purposes come into the picture.

The selection of reliable parties involved

A commodity finance bank must be selective to decide who are the targets parties for warehouse finance, not only to whom the bank has provided finance for but also who the client is working with.

In warehouse finance, the parties involved in the flow of goods such as suppliers, buyers, warehouse keepers (collateral management companies), transportation companies, and surveyors must be reputable companies, with track records checked and confirmed.

The selection of warehouses

As mentioned, warehouse finance is using goods in the warehouse as collateral which is the base for the lending. The selection of the warehouse and the collateral management company which monitors the collateral is the critical point of the structure. The care a bank should take over the selection is the same when a bank is selecting its own employees. This is because the collateral management company can get access to the securities which are supposed to belong to the lending bank before the loan is repaid.

The authority of the warehouse to produce warehouse receipts should always be checked if the warehouse receipts are to be used as title documents. The legal binding document between the financing bank and the warehouse should be established.

Usually the credit department will give a guideline on the list of acceptable warehouses.

Quality of commodities as collaterals

The quality of commodities is important. Commodity finance banks have preferred categories ranking in terms of quality of commodities in using them as collateral.

First of all, commodities used as collateral must be identifiable and preferably segregated. Commodities of proven quality that are certified to be commodity exchange deliverable is preferred, as the bank has full title and control over the goods, as well as the liquidity of the goods.

The second is the commodities for which the bank has various contacts in the market to sell them. The bank must have a full set of BLs or commodities specially pledged to the bank.

The third is commodities for which the bank may have some contacts in the market to sell but the marketability is not certain.

Lastly, liquid commodities for which the bank has little contacts available to sell will be considered.

Inferior quality delivered to the warehouse or the deterioration of the quality of the goods during the storage period will both have an impact on the value of the goods and total amount of the lending facility thereafter.

For collateral control, some other factors must be taken into consideration, such as perishability of the commodity, costs in maintaining the storage, possible restrictions in selling (e.g. whether import and export licenses are necessary and available), commingling and so on.

Monitoring of the collateral

The nightmare in warehouse finance is that goods are released/moved without the knowledge of the financing bank. It is essential that a clear link should be established between the financial and physical flows within the transaction structure. This should be taken at the very beginning of the deal and throughout the facility procedure. Especially in higher risk countries (emerging markets) where the financing bank does not have title documents, goods financed may be moved without knowledge of the financing bank.

In such cases, an independent and reliable collateral management agency or inspection agency may play a crucial role. Such an independent party is called the collateral manager/agent. They are in control of the goods in the warehouse on behalf of the financing bank. Only after the finance bank's instruction to the collateral management agent, may the goods be released out of the warehouse for loading on board or for forwarding to another place.

A Collateral Management Agreement shall be reached between the financing bank and the collateral management company. The collateral management company provides the financing bank with full information about the movement of goods on a periodical basis. Sometimes physical checks on the spot by the bank itself will be necessary.

In the monitoring of the collateral, proper insurance is a must. The insurance is supposed to cover fire, theft and other damages. In the absence of proper insurance, there will be loss or damage to the goods in the future with no possibility to claim.

Ratio of finance and the margin in the collateral value

As discussed earlier, stocks in the warehouse are never advanced at 100%. In most cases the finance-to-collateral asset ratio is maintained depending on the quality of the commodity, the liquidity of the commodity, the liquidity and transparency of the market, counterparties involved and so on. The valuation is either on the market value of the goods or in a marked-to-market form (that is, the market value is being assessed periodically).

The margin in the collateral value is a very important risk mitigant as it is the cushion for potential shrinking of value and/or miscalculation of the value. Sometimes, when the collateral margins fall below a certain minimum, the customer is requested to provide additional collateral to enable the lending to continue.

Legal documentation

Proper legal documentation will ensure your right on the goods, the perfection of your right, the seniority in the process of liquidation, and the control of the collateral.

The solidity of control of collateral very much depends on the solidity of the legal documents. Holding certificates, for example, are non-negotiable, non-title documents, provided by suppliers of the borrowers such as mining companies or smelters.

In some countries, especially in South America, holding certificates can be provided by the warehouse or the transportation companies. Holding certificates mostly relate to metal concentrates covering goods stored in the port of the exporting country waiting for shipment within a certain period of time (usually 30 days).

It goes without saying that the legal arrangement for the pledge is arranged and signed at the very beginning, that is, before the lending. If there is no pledge agreement signed, the financing bank may not have the right to hold or liquidate the goods when necessary. The lending is thus not secured.

Risk management in commodity finance: the instrumental approach

Despite the risk management efforts from the lending bank, a commodity bank cannot do each and every deal for its clients, especially when the amount involved is huge. There are instruments used in risk management either to shift the risk to another party or to enhance the credit status of the borrower, or reschedule the structure of the borrowing facility.

Risk coverage instruments

Banks set limits for the lending to the counterparty. When and if the risk appetite is reached, or credit facility offered is full, or for any other portfolio management purposes, and a bank intends to reduce its risk asset exposure, some instruments are available to offload the risk, or enhance the credit status of the borrower.

Forfaiting

Forfaiting is direct debt right transfer and supposedly risk transfer as well. Traditionally, forfaiting is to provide a source of finance to buyers and permits immediate payment to the exporter on a non-recourse basis. It is more often used in an interbank market.

Export credit agency cover

Most countries have a government or government-supported insurance scheme whereby exporters may insure against an importer's failure to pay. Bank loans under the trade finance category may also be under guarantee. Examples are ECGD in Britain, Coface in France, Hermes in Germany, and Eximbank in the USA.

The ECA's cover is traditionally acceptable as they are established in an industrialized country to facilitate the export of capital goods in the relevant countries, often backed by public funds. Risk is thus covered directly by and insured with a sovereign.

Due to high risks in medium- and long-term financing for debtors located in emerging markets, ECA's coverage becomes indispensable for these transactions.

ECA cover can be as high as 95% or more for commercial and political risk. A default under an ECA-backed loan results in international consequences for the entire country as the defaulted loan will be taken to the Paris Club[20].

Political insurance

There are also private sector initiatives for export-linked insurance, usually on commercial terms. In case of the absence of ECA coverage, private risk insurance is an option.

Private insurance coverage is different from ECA coverage in the sense that this type of risk distribution carries the full solvency. The insurers are profit driven, leading to increased claim risk.

These agencies will provide insurance to exporters for protecting them against loss arising from the buyer's default or insolvency. This is especially common to export to countries outside OECD countries. Political insurances are used to mitigate the exposure risk for commodity banks.

Political insurance schemes vary as the agreement is negotiated between the insurance underwriters and the parties who need the insurance. Moreover, the coverage may also be different. Insurance usually has coverage on the political risk of the country. The commercial conflict between the buyer and the seller is not covered by the policy as the underwriters have no insight behind the details of the transaction.

A typical political insurance contract will have the following parts:

- the description of eligible transactions
- the insurance percentage
- the waiting period
- the information needed.

Two points must be highlighted in the coverage. First of all, many insurance agreements may have exclusions for risk coverage, that is, risks are explicitly not covered. This is worth attention. Exclusions can very often be linked to a commercial dispute between the insured and its customer, or an operational risk where the political insurance underwriters cannot foresee nor can they control, such as a documentary discrepancy. Secondly, the claim to the insurance scheme will not be honored immediately. There will be a waiting period during which no interest will be paid.

---

20 The OECD member countries founded the so-called Paris Club to streamline and unify the debt restructuring. It is an informal consultative body of OECD. The mission is to arrange settlement and restructurings for countries that have defaulted on loans. The Paris Club cooperate closely with IMF and World Bank.

Before the political insurance underwriters can work, they may first of all request a package of information for the risk management competence of the bank. This may include the credit process, bank and country analysis capacity, transactions approval procedure and governing rules. Such an information package will ensure the risk underwriters that they are dealing with professional parties.

Coverage from development banks/import-export banks

Development banks such as the World Bank Group, IFC and its regional peers are playing a growing role in facilitating trade finance flow by offering their coverage.

At times of political uncertainty, offshore suppliers that sell much will need imports as raw materials. But they may have difficulties in obtaining confirmation of LCs issued by some countries which are experiencing domestic political or economic difficulties, or they can have the LC confirmation but the confirmation is at an exceptionally high cost. This results in the emerging market country which is in difficulties paying more for inputs used for export production, thus penalizing them vis-à-vis their international competitors due to political factors which are beyond their control.

Regional development banks may come into the picture under such circumstances and transfer this difficult risk into their regional development bank risk by offering a trade finance facilitation program to confirm bank risk in these difficult countries. Such a kind of trade finance facility will keep the difficult country open for international banks confirming eligible import LCs and ensure access to finance. This will also effectively reduce the cost of imports for export production.

Regional development banks are offering this due to their development strategy but also due to the fact that they have much bigger influence than the international banks on persuading individual countries to repay outstanding debts.

Under such a risk coverage scheme, the regional development bank guarantees the confirming bank that if it suffers a loss from the issuing bank's failure to make payments under the approved LC, then subject to certain terms and conditions, the regional bank shall pay to the guaranteed bank the guaranteed amount.

This kind of guarantee is often subject to certain conditions. For example, the facility will explain what kind of political risks are covered. These risks are often related to the transfer risk and/or the sovereignty risk of the country.

Examples can be the imposition by the government to regulate the capital outflow, amendment by the government to any existing exchange control regulations which result in an often more restrictive outflow of hard currencies or failure of the government to provide any lawful approvals which affect the availability, convertibility or transferability of foreign currency.

Non-payment under LCs can also be debt moratorium. The government in that particular country may announce a moratorium on the payment of any class of external indebtedness of any residents or nationals in that country.

A guarantee may also cover some less serious situations such as change of laws or regulations, or change of economic or monetary policy which adversely affects the timing, currency or manner of debt payment.

Some typical political risk should also be included, such as riots in the country, any expropriation, confiscation, nationalization and discriminatory legislative actions.

Usually not all the LCs will be eligible for such facilities. LCs must conform to UCP rules. An LC should be an irrevocable and unconditional obligation to pay. Eligible tenor (usually short) and maximum amount per LC may also be indicated.

As the rationale of such LCs is to promote the export of the country in difficulties, some of the LCs are not included in such a program. Typically, LCs are excluded for arms, ammunition, luxury goods and so on.

For such a program to work, the issuing bank, the confirming bank and the development bank will have a pre-arranged agreement. A master risk participation agreement must be signed by the regional development bank and the international confirming bank to define the terms and conditions mentioned above.

Development banks are working on commercial terms. The fee charged by them should be attractive to both the issuing bank and the confirming bank. It should also reflect the country risk premium.

Countertrade as a risk mitigation measure

Countertrade is the funding program which involves the exchange of commodities as the basis for a commercial transaction between two parties.

Banks are requested to provide finance on a 'with or without recourse basis' between the delivery of goods on one side (import) and the repayment from delivery of goods on the other side (export). Countertrade was popular especially in the 1970s and 1980s, when there was a lack of hard currency for the former Soviet Union block. Countertrade effectively covers the currency risk and price risk.

In countertrade deals, linkage between importer and exporter is crucial. Linked to countertrade, a kind of escrow account is established to facilitate the cash flow.

Fraud risk in commodity finance

Fraud risk and its impact

If we talk about risk management for commodity finance, fraud risk is certainly worth a special discussion as it is a nightmare for commodity finance banks. Typically, a fraudulent deal has the general characteristics of legitimate transactions of commodity flow, but with the critical difference that, while an honest party provides genuine value, the fraudster provides little or none. A fundamental fact which we cannot change is that, for banking finance, banks are working based on document. Even trade itself is based on contract.

Nowadays, there is a greater awareness of operational risk in general and fraud risk in particular for commodity finance banks. Nevertheless, unless very close control is imposed by the bank on fraud identification and prevention, fraud will occur over time.

Even in banks where precautions are taken, fraud cases unexpectedly still occur. It is often difficult to make a distinction between accounts and transactions associated with fraud and those that have a legal and sound basis. This is particularly true when dealing with substantial trade volume and commodity companies with complex business transactions which are often cross border with emerging markets.

Although there is a lack of reporting and statistics of losses to commodity finance banks due to fraud, no commodity finance bank can claim that they are fraud free.

Although transactions involving fraud may follow some patterns of behavior common to other criminal activities such as money laundering and so on, existing literature and cases give no guidelines for avoiding fraud in the future. Rather, they just inform us what fraud cases occurred in the past which may shed light on potential deals in the future.

Some of the world's largest banks, with very sophisticated bank management practices have fallen victim to fraud. Several banks simply withdrew from the commodity finance sector because their fingers were burnt by fraud.

One key fact is that banks always take the view that they are financing the commodity flow on a documentation basis. They are not supposed to assume responsibility for the existence or quality of the commodities traded. This is true.

But commodity finance, or international trade itself, is paid for under the documentary credit system. The title documents we discussed earlier gives the financing banks right as an owner when they are financing the commodity flow. The convenience of the commodity finance system is that the financing banks are dealing with documents. But fraud occurs simply because documents can be forged.

Hence the possibility of potential fraud arises from the fact that, typically, documents used in a trade finance transaction have few security measures built into them. None of these documents are immune from forgery, more so with the technical progress in scanners, color printers and laser printers.

The famous sugar fraud case is often used for discussion of commodity finance. The story goes that, once upon a time a Bulgarian buyer paid US$3.8 m/m for 13,100 tonnes of Brazilian sugar by LC. The payment was released by international banks on the basis of complied documents under LC. Nothing seemed to be wrong at that moment. The documents proved that the sugar was loaded with the name of the port and the name of the ship, bound for Vama, Bulgaria.

It turned out, however, that neither the ship nor the sugar existed and the fraudsters disappeared once they had the money in their hands. There is nothing peculiar about sugar which leads itself to fraud: it is simply one of many commodities and trades which are used in similar fraudulent routines. There is also nothing wrong with the international banks that paid as they followed the UCP practice.

As we discussed, a LC payment system is a relatively well-established system in trade finance. This system is based on the belief in the authority of paperwork. When diamonds can be faked and antiques can be forged, title documents can be fraudulent as well (see Figure 5.3 Fraudulent certificate of proof of product).

When a system is working on papers and papers can be forged, fraudsters are finding their way to take benefits from bureaucracies everywhere. Can we establish a new system which is based on physical assets? There must be suggestions as such but this is hardly workable for banks. How can a bank safeguard the commodity from the beginning to the end? It is therefore only natural that UCP is silent on fraud. Nevertheless, business must go on.

Figure 5.3: Fraudulent certificate of proof of product

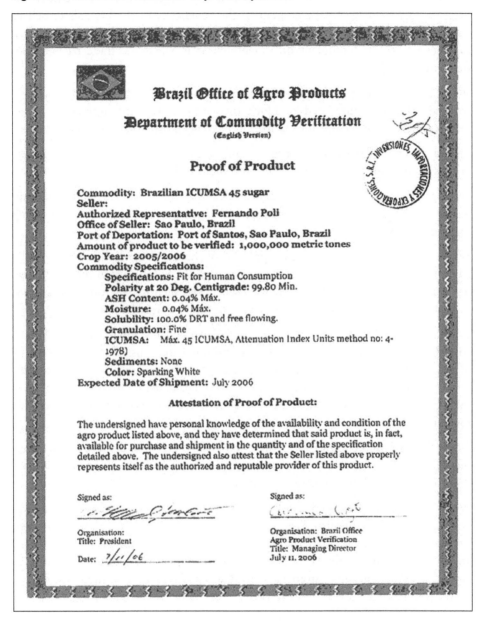

The strict obligation of banks issuing an LC under the concept of the autonomy of the credit is, to some extent, counterbalanced by the rights of the banks to refuse payment where documentation tendered is identified as fraudulent. Notwithstanding the fact that documents tendered are on the face of it in strict compliance with the terms of the credit, payment can be refused under the 'fraud exception' – when there is clear evidence of fraud, the bank has clear notice of the evidence of fraud and the bank is aware of the fraud in time.

An LC fraud can be established if the beneficiary forges a shipping document or presents documents with false content. If the beneficiary of the LC fails to deliver goods maliciously and the physical damage is evidenced, or the LC parties work together to present fraudulent documents without a genuine trade background, fraud will be claimed.

When a fraud is alleged, the payment obligation of a bank is, at least, temporarily blocked. The procedure used to block the payment is 'legal injunction' – the intervention of a local court for the irrevocable obligations assumed by banks.

This stop payment situation can, of course, only be used in 'exceptional circumstances'; otherwise the trade flow system is easily disrupted and distrusted.

Fraud as a threat to a commodity finance bank is also due to the fact that commodity deals are often in large amounts. The fraudsters are more motivated in manipulating the system to their advantages.

When and if fraud does occur, the applicant of the LC (buyer) wishes to stop the paying bank making payment on the ground that the beneficiary of the LC (seller) has been guilty of fraud. The beneficiary(seller) will sue the bank on the basis that the bank has refused to make payment on the ground of fraud.

Eventually the fight starts among banks: the LC issuing bank will refuse the payment with the excuse of legal injunction. The confirming bank – usually a correspondent of the issuing bank – that may have paid out in all innocence will defend their position towards the issuing bank. The confirming/financing bank will also check the legal relationship with the beneficiary/buyer to see if recovery can be possible towards the beneficiary.

Under the legal injunction scenario, one complication is how to define a fraud. Given the differing views taken by national courts regarding fraud, allegations of fraud are thus to be dealt with by the national courts instead of UCP rules.[21]

When and if fraud does occur, the financing banks will lose in one way or another, depending on the situation and the agreement with its customers. To add to that, the legal costs will occur, plus internal reporting, provisions and court hearings which are really irritating. At the very least, the fraud case will frustrate the relationship between the bank and its customers, or the correspondent bank in the LC chain.

---

21 King Tak Fung, in his book *Leading Court Cases on Letter of Credit* has a lengthy discussion and various cases in Chapter 5 Fraud and Injunctions. This includes questions like: Under what circumstances can the fraud exception apply?; and, Does the fraud exception apply if illegal actions are committed in a foreign country?

Considerations in fraud risk management

Whereas fraud cases vary from one to another, some patterns of behavior can be identified.

The IT development in communications enables criminals to operate by remote control and construct a web of fraud transcending boundaries with ease. But to a fraudster, to find a victim is the first step as there must be a victim in any fraud case.

The victim can be an individual or a company, or a bank. And there must be substance or pretext to entice the victim – whether it is counterfeit commodities or forged title documents.

The fraudster then needs the mechanism to obtain something of value in exchange for his fraudulent documents. Last but not least, he needs to evade arrest for his crime.

Hence, entrance control and client selection is the sure way to prevent fraud. Dealing with well-known, long-established entities definitely helps fraud prevention. Fraudsters are thus prevented from entering the door. Many international commodity banks are aware of fraud risk and have established a very strict 'know your client' policy.

As discussed in credit risk management at the beginning of this chapter, well-known, long-established companies, especially those with a decent credit rating, have themselves strict corporate governance. They also select their clients on a critical basis.

Clients with proposals of a strange structure, unusual roundabout ways of business, certain geographical areas where fraud cases are repeatedly reported, or commodities with irregularities (steel, scrap, fertilizer and so on) are all signs to watch. Yes, sometimes you just need common sense in judging a case.

Adhering to customer due diligence policy, including transaction monitoring policy procedures and control, is crucial. That is why the function of a commodity support group is an indispensable part for a commodity finance bank – a point on which we will elaborate in Chapter 6.

Everything against common sense can be a door a fraudster intends to enter. It is important to develop risk insights into types of clients representing higher fraud risk. The following may offer some tips for fraud prevention.

- **Unusual price**: Very 'generous clients' urging the bank to finance are worth our attention – victims of fraud are almost always attracted by expectations of exceptional profit. A deal which is too good to be true, probably isn't true.

- **Soliciting as many references as possible**: Nowadays every bank has its due diligence policy: 'know your customers and know your customer's business'. But fraud risk management is beyond that. You have to dig deep and check more when and if you have doubts of fraud. Soliciting as many as possible references can be useful to have a judgment. Checking with the client's competitors in the market often can tell more as market reputation indicates the integrity of the client. Upstream and downstream checks may reveal some points to watch.

- **Overseas deals and in-house legal experts**: Most commodity finance deals are emerging market linked. The difference in the legal environment often gives opportunities for fraudsters. In-house country specialists and proper legal advice will reduce the chance of stepping into fraud due to legal loopholes. Limiting the number and dollar value of non-domestic title documents that are presented as collateral also helps. Establishing and implementing a routine tracking system for the transactional lending, to monitor receivable due dates is necessary. It may serve as a net for fraud prevention.

- **Physical control and check**: Although it is true that banks are dealing with documents, occasional spot-checking warehouses and steamship lines to verify the physical presence of the commodities may help to protect the financing bank. Most commodity flow is via sea routes. Check with the steamship lines, by phone for example, on the existence of the goods, or the existence of the shipping line itself offers comfort. In the above-mentioned case of sugar fraud, by contacting Lloyd's Register of Ships, the financing bank would have found out that the ship was nowhere near the Brazilian port of Santos where the sugar was supposed to be loaded. The ship was in fact renamed in 1983 and broken up for scrap in Pakistan in 1984!

To hire an outside auditor to check an inventory on the spot and check the company's bookkeeping does add value in reducing fraud risk.

Defaults and bad debts management for commodity finance

Defaults and bad debts in commodity finance follow the development of business, especially for business in emerging markets. Loss due to fraud is only part of it.

One positive thing for bad debts is that people learn quickly about where the real risk lies. Defaults and bad debts are, nevertheless, painful to any commodity banks.

First of all, the costs associated with problematic exposure can easily wipe out the hard-earned profits. Added to that are the potential attorney's fees, time spent and opportunities lost and internal frustration and, sometimes, total standstill of this part of business in the bank's business.

The best problem solving is, therefore, problem prevention for which we have discussed. However, when all has been said and done, the problem may still arise despite the bank's various efforts. One of the competences for the success of the business or continuation of the business is the ability to resolve problems.

There are two crucial elements in securing the success of handling defaults and bad debt. One is a good and thorough appraisal of the case and the counterparty. The other is a good communication line with the counterparty.

Once a problem of payment occurs, the fundamental rule is to get organized as soon as possible. This is because the longer you wait in addressing a problem the more serious a problem may become.

Defaults and bad debts can be linked to counterparty bank failures and corporate failures. The way to handle these two categories of problems may vary. But, internally, an initial response and legal opinion of the position should be quickly in place.

For corporate exposure, searching for collateral is almost in all cases the rule of thumb, especially if financing is made against collateral. In this way, the commodity bank financing the counterparty can secure its position, even though the final settlement may depend on legal action. The financing bank can also off-set some deposits it may hold of a defaulting borrower, if a pledge agreement allows that.

Case appraisal and solution search

Solutions come from a good and thorough appraisal of the case and the counterparty. To analyze the problem and see if it is a temporary liquidity issue or fundamental insolvency is also critical. Very often the reasons given for delayed payment/non-payment on paper are only superficial.

Under an LC, for example, a discrepancy argument is very popular as a trade finance problem. Issuing banks are arguing for 'discrepancy' to 'legitimately' defend their non-payment attitude. But the fundamental causes could well be 'price of the underlying goods', 'quality of goods', or any other commercial conflict between the buyer and the seller.

Professional knowledge and network, and the first-hand information from relevant colleagues around the deal, will give access to the core of the problem and help to analyze it.

However, sometimes colleagues, due to the anger towards non-payment, may be emotional or may interpret the case in their own way. It is necessary to cool down to a rational attitude to analyze. At this moment, it is better to study similar cases in depth from the past.

A careful review of the case and relevant documentation files will earn you a better understanding of what is happening and why. Reading detailed correspondence, sometimes boring, between the fighting parties, particularly reading between the lines, may give more clues to a solution.

Legal advice, internal and external, is overwhelmingly important because they may be in a position to point out different scenarios for negotiation, litigation and arbitration. But more often than not, to let legal opinion replace your own opinion and analysis may lead to deadlock in possible solutions.

Legal opinion, at its best, can hardly include country-specific cultural aspects (especially for emerging markets) as well as relationship considerations. Out-of-court settlement is usually more preferred to legal actions.

Once you have an appraisal of the case, negotiation can start. In cases of disputes, banks often start negotiation by arguing who is right and who is wrong. This can be very misleading. Many banks are too brutally frank and too quick to propose a legal solution, and the negotiation will easily end up with 'seeing each other in court!'.

As a matter of fact, any negotiation is, in the first place, for the purpose of recovering your money rather than your face. You will have time afterwards anyway to sort out who is right and who is wrong, or perhaps the question will become irrelevant altogether.

The settlement can be 100%, 50% or less. This is up to your negotiation skills and it depends on how strong your position is. Hence, good legal opinion has its weight.

During the course of negotiation, it is better to identify quickly how a decision is made in the hierarchy of the counterparty with whom you are negotiating. It may happen that one of the persons at the operational level is a key person in the process. The decision is, of course, taken by the senior decision-maker, but the operational staff have an input anyway.

From time to time, banks adopt an up-looking attitude for negotiation – trying to push payment by approaching the top management of the counterparty – which is not always effective.

Payment, if any, must be made by the proposal of the operational department. Moreover, contact with the operational staff will give you useful information on the background of the problem, so that you will know what really went wrong, which is the starting point of your negotiation. If no settlement is reached after negotiation, there are options for various actions.

Strange enough perhaps, to 'take no action' can be one of the options. In several difficult cases, the real problem turns out to be that the counterparty needs time to sort out their internal problem. If this turns out to be true, the solution is simply to give time but insist on your right that their commitment for payment be in place. To push immediate payment could push the counterparty to deadlock, so that court solution becomes the only option.

Occasionally, a payment problem may cure itself once time is given. This, however, does not mean that you just sit and hope. In the case of a legal court injunction, for example, you cannot take any action but you still have to follow the development in court.

Sometimes when a deal involves a large amount or several parties, a steering committee is established to work on general solutions, but you may have to provide different documents to the authorities. Ignorance of some deadlines may have consequences on your legal right.

Litigation

The fact that legal action is not preferred can be explained by a couple of reasons.

First, it usually takes a very long time from 'writ serving' to 'scheduling the date of hearing'. Sometimes it may even take years. Legal documents usually need to be translated into the local language used on the other side of the world and different countries may have different legal procedures.

Second, legal action can be a source of embarrassment and usually can have bad publicity to both parties. There are also complications linked to foreclosure.

Last but not least, it is difficult to predict the result of a court decision. Some banks have lost cases due to some negligence of legal procedure rather than plain facts.

Legal action should be taken as a last resort and only after careful deliberation. A couple of issues should still be addressed before going to court:

Does the counterparty have means to pay anyway?

If not, the court decision only gives you the comfort of who is right and who is wrong. There is little commercial sense to your file. Of course, the case may serve as a model for similar cases in the future.

Is the relationship with the counterparty important enough that you have to think twice for a legal action, to avoid cultural harm to the relationship?

It is not unusual that, when a court file is prepared, the business relationship is frozen. This is not necessarily good for both parties, unless you definitely want to delete the counterparty as your business partner, at least for a period.

It is good to separate individual business disputes from the overall business relationship. A phenomenon worth noticing is that when two parties are under legal settlement procedure, the chance for 'business accidents' will be less as both parties are on the alert. Commodity banks will have to bear this in mind and try to minimise the cultural harm to the overall relationship.

How certain is the result of court?

The result of court is difficult to predict, an estimation is however possible. Nevertheless, do not rely on this estimation. Logic and common sense may not always work in a court.

Is there any similar alternative for a solution such as third-party arbitrage?[22]

Sometimes, an alternative from a similar case, if quicker and cheaper, can be of reference.

How to facilitate the post-solution relationship

There are a lot of cases where dispute and conflict become emotional and both parties finally become, unnecessarily, 'enemies'. Handle the relationship carefully whether you win or not. Under many circumstances, your efforts for a positive relationship will be rewarding in the end.

If the final decision is litigation or arbitration, questions as follows remain:

Is the judgment of court enforceable to the other party?

If the verdict of the court is not enforceable, the verdict is only a judgment of who is right and who is wrong.

Which court suits your interest most?

If there is no mention of applicable law in the agreement, what has to be noticed is that the same fact may lead to different judgments due to the applicable law. A typical example is the discrepancy argument among banks. Under certain circumstances, some courts may give favorable judgment if material conformity is there, despite documentary irregularities.

Which law firm is the most specialised one in this regard?

Usually a large law firm may have law experts available in different countries. But some law firms may be particularly strong in the field to which your case is relevant – strong not only in this professional law subject but also in the cultural and network in the country of the counterparty.

---

22 Hopward Palmer in his 'Bank Risk Analysis in Emerging Markets' mentioned his principles: legal action can work if: The debtor has money or saleable assets; The debt is acknowledged; The law is agreed; Exchange control formalities are in order; There is reasonable certainty about the law; and Exchange reserves are available for repayment.

Debt sale and debt collection

When default and bad debts are certain and provisions are provided, there are still options to reduce total loss.

Some debt agents (including some investment funds) may buy 'bad' debt either as final investors or trade it in the secondary market. The motivation for them to purchase is to collect the bad debts but finally to recover them through their own ability, or via special debt collection agents.

If a sale is ever possible, it will understandably be at a discount. Any difference between the real debt and the recovered part of the debt will be booked as loss to the bank. Sometimes it is possible to claim a tax refund on that.

The motivation for a third party to buy can also be that the investors (investment funds), after buying it at a good discount, keep the debt and wait. They expect some political changes for the obligor of the debts in the future, which raises the hope of the repayment of total debts or part of it.

When trading, the debt agents assist in the monitoring and managing of the transaction including the conduct of negotiations with the investors and asset traders and the repackaging and/or securitization of debts to facilitate the sale.

If the decision of the sale of distressed debt is made, there are issues to be discussed and agreed upon by relevant parties. For example, whether the procedure should be confidential or not, that is, can it be released to the third party or even to the public. The confidentiality terms will be made to clarify the commitment of relevant parties. The original loan agreements will be carefully studied.

A key issue here is if this debt can be further transferred according to the original lending terms. If the loan agreement specified that the loan would not be allowed to be transferred, the buying party may only offer a solution on a 'participated' basis, with all the future administration remaining in the hands of the selling bank. There are also issues of tax and so on. The bank may get some refund from local tax authorities for the part of loss.

The sale of distressed debt will enable the lending banks to remove the debts from their balance sheet. The sale of distressed debts will also provide immediate cash to the bank.

Once the selling price is determined and the selling contract is signed, the nightmare of bad debt will be out of the book. No argument, no re-negotiation, out of sight, out of mind.

But not every deal is saleable – either due to a lack of any suitable buyers, or because legally it is not allowed to transfer the debt right to another party. If the decision of the sale of debts is not the best anyway, another option is then to appoint the debt solution agency to collect the debt on your behalf.

Debt collection, alternatively, takes time and you will be constantly engaged for the whole period. Return on debt collection is also uncertain, although it may be higher than the direct selling price.

Debt collection typically involves assets tracing. Litigation is often a must. Any debt collection agency must have experienced lawyers and country specialists available, who have both country knowledge and a high-level contact for effective debt repayment negotiation. They will thoroughly analyze the debt in question, so the relevant professionals will be appointed.

As bad debts can be anywhere in the world, a good debt collection agency should have an efficient international network of lawyers or law firms, who offer services from the local perspective.

Alliance with local professionals, including local lawyers, is crucial to the success of the collection, as the local professionals will eventually act as real debt collectors. That is also the reason to choose the right debt collection agency for the specific bad debt.

Final recovery of bad debts is very often through the use of legal remedies. It is important to identify and trace attachable assets in favourable worldwide jurisdictions, to ensure that the judgments obtained can actually be enforced.

In some cases, further lending to the existing debtor could be a possible action. But several conditions must be met:

- This new lending may give the defaulted party more time to sort out its problems and to weather the immediate crisis.

- The lending should give momentum for a dynamic motivation, i.e. new income may be generated if and when the new lending is in place.

This action of new lending must be carefully weighed as the new lending should be safe and secured in a way that assures you can be paid (for example, control of collateral, secured flow of future income, etc.).

For emerging market counterparties, new lending should be linked to hard currency income as off-shore income is important for an emerging market debtor. If possible, the new lending should have a senior position among all existing outstanding. There should usually be restrictions to the utilization of the new lending, as it should only be used in places where new income can be generated.

CHAPTER 6

Commodity Finance and its Infrastructure

The organizational infrastructure of commodity finance in a bank

Not every bank can be a commodity bank. Some banks are doing commodity finance deals but they are not a commodity finance bank.

Commodity trade and the finance of it started centuries ago. The past 10 to 20 years have seen China's rush for commodities. But the quest for commodities can be traced as far back as the Roman campaigns in the first century (tin, olive oil, grains, etc.), via the Spanish, Dutch, French and subsequently British empires and their quest for gold, silver (Spanish), spices (Dutch), sugar, tea, cotton (English); and to the rise of modern English and American corporations since the 1860s on the back of the Industrial Revolution which powered the economies and created an enormous demand for commodities. Hence, it is not surprising that the accumulated banking know-how on commodity trade and commodity finance has been concentrated on Spanish, Dutch, French and English banks, although it is definitely spreading to more banks.

Commodity finance is a cross-border banking business. A full-fledged commodity finance bank offers financial products throughout the entire commodity supply chain, which ranges from the production of raw materials in the country of origin to the delivery of the final product to manufacturers. Financial products include the pre- and post-financing of commodity flows, inventories and receivables finance, etc.

Banks with the ambition to service commodity clients need internal and external resources to support the whole commodity value chain. Equally important is the know-how and the risk management of this niche banking. In fact, as a niche banking activity, commodity finance is unique in many ways. Accordingly, a commodity bank therefore needs some unique qualifications.

First of all, commodity finance is a type of asset-backed finance with risk components that are often beyond the traditional balance sheet credit risk. A commodity bank must have qualified and capable credit professionals in place to estimate relevant risks of the products or the risk components of a deal.

Second, commodity producers, traders or customers often need more banking services than financing the transaction, such as financial market products and price hedging services.

Third, because banks use collateral to mitigate risk and many deals are self-liquidating with quick turnover, a good support group is necessary in order to handle, monitor and control the underlying commodity flow and the change of collaterals, so as to check the mark-to-market value of the collateral.

Also, a commodity bank must have commodity knowledge competence and research units, not only to follow industry developments and have a forward-looking view on the market, but also to enable a commodity finance bank to choose its right clients, or choose the right facility it is going to offer.

Unless the entire necessary infrastructure is in place, a bank may not be qualified as a commodity finance bank.

We will discuss in more detail in this chapter what departments are necessary, what they are supposed to do and why certain competences can be critical for a commodity finance bank.

The organizational setup of a typical trade and commodity finance department within a commodity bank usually can be summarized as follows:

Table 6.1: A trade and commodity finance department set-up

Directly involved		Indirectly involved	
Team name	Responsibility	Team name	Responsibility
Relationship management	• Focuses on a sector. • Communicates with the client. • Is the first risk filter.	Credit approval department	• Approves, disapproves or modifies proposals. • Is a part of the central credit committee.
Credit analysis department	• Assesses client and deal risk. • Asks questions accordingly. • Prepares financing proposals for the credit committee.	Legal department	• Drafts offering letters, deal documentation, assists in disputes. • Co-operates with external and local counsel as well.
Risk management	• Advises on credit facilities. • Checks and approves products. • Imposes special terms.	Bank and country risk analysis department	• Sets credit limits on banks and countries.
Financial institutions	• Creates bank and country limits. • Manages bank and country risk.	Industry research	• Researches trends in soft, hard and energy sectors.
Support group	• Monitors collateral position. • Checks client requests and positions.	Corporate social responsibility department	• Interprets and implements the bank's guidelines on social responsibility.
		Commodity hedging desk	• Hedges commodity price risk. • Is a part of the global financial markets.

Source: Author.

Front desk: relationship management

The relationship managers are supposed to acquire suitable clients and transactions for the bank. They communicate directly with clients and prospects. They are so called 'front desk'.

The front desk is also the first risk filter by deciding which corporate to accept. They will estimate and recommend a suitable product for the client.

Relationship managers must have commodity knowledge and market information. According to their special knowledge and background, they are divided into different sectors: hard commodity, soft commodity and energy.

The relationship management should be the access point for prospects to the bank service. They will have initial meetings with prospects or clients to assess if a mutually beneficial relationship can be established, and deals can be created that would fit the strategy of the bank and the department.

In most cases, the borrower and its representatives will be known to the relationship manager. In cases which concern a new client, the relationship manager will start up a pre-check including EU/USA sanction list by fulfilling the know-your-customer-checklist, to determine in adequate detail the exact finance needs and outline the deal structure of the potential borrower.

Credit analysis team

The credit analysts, usually with financial analysis skill and training, work hand-in-hand with relationship managers to assess the risk of the client/deal and prepare the financing proposal to the credit committee. The credit analyst is responsible for the standard risk filter using financial analysis, rating, and risk return calculations.

The team is also responsible for collecting and capturing default data, and is supposed to analyze potential risks underlying the deals and ask questions accordingly. Often, but not always, the analysts also join the visit to the client.

Risk management team

This team, the members of which must have plenty of experience and exposure to commodity finance, has an independent and crucial function in evaluating the risk of a client or a deal for the client. They advise on credit facilities, check and approve products and structures offered to clients, and handle emergency cases. The risk management team can impose special terms and conditions on the facilities offered to clients to protect the position of the bank. They are supposed to evaluate and approve new products and the excess of credit limit, if necessary.

Commodity support group

The Commodity Support Group (CSG) or the 'mid-office', as it is often called, monitors, amongst others, the collateral position of the bank and execution of the credit facilities. The CSG has a pivotal role between the front-office and back-office: the CSG checks whether clients' outstanding positions and drawing requests fall within the approved facilities. The CSG also checks if sufficient collateral is available.

Financial institutions

The commodity finance business is very much linked to bank and country risk, either because a corporate risk is often converted into a bank risk or because the exposure must be booked under country risk. The business unit of financial institutions (FI) is established to fulfill this function.

The FI department estimates and manages the bank and country risks within commodity finance. It is also responsible for creating credit limits per bank and country. Eventually, the FI unit also handles problems related to banks and countries.

There are other departments in a commodity bank linked to commodity finance activities, such as:

Credit approval department

The credit approval department is the department which approves, disapproves or modifies the financing proposals received from relationship managers. This department is part of the central credit committee of the bank.

Legal department

The legal department offers legal services such as drafting the bank's offering letter, drawing deal documentation and assisting in potential legal disputes with clients or banks.

The documentation is drafted by an in-house legal counsel. In case of complicated deal structures, external counsel will be invited.

Once legal documentation has been accepted and signed by the client, the legal department checks all facilities and makes sure security documents (such as a pledge) have been received correctly.

Given the nature of multi-jurisdictions and conflict of laws, for commodity finance, the legal department should be a competence center for legal services, including outsourcing such a service via its network in different countries when a dispute of commodity deal emerges.

When and if a legal solution is a must for a commodity deal dispute, the legal department is fully responsible for possible steps and analysis of different scenarios. Throughout the handling of problem, legal service will be needed. To contract external lawyers is sometimes necessary.

The department also serves to avoid the risk associated with changes in and compliance with legislation and regulation, potential threats to the bank's legal status, including the possibility that contractual provisions are not enforceable or not properly documented.

On specific or complex products, a legal opinion is offered by this department, in order to assess the legal position of the bank. A second opinion from a local lawyer in that jurisdiction is often a must, since the knowledge of the local legal practice is key in emerging market deals.

Bank analysis department

Whereas the FI department proposes a bank credit limit, this department evaluates and sets the credit limits for banks with which trade and commodity clients do business. Commodity clients doing bank risk products (such as the confirmation of LCs) will all be booked under the bank limit. The FI department approves the excess of individual bank limit, if necessary.

Country risk analysis department

This department sets credit limits for countries with which trade and commodity clients do business, because commodity finance deals often involve country risk (such as pre-export finance, export finance, and so on). They approve the excess of individual country limit, if necessary.

Industry research department

The industry research department researches trends and developments in the soft and hard commodity markets and energy sectors. This department also does research and forecasts the supply and demand in commodity market and the prices. These reports will provide both clients and relationship managers with input to formulate a vision of developments in the commodity market.

Corporate social responsibility department

This CSR unit is devoted to the interpretation and implementation of the bank's guidelines on social responsibility, because some of the commodities' production processes have an impact on the environment.

Commodity price hedging desk

Commodity price risk is critical to commodity clients and banks. Hedging the price risk is thus important. This task is usually executed by a future/forward desk of the global financial markets team. It may also be outsourced to special external agencies.

Commodity finance and commodity market research

For a bank to do commodity finance, it must follow the development in the markets for commodities, since the markets are dynamic and volatile. Therefore, a commodity bank needs a competent research team.

This team not only provides in-house expertise on the relevant industry, but also helps to formulate strategies in different sectors. This will allow the bank to have a global vision on the market.

Such a commodity market research unit serves several purposes. First, a strong research department will boost the professional image of the bank. Second, it will help facilitate the business plan inside the bank: a forward-looking attitude enables the bank to plan its business and determines its risk appetite.

The future cannot be predicted. Nonetheless, efforts are made to forecast trends that are related to the production and trade flow of commodities. For example, in the agricultural sector, scientists have developed a variety of tools, ranging from the simple extrapolation of historical data to computer models predicting future weather patterns.

A model is a simplification of reality and its outputs are not better than the quality of its inputs. Researchers create simple or complex models, each with its own assumptions, uncertainties and limitations.

When the predictions of several models point in the same direction, the likelihood increases that this direction may be the actual trend, which will impact commodity trade. Hence, both commodity trading houses and the banks that serve them are interested in such kinds of research.

Research on individual commodities has been around for a long time, especially for those listed on commodity exchanges. These studies often focus on the supply or demand side of commodities. Big commodity finance banks or commodity traders employ their own research teams to support their business.

Given the rising importance of commodities, many universities and institutes also undertake commodity research. Understandably, their research is more general.

The following table is only an example of a study on the world iron ore trade. It depicts the results of research indicating the future trends in the global production and consumption of iron and ore. This kind of information will greatly help the commodity banks in their planning process. Such a table may help the commodity traders and their banks understand the trend and estimate the volume of iron ore available in the market.

Table 6.2: Outlook for world iron ore trade (million metric tons)

	2009	2010	2011 estimated	2012 estimated
Iron ore imports				
European Union (27)	92	133	145	154
Japan	106	133	133	149
China	628	623	642	694
Republic of Korea	42	53	57	60
Chinese Taipei	12	15	16	17
World total	948	1,036	1,071	1,155
Iron ore exports				
Australia	363	402	414	459
Brazil	266	308	324	358
India	97	89	87	83
Canada	31	34	35	36
South Africa	45	47	52	56
Sweden	16	14	15	15
World total	948	1,036	1,071	1,155

Source: The Australian Bureau of Agricultural and Resource Economics and Sciences.

Commodity finance: the support group and the trade service department

Commodity finance activities in a commodity bank also need the mid-office, back-office, Trade Service department, and a tailor-made IT system.

The support group, or the mid-office, is important because commodity finance is self-liquidating and collateral-based finance. Therefore, the collateral position of the bank vis-à-vis borrowers is of critical importance. Just imagine a commodity bank financing its clients with US$25 m/m limit based on US$50 m/m worth of warehouse storage of copper. However, if the storage reduces to 25 m/m, the bank must call for extra security. Otherwise the bank's position is not protected. The CSG is, amongst others, tasked with the monitoring of the bank's collateral position.

In the organizational structure of a commodity bank, the CSG has a pivotal role between the front-office and back-office: the CSG checks whether clients' outstanding positions and drawing requests fall within the approved facilities. The CSG also checks if sufficient collateral is available.

Each drawdown is presented on a case-by-case basis under a framework pre-agreed between the bank and the client. Before the drawdown occurs, the mid-office verifies whether the transaction complies with all the terms and conditions of the granted facility. Such terms and conditions can include an upfront presentation of transport documentation, insurance and a sales contract. Terms and conditions may also include a list of acceptable names, lists for warehouses, shipping lines, etc.

The CSG monitors the movement of the goods throughout the life of the transaction. For example, the group monitors the transfer of title documents until borrowers receive the proceeds of the sale from the off-takers.

Financing commodity trade involves high risk, because of the huge amount of transaction size. One shipment of soybean is around US$40 m/m–US$50 m/m, iron ore US$25 m/m–US$30 m/m, let alone energy commodities.

Obviously, most commodity trading companies are considered as thinly capitalised and considerably leveraged, due to the liquidity of their assets. Thus, operational risk is one of the major risks in commodity finance.

The CSG therefore plays a role in supporting the bank's commodity finance initiatives. The CSG provides dedicated, specialized and quality administration for commodity clients on a daily basis. Transactions are followed, scrutinized and managed with a hands-on approach.

The CSG is responsible for tracking the collateral under secured faculties and following individual transactions under transactional facilities. Such a task involves monitoring the movement of commodities, release of stocks, payment/receivables due, and shipment details.

They also check different credit limits offered to clients, such as collateral limits, tenor limits, credit exposure limits, collateral caps, approved buyers/sellers, warehouses, charterers, insurers, market value of collateral and the timely collection of proceeds.

In commodity finance this support function is never over-emphasised. An information mismatch, such as the lack of prompt reactions to payments or receivables, will lead to a direct loss. Many commodity finance banks suffer losses due to their ignorance of a change in collateral or their failure to trace negative developments of their clients.

As a matter of fact, for all commodity finance customers and products, the CSG acts as an internal central 'checkpoint'.

Before any change in exposures (such as transferring funds, loan drawings and/or the issuance of LCs and guarantees) is executed, the CSG is informed. Additionally, repayments, reductions in exposure and changes in facilities need to be reported to the CSG, because this team checks any new drawing under the approved facilities on (sub-) limits, available collateral and other restrictions. The CSG should be able to provide relationship managers, risk management and client's information on gross and net exposure per customer at any point in time.

Sometimes the commodity finance support group's function is mixed-up with pure back-office. Traditionally, the back-office executes transactions, such as the issuance of an LC, wiring a payment due, receiving payments and registering those. However, the CSG has more responsibilities.

The CSG team has the position to hold or release title documents, such as a bill of exchange and warrants. Also, the department communicates directly with the front-office to remind it either of some negative movement, or a decrease of the collateral's market value. The CSG also monitors the relevant legal documents, such as pledge agreements.

A significant task of the CSG is that it is responsible for tracking the accurate exposure (such as gross, net, secured and clean maturity dates) per client and to feed that information through, both to the local commodity finance department and the global head office.

The CSG ensures that a detailed and accurate information report is provided to the relevant people at the relevant level, such as management, risk managers, relationship managers and internal auditors. Such a report will describe details per obligor, region, market, product and tenor horizon.

The accuracy and quality of information has a direct impact on a commodity bank's professional position.

As such, the CSG reports on a regular basis on limit excesses and collateral deficits. Any material deviations exceeding a pre-determined amount, or delay and defaults should be reported immediately in order to take remedy actions.

The vast majority of commodity finance credit facilities are split into sub-limits and available against collateral and/or detailed transaction information. Transactions and/or collateral need to be monitored on a daily basis. The CSG is responsible for the daily monitoring of outstanding exposures under approved credit facilities, related collateral values and individual transactions under transactional secured and unsecured facilities.

As mentioned, the most important task of the CSG team is to administer the collateral value. They are different from pure back-office as they communicate with customers and third parties regarding collateral specifics (quantity, quality, location, warehouse, shipping company and insurance). The CSG is also responsible for initiating quality inspections, monitoring collateral, ensuring the security will be perfected, checking title documents on completeness, asking for additional or releasing collateral against payment (in accordance with the terms and conditions of the approved facility). The release of collateral requires 'two pair of eyes' and signatories from the CSG.

In a nutshell, the CSG is responsible for the full overview of the facilities (committed and uncommitted), exposures (gross and net), collateral and covenants.

Collateral management is understandably important because of the asset-backed nature of commodity finance. Collateral management thus becomes an indispensable part of commodity finance: it supervises the storage and logistics of commodities.

Although the CSG monitors collateral, many commodity banks are aware of the importance of collateral and therefore involve collateral managers. These managers look after collateral on behalf of the bank, especially in the case of inventory finance. By using a collateral management agency, the commodity finance bank makes sure commodities stay under control in case anything goes wrong. If the borrower defaults on interest payments, the bank may sell the commodities to cover its position.

Last but not least, a good CSG needs a tailor-made IT system to keep track of the collateral and perform daily mark-to-market calculations. As the business has become more and more reliant on technology it is clear that a stable IT system is crucial for transaction processing, monitoring and reporting. By having an overview via the information system, a good insight for all deals is provided.

The IT system should be able to monitor different and detailed types of credit facilities, such as:

- secured transactional finance
- forfaiting and discounting
- borrowing base
- commodity repos
- hedged structured deals.

And all kind of collateral types, like:

- financial collateral
- documentary collateral
- physical collateral
- performance collateral.

Of course, a number of limits regarding credit risk are to be recorded and controlled such as:

- collateral limits

- tenor limits

- credit exposure limits

- collateral caps

- approved buyers/sellers, warehouses and charterers.

Similar to the CSG, the trade service department, or documentary department as it is sometimes called, is critical for the success of commodity finance banks. It is another operational part of commodity finance activities.

Although different researchers seem to indicate that documentary credit is on the decrease and bank payment obligation (BPO) is widely promoted, in the field of commodity finance, documentary credit seems, stubbornly, resistant to disappearing. This is particularly so when there is a financial crisis.

Special competence for the trade service department

The trade service department's importance is linked to the instrument often used in commodity finance: the LC. The department is supposed to handle documents used in commodity finance. For a good trade service department, it must meet several special requirements.

First, they must do their document handling quickly to serve the commodity clients, as most of them need the proceeds to manage their cash flow. Some banks do have a 'day in day out' guideline, when possible.

Second, the department must have sound knowledge of the commodity finance title documents. For example, when the amount of LC does not sound logical, they would contact the relevant relationship manager to cross check.

Third, they have to fulfill the compliance function for the bank, such as check the sanction list. They also have other due diligence responsibilities.

The function of this department is beyond the regular handling of documents in a normal trade finance bank, because there are documents mainly or even exclusively used in commodity finance.

Commodity finance very often consists of secured lending to trading companies. Various instruments are used to control the eligible collateral, from BLs to warehouse receipts. These title documents represent the ownership of the collateral. Sometimes some instruments are subject to local legislation, but many of them have common characteristics.

It was discussed that the LCs are often used in international trade finance so as to replace the payment risk of the buyer by the risk of the issuing bank. Under an LC, documents should comply strictly with the terms and conditions of the requirements of the LC. Several kinds of title documents are used to represent the ownership of the goods. Losing control of the documents implies losing ownership of the goods and subsequently losing control over collateral.

Major documents handled by the trade service department for commodity finance include BLs, trust receipts, letters of indemnity, and warehouse warrants.

Bill of lading (negotiable)

For commodity trade, the basic document for controlling goods is a BL. When goods are loaded on board a ship or on a carrier (train, airplane and so on), the driver of the vehicle issues a document called the bill of lading for sea transportation, and railway bills and airway bills for train/plane transportation.

A maritime BL is the contract of carriage between the shipping company and the exporter to transport the goods by sea. The BL outlines the terms of contract of the carriage and acts as a receipt for the goods. It also constitutes a negotiable document of title to the goods. As such, the seller or the buyer holding the BL may transfer ownership of the goods if and when he endorses the new holder of the bill. The carrier must deliver the goods to the new holder of the BL. The bill can also be endorsed to a bank that finances the holder. This endorsement enables the financing bank to use the goods as collateral to its financing. The carrier is not entitled to hand over the goods to the buyer without the consent of the bank. Despite the fact that container transport is growing, the BL remains an important title document, especially for export to Africa, Asia and the Middle East.

If the goods are transported by airway or by train, the airway bills or railway bills will be used. Rail, road and air transport documents are issued only in non-negotiable form, with the goods consigned direct to a named consignee. This presents some irregularities. For such documents, the seller may require 'accepted as presented' to avoid discrepancy arguments under an LC.

Trust receipt

When a bank finances a trading company which imports commodities abroad, usually the bank uses the purchased goods as collateral for its security. The bank will release the goods before the reimbursement of its loan in return for the signature of a trust receipt by the recipient. This trust of receipt is the acknowledgement of the importer that, pending reimbursement of the loan, he holds the goods in trust for the bank.

The trust receipt is commonly used in commodity lending as a means of releasing title documents (such as bills of lading and warehouse receipts) to the borrower, so that he can take possession of the goods. By signing this document, the borrower gives certain undertakings to the lending bank; in effect acknowledging the bank's line on the goods or proceeds coming forth out of the sale of goods to the end-user.

Letters of indemnity (LOI)

An LOI is the typical financing instrument used in the oil industry, because oil shipments are not made on the shipping liner's bills of lading, but on chartered party or tank ship bills. These documents have distinct conditions attached to them. Hence, they are handled differently under the UCP rules.

An LOI will enable the supplier of goods to receive payment under an LC, prior to the supplier providing the buyer's bank with the original title documents in respect of the underlying goods.

Essentially there are two types of LOI. One is the oil LOI which we have discussed. The other is the maritime LOI (what banks commonly called shipping guarantees) for which the format is provided by shipping companies (recommended by their P & I Clubs) and countersigned by banks for:

(a) delivery of cargo without production of the original bills of lading;

(b) delivering cargo at a port other than that stated in the bills of lading; and

(c) delivering cargo at a port other than that stated in the bills of lading and without production of the original bills of lading. [23]

The use of LOIs in oil trading can be traced back to the early 1970s when OPEC boycotted oil export. Control of the movement and sale of oil cargos was largely in the hands of the major oil companies. The monopoly position of OPEC in oil production and export created an opportunity for independent trading companies. When independent traders have influence and control on producing companies, they have much more power to influence the price. However, the oil trading companies sell the oil purchased by them. Control of the shipped oil is then the major concern of the oil trading company. It is imperative to hold the shipping documents for a sale party, because oil frequently changes hands. A delay in the receipt of the original bills of lading means that the trading company is not able to obtain the proceeds of his sale. The LOI became an alternative method of transferring title for the purpose of payment effected in time (before the arrival of a BL).

The problem with these kinds of documents is that, when a bank countersigns a payment indemnity for its client onward sale, the bank in the meantime is asked to countersign an indemnity for discharge of cargo in the absence of bills of lading. But in practice, the bank's client is responsible for discharging the vessel. The issue for risk management control is that indemnities are released against presentation

---

23 Special thanks to Yong Meng for his knowledge contributed here. People interested may wish to refer to the following publication: *Letter of Indemnity – a guide to good practice* authored by Stephen Mills, Ben Roberts and North of England P&I Association (2005).

of a full set of original bills of lading. One set of original bills is used to create two indemnities that are issued to two different parties.

The solution is to adjust the text of the relevant indemnities. Very often the payment indemnity is amended to 'all for release against 2/3 of the original BL plus the vessel owner's/agents' receipt for 1/3 of the original bill', while the indemnity to the owners is amended to allow release against either '1/3 of the original bills of lading or 3/3 of the original', with the owners returning their receipt for the '1/3 of the retained bill, plus in the latter case the other 2/3 of the original'.

Missing an original BL is a potential risk that creates problems for the owner's claim to the goods.

Warehouse warrant

A warehouse warrant is issued by a warehouse that confirms the quantity and quality of a stored commodity. This warrant is used as an instrument to transfer ownership in both cash and futures transactions. A warehouse warrant is a title document.

Some LCs may require such a document as proof of the delivery of requested goods. For example, LME warehouse warrants are well accepted as title documents. Such a document is a convenient way for the commodity traders and users to pick up their goods at the nearby exchange. Warrants are negotiable documents. They may change hands with or without the knowledge of the applicable warehouses.

Similar to warehouse warrants, warehouse receipts are issued by a warehouse listing goods received for storage. However, these cannot be tended to the commodity exchange. Furthermore, warehouse receipts are non-negotiable documents and cannot be used to pass title from one trader to another.

The trade service department is directly involved in some unique operational risks of commodity deals, because the department wires payments to the client. These operational risks, if improperly handled, will lead to potential losses for a commodity bank.

In handling these operational risks, the following list of questions are very often encountered by the trade service department. Hence these questions may present hints of challenges to the trade service department in a commodity finance bank.

1. Which clients are eligible for 'discounting before acceptance'?

2. When has the bank the right to invoke the clause of 'recourse to client in case of fraud and legal injunction'?

3. Where to book a guarantee? Under the corporate line or the bank line?

4. How can one check the text of a guarantee to see if it is a funding or non-funding guarantee?

5. Should the bank pay under documents which are with reserved discrepancy?

6. How should the bank handle exotic LCs such as 10%–90% payment, warehouse warrants and LOIs?

7. Where and how should deep trade service check the sanction clause?

8. How should the bank deal with new and special products, such as avalized drafts and pre-export in countries with different legal environments?

There is no doubt that the quality of the service offered by the trade service department has a direct impact on the bank's business. They are the 'face' of a commodity bank.

On a daily basis, the operational staff of a commodity trading company, that is, the client of the bank, deals with both trade service and the support department of a commodity bank. After the relationship manager introduced the client to the bank, the above two departments represent the bank for real business handling, including in and out of funds.

Negligent handling of some document details may lead to substantial losses for the bank. Some banks depart the commodity finance business due to the fact that they fail to have such infrastructure in the bank when a loss emerges.

Commodity finance, global market operation and price hedging

Commodity finance business is international. Transactions are fundamentally cross-border. It is only natural that customers of commodity finance, who are financed by a commodity bank, may need services for their cross-border activities such as short-term working capital, in different currencies.

For international customers, a credit facility arrangement can be served under a global limit provided by the commodity finance bank. Both the company's head office and its overseas branches may utilize part of the total facility. The loan can be made in local currency as well. Hence the need for a foreign exchange product is only natural for commodity finance clients.

The relationship managers of commodity companies are able to draw on the resources of the bank's international network in order to provide sound advice and innovative ideas. That will help facilitate the client's success in today's domestic and cross-border markets.

Short-term products, such as call deposits (which intend to help clients maximize interest income on their deposits), negotiable certificate of deposits (which intend to help clients to improve their liquidity position) and long-term deposits, are all products familiar to commodity trading companies and commodity producers. The frequency of interest payments, either periodically or on maturity of the deposit, is tailored to suit the depositor.

Foreign exchange products are important for commodity companies, because these products allow for hedging current, future and potential foreign exchange and interest rate exposures.

To serve the commodity clients, the global market department may offer different products:

- **Spot foreign exchange contracts** are offered on currency notes through to import/export requirements, in all major currencies. Transactions are generally settled on a 'value today' or 'value tomorrow' basis.

- **Forward foreign exchange contracts** are offered in most major currencies, to protect exporters and importers subject to exchange risk in the course of their international transactions. The bank offers fixed and optional term contracts for both buyers and sellers.

- **Foreign exchange options** are offered in all major currencies.

The global market department also offers interest rate products to help clients structure and manage their interest rate exposures.

However, for the global market department, the most unique role lies in hedging price risk for commodity clients.

Special competence for global financial markets department

Both for the lending bank and for the borrower, the commodity trading houses, to mitigate commodity price risk is vital.

When commodity traders are subjected to volatility in commodity prices, they have difficulty in maintaining steady cash flows and do not have excess capital for new investments[24].

The objective of hedging commodity price risk is to offset exposures and reduce earnings volatility. Both over the counter (OTC) and exchange traded derivatives are considered functional for purposes of hedging commodity price risk. In this aspect, banks offer both types of derivatives. Exchange traded derivatives are traded via central exchanges.

The instruments used in commodity finance price hedge are forwards, futures and options. The contract specifications for future contracts can be found on the websites of the exchanges, together with the rulebook, which specifies all contractual details.

---

24 *World Grain* magazine, October 2009, www.worldgrain.com.

Forward contracts

A forward contract is a bilateral agreement, privately negotiated between two parties, to deliver a specified quantity and quality of a specified commodity at a specified future date. The central point of such a contract is that, the agreement has an upfront agreed-upon price. This kind of contract intends to physically deliver the commodity in the future. These contracts are also known as physical forwards, because they guarantee the future delivery of a commodity against a fixed price. The contract gives the producer certainty on his future income.

A futures contract takes this one step further. It is a standardized forward contract, which is traded on the futures exchanges market. A standardized contract means standardized terms, such as the amount of the commodity, the delivery period (30, 60 or 90 days) and qualitative commodity criteria.

Such a contract offers opportunities to hedge a commodity price as, like in a forward contract, the commodity delivered in the future will have a fixed price. Consequently, delivery terms are determined by the commodity market exchanges. These terms are not negotiated by the two contractual parties. Through the involvement of many parties, futures contracts often result in cash offsetting rather than the commodity's physical delivery. This increases the speculative nature of the contract and creates the need for a party to monitor the development, so that final settlement is possible. This task is done by a commodity exchange.

At the beginning, commodity exchanges such as the Chicago Board of Trade witnessed an increasing number of forward contracts. The Board decided to standardize these forward contracts to improve efficiency and remove the need for negotiating and fulfilling individualized contracts. Traders were asked to enter into the non-standardized contracts and leave price as the major issue to discuss.

This standardized contract offers liquidity in the market, since standardized futures contracts are easily tradable, because all traders simply renegotiate prices. These contracts thus change hands many times before expiration.

Futures contracts

A futures contract is an agreement to buy or sell a specified commodity of standardized quality at a certain date in the future. The contract has specific basic terms, amount, type, price, timeframe and location of delivery. A futures contract does not apply to any specific transaction and can be traded at futures markets around the world. Future contracts are the most common hedging derivate used by commodity traders. Nowadays, future contract exchanges are characterized by high liquidity and volatility.

- Pros:
  - centrally traded at an exchange and no need to know the counterparty
  - highly liquid
  - transparent and understood
  - no counterparty risk as the clearing corporation assumes the risk. The only reason that people are willing to buy and sell futures contracts with anonymous counterparties is because the exchange guarantees all trades.[25]
  - not necessary to hold until maturity or expiration.[26]
- Cons:
  - daily margining (high volatility can cause large payments)
  - only available during exchange hours
  - only quoted in base currency
  - client might need to manage position on multiple exchanges.

The effect of a futures contract is best explained by a sugar long futures hedge example, based on an example by CBOT.[27]

Case study of a futures contract

Scenario

A candy manufacturer has profit margins that are extremely sensitive to the cost of sugar. In August, he/she contracts to sell candy for delivery in November at a fixed price. The manufacturer will need 224,000 pounds of raw sugar (equal to 2 Sugar No. 11sm futures contracts of 112,000 pounds each) to make the candy. In order to maximize profits, the candy maker needs to buy sugar for October delivery at a price of 7.20 cents/lb. or better. By purchasing the futures (currently trading at 7.20), the manufacturer can lock in raw material costs and protect his/her profit margin.

Strategy

On August 10, the manufacturer sells candy for November delivery with 224,000 pounds of raw sugar content. His/her profitability depends on purchasing sugar at

---

25 http://www.finweb.com/investing/forward-and-futures-contracts-pt2.html

26 http://futureoptionsbasics.blogspot.com/2008/11/advantages-of-futures-contract.html

27 *Understanding Futures & Options*, Copyright 2004, New York Board of Trade.

no more than 7.20 cents/lb. At the time the manufacturer contracts to sell the candy, he/she buys 2 October Sugar No. 11 futures at the current price of 7.20 cents/lb.

Result

On September 15, the candy maker closes out the futures position by selling 2 October Sugar No. 11 futures at the current price of 9.92/cents/lb. for a 2.72 cents/lb. gain. This means a futures gain of US$6,092.80 (112,000 lbs. x US$.0272 = US$3,046.40/contract x 2). On September 15, the candy maker purchases raw sugar in the cash market at 9.92 cents/lb., paying 2.72 cents/lb. more than planned, meaning an unexpected US$6,092.80 shortfall on the manufacture of the candy. When the futures gain is applied to the cash market shortfall (2.72 cents/lb. futures gain minus 2.72 cents/lb. cash market loss), the manufacturer has in effect purchased sugar for 7.20 cents/lb. – the target purchase price that had to be locked in to protect the profit margin. If sugar prices had fallen to 5.10 cents/lb., the futures market loss of 2.10 cents/lb. would be off-set by the gain of 2.10 cents/lb. from the lower cash market price of 5.10 cents/lb. The end result would still be the target price of 7.20 cents/lb. While it may be tempting to view the long futures hedge in a declining market as a loss, it is important to remember the purpose of the hedge – to lock in a price. Had the manufacturer remained un-hedged, he/she would be speculating in the cash market and risk losses when cash prices rise. Protecting the bottom line is sound business management. The target price that represented a profit in August still represents a profit in September.

Option contracts

A hedger can use put options to establish a price floor (a kind of price protection) without sacrificing gains in a favourable cash market. For example, an orange juice processing company might wish to protect a purchase of inventory against a price decline. The contract specifications for options can be found on the websites of the exchanges. The dynamics of an option are best explained by an option example, based on an example by CBOT[28]:

Case study of an option contract

Scenario

In October, a juice processor seeks to hedge an inventory purchase of 30,000 lbs. of FCOJ. January FCOJ-A futures (representing 15,000 lbs.) are trading at 96.40 cents/lb. A put option on a January FCOJ-A futures contract with a strike price of 95.00 is available at a 1.45 cents/lb. premium. This means the processor has the right to sell Jan FCOJ-A futures at 95.00 cents/lb.

---

28 *Understanding Futures & Options*, Copyright 2004, New York Board of Trade.

Result

On December 14, Jan FCOJ-A futures are trading at 84.05 cents/lb. The processor sells the inventory at 84.05 cents/lb. Simultaneously, the processor exercises the two Jan 95 put options for a net futures market gain of 9.50 cents/lb. (95.00 – 84.05 – 1.45). The processor therefore has received an effective 93.55 cents/lb. for the FCOJ inventory. Had the cash market moved upward during the period, the processor could still profit from the gain (less only the cost of the option). By comparison, a straight futures hedge would have meant selling 2 FCOJ-A Jan futures on October 18 at 96.40 and closing out the position on December 14 at 84.05 for 12.35-cents/lb. futures gain. When the 12.35 gain is added to the lower cash FCOJ price of 84.05, the processor would receive an effective 96.40 cents/lb. for the FCOJ sale. Conversely, the options hedge protected the processor against a downward move while preserving the ability to benefit from a rise. The advantage of locking in a higher price for the FCOJ (with its accompanying margin commitment) must be weighed against the flexibility of the option purchase in offering an upside potential in a favorable cash market. Unhedged, the processor would have been left with an 84.05 cents/lb. price for FCOJ. Options with different exercise prices (and different premiums) provide different levels of protection. For example, a Jan 90 put option might carry a lower premium of 0.45 cent/lb., but it would reduce the protection by 5.00 cents/lb. With a 90 strike price, the resulting futures market gain of 5.50 (90.00 – 84.05 – 0.45) would provide a reduced level of protection and leave the processor with an effective 89.55 cents/lb. price for FCOJ.

Commodity finance, risk appetite and credit mentality

Commodity finance differs a lot from normal corporate finance, because of the large (nominal) volume of turnover and collateral under the lending facility. This presents challenges to risk management.

Many commodity finance banks serve commodity traders both by the corporate finance and trade finance approach. Corporate finance is often done on a balance sheet basis: the financial strength of the borrower is at the centre of evaluation. Commodity trade finance, however, is based more on collateral and the quality, quantity and liquidity of collateral. This elementary difference creates different discussions on credit mentality.

It is not unusual that when the chairperson of a credit committee in the bank changes, credit mentality changes, which result in a discussion regarding the amount of limits. This leads to a change of the limit offered to a client.

As commodity trade finance credit is more linked to collateral and collateral management, the credit evaluation and credit mentality can be very different.

A client's financial strength can be evaluated with standard instruments and rules. After all, lending has been a traditional banking business for hundreds of years. Commodity finance, however, requires credit analysts to move further into the risk structure and find sophisticated risk mitigation mechanisms.

Special competence for the credit department

A fully-fledged commodity finance bank, at its best, has a specialised commodity trade credit mentality. In some banks this point is underestimated. And tension between the credit committee and the front-desk will arise.

To analyze a commodity finance deal, one needs at least the following qualifications:

- market knowledge of the commodity and business cycle

- trade flow patterns and instruments used in commodity trading

- risk mitigation knowledge

- risk mitigation tools: amount, tenor, liquidity, country risk, characteristics of commodity, etc.

Much of the above exists only in the accumulation of experience rather than a ready-made handbook.

The essence of commodity finance lies in supposedly liquid assets. The lending amount alone cannot determine the risk a lending bank is taking. A commodity finance bank may lend out a large amount of money with no loss, but may suffer large losses if there is a lack of understanding of commodity risk and its risk mitigation.

The risk a commodity bank takes thus depends on the control of the commodities and the flow of proceeds of the commodity trade. The higher the level of control over the underlying assets, the lower risk a financing bank takes.

This reasoning is straightforward: the risk of the obligor defaulting is mitigated by the assets that can be potentially liquidated.

Unlike the case under the balance sheet approach, the size of the commodity deal is not necessarily the amount/risk the bank is supposed to take. Two key phrases here are 'risk weighing' and 'risk mitigation'.

For example, a US$5 m/m sight LC under which the chance to trace the underlying goods is much bigger than a US$5 m/m usance LC. Hence the risk for sight L/C is smaller. Financing a US$50 m/m oil trade is again different from financing US$50 m/m of steel scrap. The liquidity of the commodity is reflected in its price movements.

On the other hand, the liquidity of the commodity offers an opportunity for commodity traders to change ownership for profits to buy and sell many times until the ultimate user uses the raw material. Change of ownership of commodity presents business opportunities, but also more risks.

Under a pre-export financing structure, an advance payment against a decent bank refund guarantee is more acceptable than an advance against the guarantee of a corporate. The delay and default risk is mitigated by a bank guarantee. Furthermore, a bank should know from the text of the guarantee whether it is a first demand guarantee or not. Under certain circumstances, risk is mitigated by selling it to a third party, insuring it, or finding a guarantor (such as the IFC). There are obviously differences in the quality of risk mitigation between government or government-linked agency coverage and private underwriters' coverage, as was evidenced during the financial crisis.

A bank aiming to enter commodity finance must have the credit professionalism in place to judge, monitor and facilitate the credit proposal and its limit. Without a commodity finance credit mentality, both the credit committee and the commercial front-desk are twisted in their discussion of risk: the bank will end up being too restrictive to risks that are in fact mitigated and too loose to the real risk existing in executing the deal.

The following conversation can be an indication of some understanding and misunderstandings that emerge during the discussions of deals with regard to LC confirmation and discounting in a commodity bank:

Is there any link between the traded commodity and the tenor of the LC?

The tenor of an LC is what the buyer and seller agree upon. The parties put these terms first in their contract and apply for an LC afterwards. Usually the settlement of the trade is limited to 180 days. However, oil LCs can have a tenor of 360 days.

Do we finance the bank, the buyer or the seller in LC deals?

When a bank confirms and discounts an LC issued by another bank, the bank provides funding to its client. The confirming bank first 'advances' the payment and are reimbursed by the issuing bank later. The bank does not provide funding directly to the issuing bank.

Why do we see more small banks issuing LCs in trade finance?

A commodity bank may indeed have more chances to confirm and discount LCs from small banks. Well-known names are known to the confirming bank and its clients as well. Therefore, clients do not need the confirming bank to take over the payment risk. That explains why there are more small banks: it is the clients who choose the name of the issuing bank, the bank is left to say yes or no.

Are food and agricultural goods safer than other commodities?

The risk in commodity finance is partly mitigated through the listing of many commodities on a commodity exchange (like stocks). This provides liquidity: as long as the bank controls the physical flow of commodities, it may sell them in the market in case of emergency. If one of the food and agricultural (F&A) commodities is linked on a commodity exchange, the price transparency and liquidity does provide extra comfort. If not, F&A is not necessarily safer than energy.

Is selling risk to another bank a solution when a limit is not possible?

Risk appetite and risk solution are two different things. Yes, to sell the risk is a solution to credit risk. However, the operational risk remains at the originating bank, because the buying party does not handle the documentation. Moreover, selling risk is not possible when:

- the amount is too small;

- the tenor is too short; or

- the buying bank for the risk requests a price higher than the beneficiary wants to pay as selling will lead to a negative income to the risk-selling bank.

What is the leverage limit?

Banks buying bank risks in the secondary market for income purposes. For prudence, the buying bank may insist on the selling bank to share the risk, say at least 10%. The selling bank needs at least a small bank credit limit itself.

In case of handling a marginally acceptable bank risk, the bank can apply for a limit to accommodate a deal based on offloading 90% of the risk. This is because selling 90% is only possible when the originating bank takes a minimum of 10% of the risk on its own balance sheet. Any international professional bank requests the selling bank to be aligned with the buying bank.

Is the risk in LC document presentation period and the risk in LC tenor the same?

No. We have to separate these two risks. The risk in the pre-shipment period is that the bank commits to take in risk but the fund remains in the bank. If documents are not presented, the LC is nil and void. The risk after the acceptance period is the tenor, under which the bank pays the client and funds flow out of the bank.

Why is bank credit limit utilization unpredictable in client-driven LC confirmation or discounting?

If a commodity bank serves clients for their LC confirmation or discounting, limit utilization also follows. When a bank acquires a client, the counterparty of the client has a house bank which issues the LC. The bank then receives the LC from the counterparty's bank. When the client leaves the bank, the need for the utilization of bank limit on the counterparty's bank disappears as well.

What is the pain if a bank limit is not in place?

From a credit risk point of view, bank limit to be approved is not always an issue. However, a bank has to react quickly as a commodity client usually is banking with several banks. If the commodity bank has to apply and get approval with several signatures, it may lose the deal to the competition. That is why a commodity bank always wants to maintain the limit allowed by the credit committee.

We do not like this issuing bank. Can we ask the client (beneficiary) to change the issuing bank?

This is often difficult. To issue an LC on behalf of the client is a credit facility to the client. To establish one with another bank needs a credit check and approval by another bank.

Commodity finance and financial institutions

Most banks with international operations have a financial institutions department (FI). They used to be called a correspondent bank department.

Owing to the fact that banks themselves today are becoming more and more institutional customers to each other, they become correspondent banks to each other.

Correspondent banks can offer each other services unavailable or unable to be offered by themselves, and also provide opportunities for banks to consider if the available service in the bank should be outsourced.

Trade business, for example, is under a lot of pressure globally. Bank clients look less at where the supplier of goods or services is located and more at the quality and price of the goods or service. Banks are thus constantly under pressure to improve the quality and to get costs under control.

Many banks are looking globally for outsourcing partnerships.[29] Banks nowadays call their 'correspondent department' the 'department for financial institutions'. Such correspondent banking relationships will be of a commercial nature as they may offer substantial earnings for banks on commercial activities such as custody, account handling, international trade settlement, foreign exchange and treasury products, and syndication loans, etc.

The role played by correspondent banking does not stop there. This correspondent network will change the risk portfolio of the bank by trading assets – taking in extra risk or selling out an existing portfolio via risk participation, syndication and forfaiting. It may also change the liquidity position by taking deposits from, or giving deposits to, other banks.

The 'institutional banking', or 'correspondent banking' as we used to call it, is still a kind of relationship banking. It succeeds in serving clients by reaching the places where branch networks do not exist, or that branches do exist but that cannot offer the same service.

Any bank with the ambition to provide a comprehensive service to its clients will definitely need a sizeable network of correspondents around the world. The FI department plays a crucial role in efficient utilization of bank limits, trade services, assets trading and in supporting the acquisition of new counterparts for foreign exchange and money market operations. It also supports the bank's funding by attracting financing from other correspondent banks in the form of bilateral borrowings, pre-export financing, post-financing and syndicated loan facilities.

A commodity bank, by the international nature of its business, must have such a department. However, within commodity finance banks, institutional banking is beyond traditional correspondent banking.

Special competence for the financial institution department

The FI department has some unique functions for commodity finance. The department has both a marketing and risk management function for commodity finance.

On the whole, an FI department in a commodity bank is more commodity-client driven. The understanding and performance of the financial institutions department will have added value to the overall success of commodity finance business. The department is in fact the bank and country risk portfolio manager for the bank as well.

The responsibilities of this department include, but are not limited to:

---

29 Bank of New York (BNY) is said to have globally over 50 outsourcing partnerships, of which 12 or so are North American clients. See Trade Finance report 'Trade Services: Busy behind the Scenes' a supplement to *Trade Finance*, March 2004.

Relationship management with correspondent banks

For example, an important commodity import may need a commodity bank to take over payment risk of an emerging market bank unknown to the bank. The financial institutions department must search via its correspondent bank network to find a bank to support by its participating in the payment risk.

Portfolio management

The department is to manage the trade finance portfolio with the relevant banks and countries in line with the strategy, risk appetite, risk return guidelines and economic capital allocation.

As commodity finance is emerging-market linked, in case of a limited risk appetite, this department will work through external parties to find risk-distributing solutions. This is important because commodity finance often involves large amounts of principal.

Bank and country limit management

This function facilitates risk assessment, problem handling and credit approval. The department is actively following the market development of countries which are strategically important to commodity finance business, either to increase potential risk appetite or to find an alternative.

As far as risk management is concerned, the relationship managers of this department play an important role in planning the size of the exposure of bank and country-linked business, by applying bank and country limits. This is especially the case for deals linked to emerging markets. Also, the financial institution department is alert on operational risk, which helps to prevent losses at an early stage.

In fact, in a commodity finance bank, the FI department has both institutional banking and transactional banking functions. They make deals possible.

In most cases, deals involving country and bank risk will be under the scrutiny of the financial institutions department. In LC confirmation and discounting, the size of an LC is the first risk indication, since it is the amount that the bank may potentially lose. However, there are other risk factors in commodity finance, such as tenor, status of the client, location of the country and the underlying goods.

A longer tenor indicates more uncertainty and a higher probability of difficulties. Longer tenor also indicates more risk, because the probability of getting hold of the collateral will be more difficult and remote. The structure of the deal is worth consideration as well. A straightforward deal usually bears less risk, whereas deals that involve many parties may render a future problem. Standard products like LCs have international guidance (UCP), but products like an avalized draft, supplier's credit, buyer's credit and LC refinancing can have different legal implications. The position of a commodity bank in case of a legal dispute can be more complicated.

The status of the client can be critical in approving deals. Most well-rated trading companies tend to be less likely to be involved in trade fraud, because their own reputation is at stake. The location of the country or city is also relevant for the counterparties: in many emerging markets, remote areas tend to have more delayed payments due to logistic issues and backward infrastructure.

Although the major focus of the department is institutions, this department must also have a good overview over the corporate clients. An FI department is actively involved in initiating and coordinating business within the commodity finance bank, because LC confirmation and discounting is often a starting point for the relationship between a commodity bank and the commodity trading client.

The financial institutions department works with the relationship managers for corporates to acquire clients by marketing bank and country risk products. The competence of this department is also counted for problem solving and public relation maintenance.

The financial institutions departments in commodity finance will, side-by-side with soft, hard, and energy departments, manage the bank and country risk portfolio in order to find the optimal balance between risk and return.

CHAPTER 7

Commodity Finance: Trends and Outlook

The future of commodity finance

This book has dealt with various issues in commodity finance. As our discussion comes to an end, we want to highlight some trends observed so far. Our outlook will focus on the following:

- the commodity cycle

- investment in commodities from institutional investors

- the supply chain in commodity production

- commodity finance and the impact of environmental legislation on commodity trade, new Basel regulation and its impact on commodity finance.

The world of commodities is facing uncertainty and challenges, either for cyclical or structural reasons. As always, commodity price fluctuations will continue. This is not something new. However, what are the major driving forces in the supply of commodities as well as demand for them? This will be of interest to many. Among the driving forces one stands out – the investment from institutional investors. Why and how they invest in commodities will be our discussion in this chapter. How about the China factor, which has been a major driving force for several years already? The subject of the supply chain has been discussed a lot in our previous chapters, both as a business expansion instrument and more as a risk mitigation mechanism. We will explore further what changes this SCF may bring to the commodity world.

The protection of the environment has some direct impact on commodity producers. This will change the production costs, production pattern and behavior of commodity finance banks.

Last but not least, the banking capital regulation, Basel IV or other new Basels, will regulate the provisions a commodity bank must provide versus the risk they take – a complicated subject to non-bankers, but important to banking finance in general and commodity finance in particular. We will discuss this in detail here.

Commodity finance and the commodity cycle

The global economy seems to have shifted its focus: judged by GDP, from the developed countries to the so-called emerging markets, the ratio being almost 50:50.

The upheaval caused by the Eurozone crisis and the fiscal budget issue in the USA only further stimulated a flight from developed countries, as companies are driven more by the growth and profits in emerging markets despite the ups and downs there. Both trade and investment flows are already shifting inexorably towards the new economic powerhouse in Latin America and the Middle East and in Asia, with the most outstanding case China, the waking-up lion. Corporates are extending their global reach there.

Commodity activities are no exceptions to this global shift. The global commodity market has witnessed a commodity cycle and there has been a huge surge in demand from emerging markets.

This growing demand for commodities from so-called emerging markets is consistent for all commodities including energy, metals and soft commodities, which pushes up the price level of commodities.[30] Since 2002, this has been a rare decade of rising commodity price, with only a short break during the 2008 financial crisis, and then in 2016.

---

30 The index of Commodities Research Bureau, an institution which measures 22 types of commodities indicated that general commodities price level rose 23% from 2004 to 2006, among which crude oil was roughly 200% higher than in 2004 and natural gas prices have soared by over 650% since 2002.

Figure 7.1: CRB commodity index

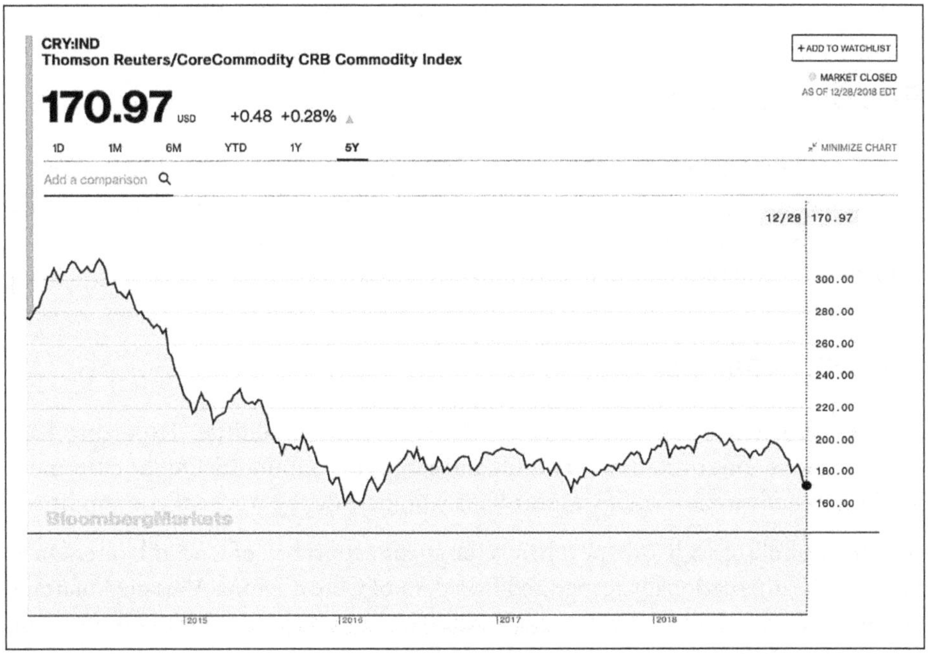

Source: Bloomberg Markets

Although factors pushing price up may vary from period to period, some of the fundamental factors for the growth of price can be identified. This may help to understand the trend for the future.

Demand from Asian countries, especially China and India

One of the major factors of increasing commodity prices, as indicated, is the demand from the Asian markets. Most people believe that price surge is mainly underpinned by the economic growth of China and other emerging markets.

The fast growth of the two big Asian emerging economies, India and China, have definitely contributed to the upward trend of commodity price. China and India have both become substantial importing countries of many commodities, especially of metals and energy. A lack of their own natural resources is the first explanation. Fast economic growth is another. As a result, such substantial import has impact on the upward pressure to the price of many commodities. As long as these two countries continue as they do now, commodity finance will be impacted.

As a matter of fact, since the start of the development of the BRIC countries, inhabitants of these countries have seen large increases in commodity prices, as well as an increase in their wealth. This eventually increases their consumption. This in turn increases the demand for commodities.

If the supply of these commodities cannot keep up with the growth in demand, it is only natural that price will increase, at least in the long-term perspective.

Population growth

Another factor that influences the commodity prices is the global population growth. We can see that population growth still is very high and will not decrease much in the years to come. If population growth continues, it will put pressure on the demand for commodities, thus increasing the prices.

Export restrictions

Another problem lies in exporting restrictions for commodities. Exporting bans decrease the volume of commodity trade and supply of commodities to the customers. While demand remains stable, export bans will increase the prices of commodities.

A good example of such an export ban is the cocoa export ban of Côte d'Ivoire. On 23 January, the internationally recognised President of Côte d'Ivoire, Alassane Ouattara, announced a one-month ban on cocoa exports as a means of increasing pressure on former president Laurent Gbagbo, who refused to leave office despite losing the presidential elections in November 2010. As Côte d'Ivoire has a market share of 40% of the global market in cocoa exports, the export ban had a major impact on the price of this commodity. In only one month, prices had risen by more than 10%.

Other factors

Technological development is also a critically important factor which is linked to the use of the commodities. Now that technology makes it possible to provide a multitude of purposes for a commodity, demand for these commodities rises. A good example of one of those goods is corn. Originally used to feed livestock, it is now used to produce bio plastics and ethanol. Again, if supply cannot keep up with demand, price will increase.

On the other hand, technology can also reduce the demand for commodities by finding replacements. Solar energy is nowadays widely used to replace oil.

In the agricultural sector, natural factors such as crop failures and disasters can always have a major impact on commodity prices. A good example is the drought in Russia in June 2010. Due to the drought, more than 20% of the wheat production was destroyed and Russia banned the export of wheat until December 2010. As can be seen in Figure 7.2, the wheat price doubled after the crop failure in Russia.

Figure 7.2: Historical prices of Paris wheat

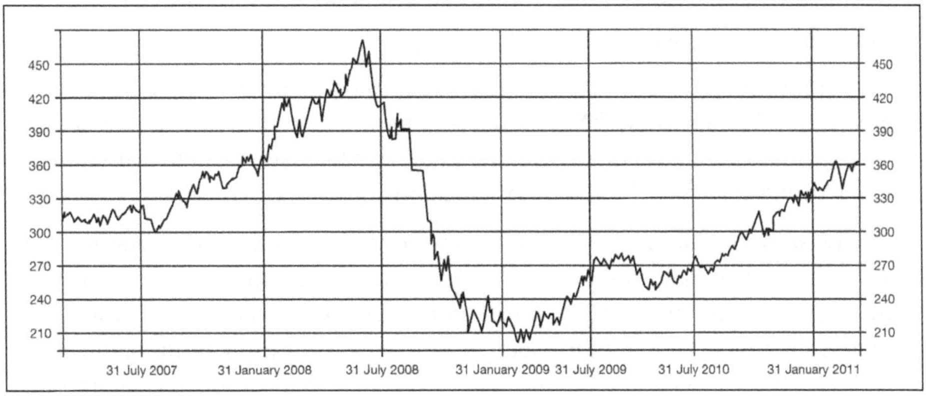

Source: De Beurs.nl

One less obvious trigger, but a very important factor for price increases is quantitative easing. In the most recent crises, central banks lowered interest rates and increased the money supply to stimulate consumer demand. Because of the abundance of money, prices in the economy will rise due to inflation. Furthermore, if central banks are intolerant of slowing growth due to fear of another recession, the possibility exists of a bubble in commodity prices. At this point it is uncertain where this issue will lead us.

We tend to believe that it depends on the policy that the central banks and governments will follow in the next years to come. The longer quantitative easing is used, the more the possibility that commodity prices rise above equilibrium levels. We will come back to this issue in the discussion of institutional investors' involvement in the commodity market, which no doubt adds more fluctuation to the commodity price.

On the other hand, it is interesting to watch the next cycle after the current 'China commodity cycle'. China's influence on global commodity flows, commodity price and commodity trade pattern is undeniable. Going forward, China is potentially facing critical challenges in restructuring its economy. If China's infrastructure investment reduces, it will likely bring down the need for some of the hard commodities such as iron ore, copper, aluminium and steel. It will drive the price of iron ore and other related commodities. This creates increasing volatility, from which most professional traders benefit.

Some believe commodities prices will return to the way they moved during the 1980s and 1990s. During this period, long-term commodity prices were stable but were punctured by short-term changes in demand.

Expectations for stable suppliers of energy and metals are based on the technological development and the rise in production capacity in China, which is so far the largest importer of copper, aluminium and other metals. [31]

The booming price of commodities has added motivation for the production of commodities. It is generally believed that China will not grow as it did in the past 20 years and the structure of the Chinese economy may also change (shifting from manufacturing export to domestic consumption).

We have seen the oil cycle (OPEC) and the China/India cycle, but the next commodity cycle remains to be seen. Roughly estimated, a copper price collapse of more than 60%, zinc cut by up to a half and oil down to US$70 a barrel, would be the fate facing world commodity markets should China's growth dip to 3% in the next three years – a scenario economists at Barclays Plc (BARC) are now examining. [32]

The imbalances between supply and demand of commodities can be explained by the fast growth of consumption on the demand side and years of under investment during the 1980s and 1990s on the supply side.

With current trade wars and changing international trade picture, the movement of commodity price level presents most uncertainty.

As we will discuss, investment in commodity is part of financial market activities, the deflationary pressure in financial assets will have impact on the price of physical commodity trade.

In terms of financing commodities, less noticeable is the country risk implication. With the globalization of the world economy, commodity production, commodity trade and commodity finance have also changed the face of country risk for emerging markets in many ways.

Traditionally, the biggest political risk lies in developing countries' immature or volatile systems. The seizure of foreign assets, among others, was a major concern. But this risk today is largely reduced – if not totally disappeared – by stronger international law and the symbiotic nature of the growth of government policy.

So far the country risk rating (also the bank credit rating to some extent) focuses on asset-seizure and contract repudiation risks. Such an approach is inadequate now.

---

31 *Financial Times*, 'Goldman Calls Commodities Cycle Shift' by Emiko Terazono, December 6 2012.

32 But some disagree with the statement that China will sharply slow down its huge commodity demand. Jean-Francois Lambert from HSBC: "Contrary to popular belief, the Chinese construction industry will carry on booming and China will still be dependent on commodity imports to feed to it for a while yet. This is because there is still so much infrastructure needed in the country. There is still a lot of underdevelopment. For example, China at present has less train tracks than the US did in 1880." See p.41, *Trade Finance* July August 2013 Issue 6.

What is missing is the aspect of policy risk – the uncertainty of the orientation of government policy and change in the regulatory environment. Legal contracts are binding and useful if they can be enforced. But shifting laws and regulations may render them void. Even when laws remain unchanged, some policy makers may circumvent them via a wide variety of means other than changing laws.

The traditional financial and contractual mechanism to mitigate political risk is also reflected in the concerns over social unrest. The Arab Spring and the unrest in Europe have led people to feel more vulnerable to the risk of terrorism and societal unrest. Without adequate protection, political violence can seriously disrupt commodity flow. Social unrest is becoming a global phenomenon and recent events have made commodity companies reassess their approach to the threat of politically motivated civil unrest.

Commodities and investment in commodities

Investment in commodities or the production of commodities usually occurs within the commodity community. Many institutional investors, however, invested in commodities. But such an interest is expanding rapidly in the wake of the 2008 financial crisis and with the global quantitative easing. In the USA, investment in physical assets has attracted attention and action again ever since.

Commodities, especially those with high liquidity, become a point of focus, not only for precious metals like gold and silver, but also for other commodities that are usually used as raw materials. Investment banks' involvement to securitize the loans pushes such a momentum further.

In 1999, the Clinton administration repealed the Glass-Steagall Act which was in part to curb speculation. Since this act has been repealed, investments by institutional investors in commodity markets have risen from US$13 billion in 2003 to between US$170 and US$205 billion in 2008. The investment of institutional investors in commodities has no doubt increased since.

For commodity bankers, what forms are used for institutional investors to invest in commodities, what is the motivation behind the investment from institutional investors, what its effects are and what impact it will have on the prices and on the volatility of the prices are all topics of relevance.

Investment in commodities

Investment in commodities can be direct or indirect. Direct investment implies buying the physical commodity. This is the most simple form of speculation and basically it means that traders hold back their commodity stock in the hope of still higher commodity prices.

Brokers can also try to corner the market by buying a large part of the supply of some commodities to drive up prices. Mostly, this is done using spot markets to evade possible regulatory limits on investments in futures markets.

As the forward and futures markets have been a long existing part of commodity markets, investment in commodities can take place by conventional speculation on futures markets.

In 1865, the Chicago Board of Trade (CBOT) launched the first commodity futures contract. Then in 1896 a cotton trader worked out a way to use futures to 'hedge' against future price changes.

Besides these commercial hedgers, futures markets have always attracted commodity investors or 'speculators' as you may call them. Furthermore, a lot of commodity traders try to make use of arbitrage opportunities in the futures markets which is the purchase of securities on one market for immediate resale on another market in order to make a riskless profit from a price discrepancy.

But the booming investment in commodities from institutional investors is definitely the contribution of financial engineering.

The idea of financial engineering is to provide new ways and new products on which futures can be traded. One could think of carbon trading and weather futures. The idea of introducing these new futures is to enable investors to diversify their holdings. Hence, investors see commodities as a new asset class for investors to make profits.

There are different and diversified derivatives in commodities which cater for the needs of different institutional investors.

OTC commodity swaps

Two types of commodity swaps, namely, fixed-floating and commodity-for-interest swaps are active for commodity swaps. Fixed-floating swaps are just like the fixed-floating swaps in the interest rate swap market. The difference is that both indices are commodity-based indices. Two of the most familiar commodity indices are the Goldman Sachs Commodities Index (GSCI) and the Commodities Research Board Index (CRB).

Commodity-for-interest swaps are similar to equity swaps in which a total return on the commodity in question is exchanged for some money market rate (plus a spread).

Index funds

Under index funds there are two sub-categories, namely, passive exchange funds and exchange traded funds. Passive index funds are funds that do not try to maximize returns via the most lucrative commodities of the moment, nor do they play the market with 'long' and 'short' positions. Instead they aim to replicate the price movements of a commodity index. Examples of such funds are the DBLCI, DJ-UBSCI, Thomson Reuters/Jefferies CRB Index, RICI and Standard & Poor's GSCI.

Although they do not actually try to outperform the market, we may well call passive index funds speculators. This is because they have a direct impact on prices, which diverts commodity prices from their fundamental supply and demand.

Exchange Traded Funds (ETFs)

ETFs are practically the same as passive index funds. The difference, however, lies in the fact that the fund is exchange traded. An ETF gathers a large bulk of money, and sometimes even matches this money with borrowings, to invest in certain commodities. Some of these funds are short in commodities, others long.

Because ETFs are exchange traded, it provides investors the opportunity to bet on the commodities market. Since they have a large volume, they have a big impact on the commodity prices. And the benefits of ETFs over hedge funds are simplicity, low fees, tax efficiency, liquidity and transparency. Hence, the market in ETFs has increased rapidly making it one of the major players on commodity markets.

Commodity-related shares

These are shares in companies that operate in the commodity sectors, such as the metals industry (mining) and oil industry (oil companies). It is an alternative way of getting exposure on the fluctuation of commodity markets. This type of investment, however, does not impact on commodity prices.

Managed futures funds

With this type of investment, a commodity trading advisor (CTA) collects funds from investors, which he then invests in the commodity markets as an investment from a single source. Managed futures funds differ from index funds in the sense that they are not based on an index. The funds are used for active trading in order to gain the maximum short-term income using the CTA's expertise.

Commodity collateralized obligations (CCOs)

CCOs are the commodity equivalent of collateralized mortgage securities. It makes use of the same slice and dice principle as the products that triggered the financial crises of 2007. It combines the prices of several commodities into a package as an interest-bearing bond. Formally, it is sold as a commodity swap, but with a 'trigger point', which means it will pay out immediately if the bond price falls below a certain point.

These are the other kinds of products that are used to speculate in the commodities markets. These various kinds of commodity investment products inevitably increase the access to the commodity markets for many institutional investors and, to some extent, non-institutional investors. Nowadays, investing in commodity ETFs is so popular that almost every investor can try their luck in this part of the market.

Of course, major commodity investors, apart from commodity traders, are hedge funds, mutual funds, unit trusts or an exchange traded fund. In a broader sense, any investors, institutional or non-institutional, should be interested in investing in commodities if their investment strategy is 'buy and hold'.

A question often asked is – how large is the market share that these kinds of investment occupy?

It is never easy to give a precise answer. But in recent times institutional investors have a larger share of outstanding commodities than other market participants. Morgan Stanley Bank estimated that the number of outstanding contracts in the corn futures market increased from 500,000 to nearly 2.5 million between 2003 and 2008 while there was no reason for farmers, merchants and agro-processing firms to increase their use of the futures market. Hence, we would expect that because of their large market share, they influence the price and volatility of commodity prices.

Another problem that arises from the large market share that institutional investors occupy has to do with the variables that affect food prices. Institutional investors are not only driven by supply and demand in the commodity market itself, but also by returns, volatility and prices in other markets. Hence, prices of commodities become less related to the commodities themselves and thus make them more unpredictable.

Furthermore, speculation disrupts the rolling over of futures contracts when the shortest maturity futures contracts expire. Just before expiration these contracts are sold by the speculators. If a merchant has to roll over his hedge he has to pay more for the longer maturity contract with respect to the short maturity contract. Hence, speculation makes rolling over hedges inefficient.

Speculation also causes problems for smaller suppliers. If prices become more volatile, exporters have to hedge their price risk. For larger exporters this should not be a problem since they can attract the knowledge. However, smaller suppliers cannot attract the knowledge and have to pay the price which could drive them out of the market. The result of this will be a consolidation of suppliers of commodities which decreases competition. In general, this leads to less competitive prices.

Investment motivation

Interest in commodities is not surprising. Investment in commodities, as in other kinds of investments, can generate benefits such as higher yields, and it also serves to diversify risks.

According to research by Barclays Capital, for a period of 35½ years from 1970 to 2005, the correlation co-efficient between commodities and the financial assets were:

Equities	- 0.28
Bonds	- 0.20
Treasury bills	- 0.01

But the S&P GSCI total return index reached 11.12%[33] during this period.

The growing interest in investing in commodities, despite gains or losses, stimulates the volatility of commodity prices, because this creates extra demand in commodities beyond the consuming of commodity as raw materials.

Some commodity-investors do go beyond the 'buy and hold' strategy. They simply trade commodities for profit purposes: major commodity hedge funds such as Red Kite for copper are trading actively. Banks like JP Morgan and Goldman Sachs actively trade in commodity futures and options.

After the credit crises, prices of shares, property and financial derivatives stopped their excessive growth, whereas commodity prices have been growing rapidly. Hence, institutional investors find commodities in the commodity market as a new and interesting asset class.

Why do institutional investors like the commodity markets? It is simply because, from the perspective of an institutional investor, it does not matter where he is making his money, as long as he is making money.

Investments as such have also been heavily discussed by politicians, as they are regarded as 'speculation'.

'Speculation' has long been discussed. It usually refers to the process of selecting investments with higher risk in order to profit from an anticipated price movement. But speculation should not be considered purely a form of gambling, as speculators do make an informed decision before choosing to acquire the additional risks. Additionally, speculation cannot be categorized as a traditional speculative investment because the acquired risk is higher than average.

Speculation is disliked especially when it has to do with the food supply. It can drive prices above equilibrium levels which pushes the prices of food up in the market. This causes problems, mainly in poorer countries since people who can barely feed

---

33 See *Commodity Derivatives*, Neil C. Schofield (John Wiley & Sons, 2010), p. 270.

themselves can buy less food for their money. Extensive speculation on the price of oil may also put pressure on inflation.

Volatility of commodity markets gives opportunities to speculators but also threats to those who mainly use commodities as raw materials. Eventually some believe in stabilization of the commodity markets.

We do not find clear consensus about the relationship between commodity prices and investments from institutional investors. There is, therefore, no definitive answer to the question whether investments by institutional investors affect prices.[34] Politicians are nevertheless very willing to take measures to stabilize the commodity price.[35]

Commodity finance along the supply chain

Both the commodity trading companies and commodity finance banks are extending along the supply chain – a topic repeatedly discussed in this book.

Buyers' desire to support and secure strategic suppliers is straightforward. The big commodity trading companies are not only buying commodities from producers, transporting and selling to consumers, but are also involving their banks to extend credit to producers ranging from miners to farmers as we discussed in various cases of pre-export finance facilities.

The commodity finance banks, for their own commercial interest and especially for risk management consideration, are also actively lengthening the commodity finance supply chain. Demand from suppliers, especially from those coming from emerging markets, for financing further up the supply chain is also noticed.

As commodity trade grows more international, trade volume increases, especially trade between developed and developing countries.

---

34 Some work shows that speculation by large or small traders does not cause sharp changes in volatility and prices (Chatrath and Song 1999); Garcia et al. (1986); Haigh et al. 2007) and some other studies show that volume of trading in commodities futures affects commodity prices (Sahi and Raizadi 2006).

35 According to Michael Masters, Portfolio Manager of Masters Capital Management, three things should be done to counter commodity price speculation: 1) Modify the regulation of pension funds to prohibit commodity index replication strategies because of the damage that they do to the commodities futures markets. 2) Act to close a gap in legislation that allows 'hidden' trading in swaps. 3) Compel the Commodity Futures Trading Commission to reclassify all the positions in the commercial category of the Commitments of Traders Reports to distinguish those positions that are controlled by 'bona fide' physical hedgers from those controlled by Wall Street banks. The positions of Wall Street banks should be further broken down into 'bona fide' physical hedgers and speculators.

At the start of international trade between these countries, there were several problems with financing these flows.

First of all, markets like the Asian market were very fragmented with an absence of one regulatory regime with one single currency. Furthermore, supplier companies were very small, hard to analyze and very risky. This made it very hard to finance trade flows. Historically, this problem could be tackled with the use of structured documents LCs in which the risk was diverted to foreign banks instead of foreign suppliers. This made it less risky to finance the international trade flows.

However, over time Asian countries have developed stronger political and legal institutions and companies there have grown bigger. Hence, there has been a change in the way these economies work.

For example, a lot of developing country firms are using the latest inventory and supplier management strategies. This has increased their efficiency but leaves buyers vulnerable to interruptions in the supply of goods. Therefore, there is an increasing demand for more sophisticated cash and trade management solutions. Financial supply chain management can help in managing and/or mitigating this risk.

SCF can certainly help in providing better information to the banks and suppliers by all means. It enables the bank to expand its business opportunities and to enhance sustainable relationships in the business. Therefore, future trade and commodity finance services will look to integrate supply chain management systems further into its activities. It also gives an insight into the bargaining power between buyers and suppliers. For example, it could be the case that a large buyer demands lower prices when the prices of commodities decrease but will not accept increasing prices when the prices of commodities increase. When the supply chain concept is properly used, these kinds of risks can be observed and an attempt can be made to mitigate it. This was discussed in our risk management part.

A point worthy of attention is that the kind of supply chain techniques necessary differ for developing and developed countries. In developed markets, there has been a need for greater sophistication in the electronic systems, whereas for developing countries there is a need for more flexibility in the financing offers in the system.

Another difference between how supplier financing is applied in Asia, Europe and the USA is in the timing of financing opportunities. In Europe, for example, we often find payables discounting as the preferred financing method, while in Asia there is more demand for financing at the pre- and post-shipment stages of the trade cycle.

SCF provides great promises to the banking sector, both in risk management and in making new business. There are, however, some requirements that need to be fulfilled in the future to make SCF work.

The first is the IT infrastructure. To make SCF work, internet and web-based information technologies should become the core of the system. These web-based hubs should be designed as a repository for information for the buyers as well as the suppliers in the chain. It should be the place where buyers and supplier meet and exchange bills and invoices. It is vital to this system that it is integrated with the client systems. This provides for a stronger link between the bank and its customer and strengthens the relationship.

The second is the legal documentation. For trade to become more efficient it is vital that the use of legal documentation is kept to a minimum. This will also reduce the complexity of trade. The downside on minimizing legal documentation is the extra risk of losing capital when a borrower defaults. However, as stated earlier, companies in developing countries are changing. This in itself can mitigate a part of the risk taken by minimizing legal documentation.

Another important point for future international trade has to do with both globalization and localization. To provide a global network for suppliers and buyers it is important that a bank has offices and connections all over the world. However, to understand the needs of its buyers and sellers it also needs to use a local approach. Hence, a commodity bank of the future should have a global strategy that is locally executed.

The last issue for the future has to do with liquidity. As multinational companies provide/guarantee liquidity to all its suppliers, to mitigate the risk of defaults, it could be the case that the risk for a bank on one particular customer could become too large. Therefore, there is a need to increase the credit volume in the market for trade financing.

To increase credit volume, new investors should be invited to the market. This indeed will increase competition in the market but it is necessary to mitigate risk on companies that have large credit needs.

We can summarize that the need of SCF comes from several driving forces, but mainly from the following:

- Shifting towards developing market suppliers that require more financial support from buyers.

- Buyers intending to lengthen the order-to-pay cycle.

- Minimizing the utilization of banking facilities of both buyers and sellers.

- Increasing the recognition of cash flow management.

- Buyers to reduce the cost of goods sold and streamlining the procurement process.

A trend less noticed in SCF is that the expansion along the supply chain stimulates merger and acquisition of commodity trading houses. As a result, such upstream and downstream expansion of commodity trading companies along the supply chain leads to less, but bigger trading houses.

Nowadays the top five commodity companies are, according to the figure below, comparable to conglomerates in the auto industry, consumer staples, banks/non-bank financial institutions, IT and telecom companies.

Figure 7.3: Invisible giants: how the top five commodity trading companies by revenue compare with other selected industries (annual revenue – US$ billions, 2011)

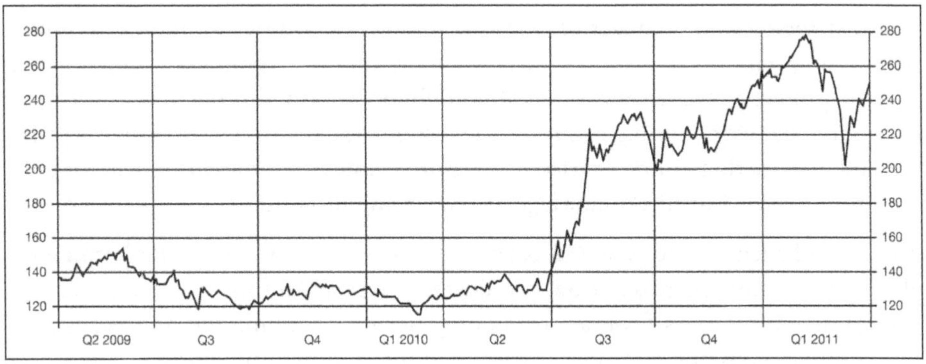

Source: Thomson Reuters.

Questions were raised that this growth of commodity trading houses would bring disruption of global commodity flows – such as a change in the supply of food. As Javier Blas pointed out, "the increasingly prominent role of large trading houses raises the possibility that some are systemically important."[36]

When big banks face serious problems, the regulator of them may stand up to rescue them. There are no parallel regulators in the commodity sector and there is divided opinion on future scenarios of this trend. Nevertheless, such worries are not totally unjustified.[37]

If further research endorses such doubts in the commodity finance world, it is only a matter of time before mechanism or regulations are established to cope with the development. When becoming big is no longer fashionable, commodity trading houses, like banks, may be asked to be split up for regulation purposes, such as the separation of insurance and banking in the financial sector.

Commodity finance and environmental protection

The production of commodities has an impact on the environment. With growing awareness of the need for environmental protection, both in the developed and developing countries, many measures are taken to address this during the production

---

36 See Javier Blass 'Have Glencore and other traders turned too big to fail?' *Financial Times* Nov 13, 2012.

37 Ibid.

of commodities. Protection of the environment is a new challenge to commodity finance and to banks involved in commodity finance.

Through the years the impact of trade for some commodities on the environment has been given much more importance. Not only are politicians constructing laws to protect the environment, public opinion is also shifting towards a more environmental way of doing business. Some countries, mainly developing countries, are still obstructing more restrictive measures aimed at reducing environmental pollution. Slowly but surely new legislation is being introduced.

The Copenhagen Accord is one global set-up in which the overall goal is keeping the global temperature increase below two degrees Celsius. All this new legislation puts constraints on the ways firms are now doing business. Commodity producers need to produce its commodities more efficiently, using less energy during this process. To achieve this they have to invest in research and new capital. This makes commodities and their transportation more expensive.

For the commodity community, two environment pollution penalty cases for commodity traders are benchmark cases.

The first case concerns the caustic washing of low-quality crude oil. The second case concerns the oil spill of the Deepwater Horizon in the Mexican Gulf.

A multinational company trading commodities was reported to be involved in the dumping of toxic waste before the coast of Côte d'Ivoire. The toxic dumping is linked with a so-called 'caustic washing' – a chemical process to purify low-quality crude oil to make it usable. This process leaves an extremely toxic waste.

In most of the countries this technique was actually banned because it is very difficult to deal with toxic by-products. However, other refining processes will be a lot more expensive. The multinational commodity company used this process on board of the *Probo Koala* with oil that they bought from a Mexican company. The company figured that by using the technique it could make a large profit on the shipment. However, the company only started to realize that it had a problem when they found out it was very difficult to find someone to deal with the waste.

The company first tried to clean the waste in Amsterdam harbor. They were, however, told that only Rotterdam's harbor had the facilities to deal with this type of waste. The company contacted the harbor of Rotterdam. However, costs were around €1,000 per m³ which was not acceptable to them. Hence, they turned to a contractor in Côte d'Ivoire which was paid only €20 per m³ for handling the toxic waste.

No questions were asked why it was that cheap to handle this type of toxic waste. In the meantime, a tragedy unfolded in Abidjan. The waste was spread around the city, and tens of thousands of people were exposed to the toxic fumes. According to reports from Côte d'Ivoire, 15 deaths were the direct consequence.

In the aftermath, it was unclear what the company's role was in the dumping of the toxic waste. The *Probo Koala* was allowed to leave Côte d'Ivoire without questions. In the weeks after the incident, the commodity company commissioned its own report regarding the dumping – also known as the Minton Report. This report was never revealed, but leaked out three years later. The results of the report were clear-cut. The waste was very toxic and should not have been dumped in Côte d'Ivoire.

Later, the Dutch government started prosecuting the commodity company for lying about the content of the waste and for the illegal export of hazardous waste which is forbidden under European law.

In 2007, they paid US$160 million to the Côte d'Ivoire government in return for the assurance that they would drop all cases against the company and its employees.

The effects of the disaster with the *Probo Koala* were that legislation in the European Union tightened. Furthermore, companies in the commodity finance sector became much more aware of what companies they were doing business with and whether their corporate social responsibility was in danger when doing business with these companies.

The second case is linked to a British oil company. The Deepwater Horizon was an ultra-deepwater, dynamically positioned, semi-submersible, offshore oil drilling rig. The rig was built in 2001 in South Korea by Hyundai Heavy Industries, and owned by Transocean.

This company leased the rig to this British oil company from March 2008 until September 2013. On 20 April 2010, while drilling at the Macondo Prospect, a blowout caused an explosion on the rig which killed 11 crewmen and ignited a fireball visible 56 km away. This was then followed by an eruption of a combination of mud, methane gas and water. The gas component of the material quickly transformed into a fully gaseous state and ignited into a series of explosions forming a firestorm. An attempt was made to activate the blowout preventer, but it failed.

After two days, without successfully extinguishing the fire, the Deepwater Horizon sank to the bottom which resulted in the oil field spilling oil into the ocean, causing the largest offshore oil spill in the history of the USA. The oil spill continued until 15 July when a temporary cap was used to close the well. Relief wells were then used to permanently seal the well, which was declared 'effectively dead' on 19 September 2010.

A report from the coastguard revealed that, although the events leading to the sinking of the Deepwater Horizon were set in motion by the failure to prevent a blowout, numerous systems deficiency, actions and omissions by the crew of the Deepwater Horizon had a negative impact on preventing or at least limiting the magnitude of the disaster.

The consequences of this spill were enormous. This company established a US$20 billion claims fund and had to sell off a major part of its assets to stay in business. Also, offshore drilling in the Gulf of Mexico has been prohibited by the USA government and the public debated the use of oil as a major energy source. Furthermore, a lot of companies dismantled their trading with these companies to protect their corporate social responsibility.

Hence, we see that disasters and environmental protection can and do have a visual impact on commodity trade and trade finance. It is to be expected that legislation and protection will take an even more prominent role in these sectors as public debate is increasingly averse to damage to the environment.

However, we need to mention that research and technology will only be introduced on a large scale if, and only if, legislation demands it. The reason for this is that commodity markets are very competitive. If one commodity supplier wants to invest in technology that places a lower burden on the environment, his prices will rise and his position vis-à-via his competitors will deteriorate. With legislation in place, the market as a whole is obliged to make this investment so that the level playing field for the competitors remains the same.

The legalization of environmental protection is progressing, notably in developed countries. Because of the large impact of oil on the carbon footprint of the earth, it is expected that environmental legislation will tighten for this commodity. The carbon-related legislation is still at an early stage but will reshape the entire oil market in the coming decades. It has the potential to reduce the demand and growth of the oil market.

In Europe, energy and climate change legislation has already been well established. The EU has established a series of energy policy objectives targeted at increasing renewable energy sources, reducing emissions and improving energy efficiency. In addition, the EU has the most comprehensive and developed program, which has had its share of teething problems, but which is now functioning relatively effectively.

In the USA, the situation with respect to energy and climate change legislation remains fairly active and fluid. There are multiple initiatives at play in the USA at this moment. The situation continues to evolve at the federal, regional and state levels with potential significant implications for oil markets and refining, across regions, the country and potentially beyond USA borders.

At the federal level, the change in the USA Administration in January 2009 heralded a more concerted effort to implement energy and climate change legislation. Under the preceding George Bush administration, at least three Senate 'climate change' bills had been proposed, but none passed the draft stage.

What the current USA administration will do is yet to be seen.

Along with legislation due to carbon footprints, legislation is also implemented due to catastrophes. One of the major disasters in the last few years was the above-mentioned Deepwater Horizon oil spill. Because of the size of this spill, more stringent regulation has been implemented which increases the costs of exploration. This will decrease the amount of drillings and makes projects economically less favorable. However, it is expected that this legislation will only impact deepwater production in the short run. In the medium and long term, offshore oil drilling continues to grow in importance as part of the global oil supply.

Although a transition is taking place in the direction of a new environmental friendly way of doing commodity business, this process is quite slow. There is still quite a lot of discussion between countries on how big the environmental challenge is and how it should be handled. Hence, in the short term we do not expect large changes, only in the long run a change will be anticipated which will also affect pricing.

Environmental issues are not only a concern for the traditional polluting industries, but also for other type of commodity companies. They have seen how the increasing cost of reputational damages affects their profits and losses just as seriously as the environmental loss itself.

Some commodity banks have promised to only finance projects that are developed in a manner that is socially responsible and reflect sound environmental management practices. To ensure that promises are being kept, a framework has been set up in which yearly reports on implementation processes and experience is required.

The above-mentioned Deepwater Horizon case is well known in this field. In 2010, the share price of this energy company dropped by 40% and its global ranking plunged overnight to 118th in the world. The international media beamed images across the world of the Deepwater Horizon disaster and the subsequent ecological devastation to natural habitats. Only after a while, did the company manage to restore its ranking to 5th place in the league table of oil companies in October 2012.

As a result of such increased environmental concerns, much capital has been spent on the reduction of undesirable environmental side effects. Big commodity producers and trading houses will get penalized if they do not comply with the rules and regulations of environmental protection.

Take the protection for the production of crude oil as an example. Refiners spent US$47 billion to meet the demand of a plethora of environmental laws. The USA government established regulations in 2006 to require refiners to reduce the amount of sulphur in both gasoline and diesel at an estimated cost of US$16 billion.[38]

Coal, for example, is perceived as a significant polluter of the environment. When coal is burnt, it releases polluters such as carbon dioxide, ash, and oxides of sulphur and nitrogen. Any associated regulations to hinder its production or consumption could have an adverse effect on the costs of the production and hence the components of its final price.

In the years to come, environmental concern and corporate social responsibility will regulate the behavior of commodity companies. Some of the commodity finance banks may shrink from deals which have environmental issues despite high returns:

---

38 Neil C. Schofield, *Commodity Derivatives* (Wiley Finance, 2011), p119.

banks simply want to avoid being under the media's spotlight which causes damage to their reputation.

Conclusion

The brief discussion on the future of commodity finance will now arrive at some tentative conclusions – tentative because commodity finance is dynamic and is driven by numerous variables; tentative also because commodity finance is not an isolated subject.

First, commodity finance holds tremendous potential, offering great opportunity to banks who are willing to take the challenge, to make business investment and to leverage the help of IT.

The potential is due to the following: vast demand for raw material from Asia in general and China in particular, imbalances in production and consumption which increased commodity price volatility, increasing political risk, especially policy risk in commodity finance, higher liquidity requirements for hedging and working capital.

The value of commodity finance activities have definitely increased, especially in emerging Asia and Latin America. This is mainly demand driven. According to an IMF-sponsored report on pricing quoted for commodity finance, most banks reported a decrease in pricing; this is particularly true for LCs.

Until today, the bulk of commodity finance for metals, oil and gas and other soft commodities is provided in the form of bank lines. Conventional standard credit facilities extended by banks are largely mitigated by exposing the credit facility to its balance sheet and to a great extent hinge upon the performance of the borrower. However, due to a plentiful money supply, margins remain very thin in most emerging markets.

Risk wise, commodity finance must face many mid-sized trading houses which may need this specialized commodity finance desperately. Very few of them will have a formal debt credit rating and even fewer will have investment grade ratings.

Both the China factor and the investment in commodities from institutional investors will have a fundamental role in the direction of price movement. As a way of reflecting this change, many commodity finance LCs are settled in Chinese currency. Many Asian banks are coming onto the horizon of the commodity world.

Second, the development in Fintech, SCF and the environment protection will in many ways change the pattern for finance and bank behaviour in commodity finance. Upstream and downstream finance for risk and earnings will motivate commodity banks to move further towards serving the needs of their clients. IT technology, such as E-presentation, will emerge in commodity finance. The possibility of shrinking

LC business and replacing it with re-lending to banks, and package services to commodity trading houses will all be on the agenda of commodity finance banks.

Now, more than ever, commodity finance banks need to re-engineer themselves to "respond to corporate demands of supply chain financing, plant expansion and upgrades, mergers and acquisitions and overall corporate building of one form or another".[39]

Third, despite the cooling down of derivatives and in the aftermath of quantitative easing, institutional investors will seek increasing opportunities in investment in commodities provided regulatory environment is not unfriendly to them. Investment banks' involvement to securitize loans in commodities will have added value to this large-scale borrowing and lending.

Fourth, there will be reshuffling of players in commodity finance. Banks will need to adjust to survive and they have to have a deeper understanding of their customers than ever before. Competing on pricing alone will not be sufficient. They will have to deliver higher value offerings that are flexible and customized to each customer's segment and individual needs.

> "The future will require new skills for the bankers. There will continue to be a move from the old-school trade finance world into the new school, where you have to be able to play with a whole new trade finance toolkit in order to play a sensible role in the market."[40]

Tomorrow's customers will be more technically savvy and demand more one-to-one service. They will expect recognition of their culture, nationalisms and migration activities as well as their age and increasingly longevity. They will be even more likely to expect banks to safeguard their privacy.

For commodity finance banks, being different than their competitors offers greater future prospects than being better. Imitating the competition is the most widespread disease in management.

With the increase in the possibilities to finance the full range of commodities from timber to soy to platinum to bauxite, there should be more than enough business to go round. What banks must do is to work to their individual competitive advantages.

Looking back into history, banks have been playing a critical role in many events: the Rothschild dynasty financed the Duke of Wellington's victory over Napoleon at Waterloo. Alexander Baring and Hope [41] financed US$11.25 m/m for the Louisiana Purchase. J.P. Morgan lent US$62 m/m in gold to Grove Cleveland's Treasury department to restore the financial health of the USA.

---

39 Jonathan Bell, 'Commodity Finance', *Trade Finance*, December 2006/January 2007.

40 Ibid.

41 Meno pointed out that this deal also involved Hope from the Dutch bank for which the author has worked.

Similarly, commodity finance banks' contribution will continue to be critical for commodity finance. Before 2008, European banks (especially the French ones) provided most commodity finance. As European banks (especially the French ones) were cut off from US dollar funding in 2008–2011, trade finance provided by European banks took a bit hit. This gap was soon filled in by American and Asian banks, especially the Japanese.

As always, new commodity finance bank names will emerge and some old names will simply depart after burning their fingers in the commodity finance business.

CHAPTER 8

Commodity Finance Case Studies

Pre-export finance

Executive summary

Bank A's client ordered four seagoing multi-purpose vessels from the shipbuilding company Shipbuilding & Heavy Industry Co., Ltd. (the 'Yard') for a price of about €6 m/m each, originally agreed to be delivered in two years' time. The respective shipbuilding contracts are governed by English law.

As usual for such deals, the deal is put under the pre-export finance framework. The contracts called for advance payments from the buyer related to the building progress at the Yard with a final payment upon delivery.

All advance payments are secured by refund guarantees with an on-demand character (the 'Refund Guarantees') from a local bank's (Bank B) branch, which is the house bank of the shipbuilding company and which understands the shipbuilding company very well.

Bank B is one of the top banks in the shipbuilder's country. It is chosen to take this role as guarantor for refund. The evaluation of the financial strength of Bank B seems that Bank B is unlikely to have a financial/liquidity problem that will prevent the bank from honoring the payment of the amount, when and if the refund request is presented.

Bank B is a good correspondent bank to Bank A, which can well accept the credit risk of Bank B and has credit facility established. Bank A has full confidence of payment with such an amount.

Hence Bank A decided to offer a credit facility to its client, so that the client can advance the funds to the shipbuilder, as a transaction normally goes.

For Bank A's credit security requirement purposes, both the contracts and the refund guarantees of Bank B were assigned to Bank A from the buyer (the 'assignments') as security for the pre-delivery financings made available by the bank to the buyer.

Notices of the assignments were given by the Bank A to the Yard and Bank B.

So far, everything is in good order for both buyer and the seller. However, over time it became very clear that due to all sorts of building delays, the Yard would not make the contractual delivery date and would exceed the same grossly.

As a result, the buyer chose to cancel each of the contracts when such became contractually possible. Subsequently, the Yard was summoned to refund the advance payments and – since the Yard did not perform – the payment was claimed to Bank B under the respective refund guarantees.

The building of hull numbers 14 and 15 was in fact never finished. Advance payments for these vessels were refunded swiftly by Bank B to the Bank A as assignees without any argument.

Meanwhile the contracts for hull numbers 16 and 17 were also cancelled (as a matter of fact, the construction of these vessels was stopped at an early stage) and a refund of the advance payments (totalling approx. €7 million plus interest) was demanded from the Yard and claimed to Bank B under the respective refund guarantees.

Surprisingly the Yard, in order to prevent Bank B from honoring the claims under the respective refund guarantees, went to the local court and obtained a 'stop-payment order', a so-called court injunction, providing Bank B with an argument that it was not entitled under the local law to honor the claims under the respective refund guarantees.

Between the buyer and the seller, dispute went on. Meanwhile the Yard, the seller, started parallel arbitration proceedings in Singapore, claiming wrongful termination of the respective contracts and damages resulting therefore, arguing that the delivery delays of hull numbers 14 and 15 were caused by the buyer changing specifications, disapproving work practices and craftsmanship, etc.

The buyer believes that the seller cannot win the arbitration case, but just tries to delay a refund of the advance payments. In the meantime, the seller is trying to find a new buyer for the partially-built hull numbers 14 and 15.

Whereas the dispute between the buyer and seller is not unusual when the market trend changes and the action of the Yard is somewhat to be expected, what is surprising is Bank B's failure to honor the claim under the respective refund guarantees given their clear on-demand character.

Further, how the local court can have jurisdiction over the matter and issue a 'stop-payment order' given the fact that the contracts, the refund guarantees and the assignments are governed by English law.

The relevant manager of Bank A in charge of the relationship with Bank B has been informed shortly after the 'stop-payment order' was issued. He was asked to coordinate the dispute.

Questions

1. What is the fundamental driving force for such a dispute?

2. What is the position of Bank B in this deal?

3. What role can arbitration play in this case?

4. Can the legal injunction be justified? What are the possible scenarios to resolve this legal injunction?

Case study – Bank M

Executive summary

Bank A's client, PC, has concluded a deal with another company, C, in Asia, selling its chemical product to them.

In February 2016, Bank M issued an LC with an amount of US$1.6 m/m with 90 day tenor. This is an open confirmation LC.

In March, Bank A added its confirmation and sent a confirmation letter to the client. After the seller shipped the goods, its house bank Bank A dispatched documents of US$1.1 m/m to the issuing bank for acceptance and payment on the due date.

After receiving the documents, Bank M however mentioned the following discrepancies:

1. Draft showing tenor maturity date unclear.

2. Invoice showing term of delivery CIF (Incoterm 2010) XXX Port for US$1,693,989 instead of US$1,122,948.50.

3. Insurance certificate not clearly stated settling agent in a country in South East Asia.

Revised documents were represented by PC, the seller. Bank M refused the documents and claimed instead non-compliance of documents. Bank A responded and reiterated that the alleged discrepancies are invalid because of the following:

1. Invoice obviously shows shipped quantity, unit price and drawing amount. An indication of total amount CIF (Incoterm 2010) XXX port for US$1,693,989 is considered as part of the description of goods mentioned in the LC field F45A.

2. Similarly, the description of goods in the Packing List and Beneficiary's Certificate correspond with the description of goods stated in the credit. The LC does not specifically indicate what to show or what not to show in such documents.

3. Insurance certificate was issued to the order of Bank M according to LC requirement. Endorsement by beneficiary has no effect and does not jeopardize the right of Bank M for further endorsement.

Most importantly, Bank A sent a letter to Bank M informing explicitly that Bank A has added their confirmation to the LC.

Discrepancy number two is not valid and Bank A enclosed revised drafts and the insurance certificate were re-presented by the beneficiary. Bank A requested Bank M to replace the documents as they are within the LC validity and presentation period.

Bank A discounted without recourse as the confirming bank because documents re-presented are compliant. Credit advice is given to the client informing them that the bill is discounted without recourse.

When the first three discrepancies were declined by Bank A, Bank M sent SWIFT disputing further acceptance of the documents. The argument further focused on the term: 'first presentation'.

Bank M: 'First presentation' means the documents must comply on first presentation. Therefore the documents still have discrepancies, although the revised documents were presented to us.

Bank A however responded that as part of the instructions to Bank A as the negotiating bank to 'reimburse yourselves from our account with Bank M Hong Kong…' nowhere in the LC does it say that the documents must comply on first presentation. The phrase 'on first presentation' is found under field 78 of the LC – 'instructions to the paying/accepting/negotiating bank'.

Bank A in the meantime searches for external experts for their opinions.

External experts all agreed that discrepancies raised were all invalid, citing ICC Opinion R715.

It turned out that the discrepancies arguments were due to commercial dispute as the applicant negotiated for US$100,000 discounting.

Given the uncertainty of the buyer's willingness to accept the goods, Company PC had also sourced six alternative buyers – with prices ranging from US$715,000 to US$817,000. The port will auction off the goods by 5 July 2016 if no one comes forward to collect the cargo.

Bank A proposed a strong message to Bank M to opt for ICC opinion or Docdex when the pending case continued.

Meanwhile, Company PC called to inform Bank A that the applicant proposed to a discount of US$80,000 which Company PC tends to accept and they will reimburse the bank on the said amount.

Bank A sent a message to Bank M stating that the 'applicant agreed to accept and take up the documents provided the beneficiary agrees to a reduction of US$80,000 from the total bill amount. Please obtain beneficiary's consent and re-present the documents under…………..for acceptance'.

The file is thus closed. Bank M did not accept documents, Company PC sent a letter of demand to the buyer on 7 May 2016.

Despite the fact that the case was settled by a reduction of the price, Bank A further applied an ICC Docdex.

After a month and a half, the Docdex conclusion came out:

'All the discrepancies raised are invalid. And the decision was rendered unanimously.'

Questions:

1. What are the fundamental underlying reasons for this problem case?

2. What are the possible solutions for such a dispute?

3. Can the discounting bank insist on compliance of documents?

4. When the Docdex conclusion comes out, what can an issuing bank do? What can the negotiating bank do?

5. What are the key success factors for solutions on such a dispute?

Haana Cocoa Board

Executive summary

Description of the deal

Haana Cocoa Board (Cocobod), established in 1947, is the 100% government-owned cocoa marketing board, responsible for the purchasing and export of cocoa beans from Haana, one of the largest cocoa producers in the world. Cocobod provides various services to the supply chain in order to improve production of cocoa and maintain quality standards.

Cocobod is the world's leading integrated cocoa bean supplier for world market demand and has a long-term proven track record. Professional management, a well-organized internal raw material supply with a focus on quantity and quality improvement has led to a strong quality image of the country's cocoa on the world market. Coupled with a consistent contract performance of Cocobod, the country's cocoa beans command a premium in the market. Privatization of internal sourcing has led to more competition for beans and higher prices for farmers.

In due course, Cocobod requested a pre-export facility of US$500 m/m and approached a commodity bank – Bank F.

On paper, Bank F's credit committee would not be able to approve such a transaction because of the country risk of Haana and bank risk (refund guarantee of a local bank). However, because Cocobod supplies to major clients of trade and commodity finance, it is essential that these players also have access to raw materials.

Off-takers of the export are large clients to Bank F, such as Company A, Company B, Company C, Company D and so on, all well-known commodity traders.

In order for these clients to be able to make payments to the Cocobod, Bank F inversely supports the off-takers.

For risk management purposes, Bank F has taken a few risk mitigation measures to re-structure the deal.

First of all, Bank F, the financing bank, has a pledge on the cocoa so that in the case that the beneficiary fails to make a payment, the bank owns the right to take control of the contracts/the flow of goods.

Second, the financing provided is repaid via payments of proceeds from sales contracts of Cocobod with reputable cocoa traders (Companies A, B, C, D, etc.) which are all important clients of Bank F, in a pledged offshore collection account governed by the collection agent in London.

Proceeds under the sales contracts will be collected via documentary collections routed via the collection agent, Haana International Bank (HIB) London branch, a 51% subsidiary of the Haana Central Bank. HIB has satisfactorily performed this role for many years.

All proceeds received by the collection agent will be transferred with a weekly sweep to the secured collection account with the offshore facility agent (currently Bank D).

In case of non-performance of the buyers after shipment, the bank will have title over the goods (BLs are routed via the collection agent) and the bank will be able to sell the goods to another market player.

Moreover, to diversify the risk, Bank F has invited other banks to participate in the deal to share the non-performance risk.

Information sheet

Buyers:

Traditionally, the European accounts for around half of Haana's cocoa exports mainly relating to purchases of, among others, Companies A, B, C, D. E, F and so on are in the Netherlands. Other important markets are the UK (Companies G and H), Belgium (Companies J and K) and Malaysia, each taking some 10% of Haana's exports. The rest of the exports are well diversified between mainly buyers from OECD countries.

Management:

The management of Cocobod appears to be adequate and competent as proven by the 20-year successful and impeccable track record of transactions with the client. Whilst the chief executive office has had much exposure to Haana's cocoa sector and Cocobod in previous jobs, the rest of the senior management is unchanged and enjoys a long experience with the organization.

Ownership:

The strategic importance and position of Cocobod in Haana is also reflected in the company being state-owned via the Ministry of Finance and Economic Planning and monitored by the Central Bank of Haana. Both are in turn closely monitored by IMF and the World Bank under ongoing strategic assistance programs.

Because of its legal inception and position in the cocoa sector, Cocobod is being assessed as sovereign risk to Haana. History has shown that the structure of the transaction is strong, that performance is reliable and that the repayment morale of Cocobod is impeccable.

Cocoa – the commodity:

Global cocoa bean exports have reached 5.0 million tonnes in 2016, an average annual growth rate of 2.8%. Total exports from Africa are expected to grow by 2.8% annually.

As mentioned, Haana is one of the largest producers of cocoa in the world, and it is setting ambitious targets to expand production for the coming years to 1 million tonnes itself.

Cocoa accounts for around 30% of Haana's export revenues. Thus, the cocoa sector has the full ongoing support of the government of Haana which has been a major investor in the past years.

To facilitate the export, measures taken include road building to improve access to/from the more remote production areas, the supply of fertilizer to improve crop yields and the creation of regional centers for crop husbandry/disease control.

Currently, Haana has low foreign reserves thus the inflow of foreign-exchange earnings from the cocoa sector helps to support the country and the local currency. As one of the main export products of Haana the push-out factor for cocoa is high.

Questions

1. What are the risks facing a bank in providing finance to an exporter located in emerging markets? Why is providing loans to the exporter difficult from the traditional balance sheet financing perspective?

2. Among the risks a financing bank is facing, which one is the most important?

3. For alternatives, what is the starting point?

4. How can a bank structure the deal in a way that all foreseeable risks are mitigated?

5. Why is structured commodity finance used for emerging markets?

Payment blocked by a local court

Executive summary

Company A in Italy buys durum, a kind of wheat, from Company G. As usual, they agree to use an LC for payment settlement. The LC is supposed to be issued by Bank B.

Typically Bank A provides discounting without recourse under LC issued by Bank B.

However, there was a dispute between Bank A and Bank B, which is a subsidiary of a major European bank. The payment from Bank B was blocked due to the legal injunction in a local court.

Bank A is concerned as they provided without recourse to the beneficiary. As such they have had numerous discussions with a European law firm which is familiar with the legal practice in that country, to find a solution.

Over the past week, Bank A has been trying to understand what is wrong, the reasons for the injunction and the possibility to have the injunction lifted.

What is noticed is that the injunction itself is between Company M and Bank B, that is, the injunction was granted to prevent Bank B from paying Company G, the supplier and the beneficiary of the LC, not Bank A. Moreover, the court injunction was granted in the court of a relatively small town in Italy in which Company A is an important company.

The law firm's advice is for Company G and Bank A to challenge the injunction. The next hearing for the injunction is not scheduled until 12 October.

The legal advice is that bringing this hearing forward may be difficult. The Italian lawyers for Company G and Bank A, in the meantime, will continue to work closely together. The process to do this is being worked through by both firms.

The ship is now due to arrive in Italy on 15 September. Representatives from Company G and XXX, a quality testing company, will both be at port to ensure that the quality testing is done according to best practice. If correctly tested, the sample taken will be large and should therefore reflect the correct blended grade of the durum.

Company G is confident that the durum will be tested within specifications and that Company M will then pay for the full shipment.

It is worth noting that Company G has also had two other testing laboratories in Australia and one in Japan undertake additional tests; all show the grain quality as being in compliance with the contract.

The shipment is broken down into high grade and lower grade durum with the injunction only on the lower grade durum (that is, US$6.3 mln). Company M is keen to use the higher grade durum as soon as possible.

Rather than seeking payment for just the higher grade durum (that is, US$12.9 mln), the current strategy for Company G is to tell Bank B not to release the BLs to Company M (that is, not to release title), which means that the durum cannot be legally discharged from the ship.

From Company M's perspective, this means that they cannot get access to the higher grade durum, and – as charter party hirer of the ship – are liable for daily demurrage costs until the BLs are released to Company M.

Bank A keeps pressures on Bank B via regular SWIFT demands for the payment due under the LC which is in conformity with UCP (importantly, Bank B is trying to find discrepancy but now admits that the shipping documents are clean).

Bank A also excises pressure to Bank B's mother bank. As the documents were clean prior to the injunction being granted, Bank B was required to pay the full amount of the LC to Bank A under UCP rules.

If payment is not forthcoming over the next few weeks and the injunction is not lifted by the court, Company G and Bank A will have other options available to them.

1. The contract is subject to GAFTA rules (the global grain industry association) and quality disputes can be decided by GAFTA arbitration. Even if this ruling cannot overrule a local court's jurisdiction, the threat of black listing for Company M could result in a resolution of this issue.

2. There may be an option to take Bank B to court in the USA, to freeze or attach to their nostro account, given the payment of the LC is denominated in US dollars where Bank B's nostro is located. This is an option but it would have far-reaching implications for the relationship between banks, and therefore would need wider consultation within Bank A. On that basis, it is not proposed for the time being.

Based on all the information so far, it is believed that Company G is not to be at fault through this process. In particular, all the quality tests have been done by very competent agencies which are widely used by the Australian grain industry.

It is also clear that Bank A is not at fault, noting the LC is now considered clean/compliant by all parties including the issuing bank, Bank B. Bank B's defense on not paying is only that a court in the country they operate in has ordered them not to.

Why Company M sought the injunction in the first place seems to be a mystery, but at the very least must be considered misguided. Equally, Bank A and Company G's legal advisors are very surprised that the local court granted the injunction.

All focus now is on applying commercial and legal pressure around getting this injunction lifted.

Questions

1. What could motivate Company M to seek the injunction?

2. Why has Bank B intended to have claim on the discrepancy?

3. If the documents are in order, must Bank B pay when there is a legal injunction?

4. Can the quality argument become a reason for non-payment?

5. Where is the solution? How do they reach it?

6. Are there lessons learnt?

Commodity fraud

Executive summary

On 25 July 1991, a Bulgarian buyer paid US$3.8 million for 13,100 tonnes of Brazilian sugar. However, neither the ship nor the sugar existed and the criminals have never been brought to the court and an LC is used in the settlement of the payment. This is the later story.

Banks, on the basis of the usual documents which proved that the sugar was loaded on 17 July in the port of Santos on the m.v. *Giovanna* bound for Varna, Bulgaria, were ready to offer finance to the deal.

In August 1992, a Paris bank released US$2.89 million under an LC on the basis of documents stating that 10,000 tonnes of white refined sugar had been loaded on the m.v. *Vladimir Ilyich* in Panama, bound for Kalingrad, Russia. Like many other deals in commodities, it went through with no surprise. The buyer bought the goods, the bank issued an LC and another bank negotiated the documents and paid out the money.

Only at a very late stage, was it found out that the documents (i.e., proofs of purchase) were forgeries and the money has never been paid.

Yes, this is fraud – a major threat which is not unusual in commodity finance. Given the large amounts of money involved and the fact that commodity banks are handling papers representing title to commodities, the motivation for fraud is higher.

Interestingly, we may identify several basic ingredients in almost all fraud cases in commodity finance: there must be substance or pretext to entice the victim, whether it be counterfeit goods, or forged documents proving title. And there must also be a victim.

Occasionally, the victim may be the market as a whole (e.g. the debasement of currencies by a government printing paper notes), but more usually the victim is an individual or business entity. The fraudster often needs a mechanism to obtain something of value in return for his exchange. Finally, he needs to evade arrest for his crime.

Unlike in other fraud cases, faked commodities are rarely seen. Diamonds can be faked and old master paintings can be forged, but commodities are easily measured and tested and are rarely of sufficient value to attract forgers.

With sugar, the fraudulent transaction is almost invariably based on a consignment which does not physically exist.

Fraudulent title paper is always the key point in fraud cases for commodities. Although surprising at first glance, this potential arises because bureaucracies everywhere have engendered a belief in the authority of paperwork. Just as worthless paper money is accepted as having value, so pieces of paper are accepted as having value and as proof that a consignment of a commodity exists.

If we think about what is happening in our daily life, hardly anybody goes to his central bank to check his wealth in gold – he relies on a statement of account on a bit of paper. By the same token, commodity documentation is taken on trust. It is only necessary for a fraudster to forge documents showing the existence of a consignment and to find someone to buy it.

The crucial point here is – a point often ignored by inexperienced merchants – banks deal solely in documents, not the underlying commodities.

Banks are protected by international banking rules (the Uniform Customs and Practice for Documentary Credits) which stipulate that a bank must honor an LC if the specified documents are presented and are correct on their face. They have neither obligation nor incentive to question the documents; only that they apparently accord with those specified and there is nothing which suggests forgery.

In fact, banks have more incentive to detect forged currency notes or checks, where they stand the loss themselves.

Another fact is that victims of fraud are unfortunately almost always attracted by expectations of exceptional profit involved in fraud for commodities. They succumb more to their own greed than anything else. A deal which is too good to be true probably isn't true. People around the world queue up every day for all manner of schemes which could not logically be genuine.

Sugar is one of the major commodities. There are several long-standing international sugar traders of the highest repute. Offers to sell sugar at less than the ruling market price makes no commercial sense – unless the real motive exactly established is fraud.

This has been a standard ploy for a long time: to make the victim of fraud believe that he has access to a phenomenal deal, so good that he wants to keep it secret. This enables the fraudulent seller to conceal detailed information about the origins and location of the sugar. The buyer thinks he is on to something no one else knows about, which will make him a quick profit, and doesn't care too much about the origins of the sugar or why it is cheap, so long as it is genuine – and the documents appear to protect him on this point.

To allay suspicions, a fraudulent seller will often offer various assurances which seem to give protection, or at least to vindicate his character. He may lodge a performance bond equal to, say, 2% of the value. He is then risking 2% in the hands of an honest buyer in order to swindle him of the remaining 98%. He may provide various attestations from banks as to his financial worth (of no legal value or protection). He may offer to supply secret information about the exact location and origins of the sugar in return for, say, 10% part payment, either as a means of consolidating the deal or simply to abscond with the part payment. Provision of unnecessary quasi-official documentation is another tactic; any bit of paper which seems to confirm the existence of the sugar provides further reassurance.

Victims are usually surprised and even outraged when they discover that the international banking system provides absolutely no protection against payments made on the basis of fraudulent documents. They often fail to understand the rules of international payments systems and the division of responsibility between themselves and the banking system. They fail to notice the exemption of payment obligation under fraud.

The common sugar fraud utilizes international trading practice of payment via the irrevocable LC. The buyer first arranges for his bank to issue an LC. This is a legal undertaking by the bank, not the buyer, to make payment when certain specified documentation is provided which 'proves' the sugar exists and is in transit to the buyer or at some agreed location – documents the fraudster of course intends to forge.

Note that it is the bank which gives the undertaking, albeit at the buyer's expense. The LC is also irrevocable – so the buyer is now entirely in the hands of his bank and the seller. Any alteration to the terms of an LC must be agreed by both parties, so the buyer is powerless even if he becomes suspicious.

It is up to the buyer to make independent checks. For example, in the case of the US$3.8 million fraud described above, it would have been simple to establish with Lloyds Register of Shipping that the m.v. *Giovanna* was nowhere near the Brazilian port of Santos in July 1991. The fact is, the ship had been renamed the m.v. *Styliani* in 1983 and broken up for scrap in Pakistan in 1984.

Prevention

The conduct of sugar frauds suggests elementary extra prudence. The following are some highlights:

1. The commodity offered is below the market price with undisclosed details of the seller or origin or any air of secrecy.

2. Performance bonds or deposits.

3. Involvement in countries previously targeted, e.g. buyers in India, China, Hong Kong, the Middle East or Eastern Europe and sugar sourced from Latin America, the Philippines or Thailand.

4. Independently checking any ship, its location, and its cargo.

5. Any unusual specification of the commodity or documentation.

The best long-term defense is to ensure that fraudulent stories are well-publicized. Any information should be given to the International Chamber of Commerce, which has taken the initiative in gathering intelligence and advising those at risk.

Questions

1. Why is sugar chosen as a target for fraud?

2. What is the starting point for this sugar fraud?

3. What are the key factors for fraudsters to achieve their goal?

4. What are the ways to prevent fraud?

Financing of railway bills

Executive summary

Under LCs, most banks use BLs as title documents. However, some inland countries will have to use railway bills as evidence of fulfilling the task of transportation.

In these transactions, banks are financing their clients based on railway bills, which are different in many ways from BLs. This creates extra risk and need risk mitigation techniques.

One of Bank A's clients, ABC Coal Ltd/Sulphur and Fertilizer Sarl, regularly exports sulphur grades from Kazakhstan XYZ Energy Company, a supplier Bank A recognizes as beneficiary in oil transactions as well to China.

They are requesting that Bank A considers silent confirmation of export LCs on the basis of copies of railway bills, as the originals will go directly to the Chinese customs.

At this moment, this client is adequately serviced by an American bank, but would like to discuss with Bank A to do a trial and potentially bring part of the business to Bank A.

Bank A thinks it will be a good and stable flow to capture, provided it is attractive (pricing, limit availability) and risk-wise acceptable (silent, copies of railway bills) from a pure bank risk perspective.

Questions

1. What is the fundamental weakness of railway bills representing the goods?

2. What is silent confirmation? What is the difference between silent confirmation and open confirmation?

3. If Bank A decides to take over at least part of this part of this business, what risks will the bank be facing?

4. What are the ways to mitigate the risks?

Court decision

Executive summary

Bank G had opened five LCs in favor of Company S under contracts for the sale of containerized scrap metal. The LCs were expressly subject to UCP 600.

Company S made a number of drawings under each of them. Bank F confirmed three of the LCs and forwarded the cargo documents to Bank G seeking reimbursement. In respect of the other two LCs, Bank F acted as nominated bank and passed the documents which Company S presented to it on to Bank G. Bank G refused to authorize reimbursement to Bank F or payment to Company S.

Bank F, together with its client Company S, applied to the commercial court seeking summary judgment against Bank G. Bank G resisted their application on a number of grounds.

Bank G firstly contended that there were discrepancies in the documents. The court rejected all but one of the alleged discrepancies on the basis that, where instructions in the LCs were ambiguous, Bank F had acted on a reasonable construction of them, or, considering the matter intelligently rather than mechanically, the documents were not in fact discrepant.

Bank G's second argument was that Bank F was not authorized to act as a confirming bank, and was therefore not entitled to reimbursement, because it could only act as the nominated bank.

This argument failed because of Article 2 of UCP 600, which provides that a confirming bank is one which adds its confirmation to a credit "upon the issuing bank's authorization or request".

In this case, each of the confirmed LCs stated in the confirmation instructions that Bank F "may add" its confirmation and in the additional conditions that it 'may be confirmed at the request and cost of the beneficiary'.

Bank G argued that in the three cases where Bank F had added its confirmation at the request of Company S, it had done so without Bank G's authorization, so rendering the confirmation silent and therefore outside the scope of UCP 600.

The court rejected this, holding that the term 'may add' in the confirmation instructions meant that Bank G had authorized the confirmation.

Bank G further contended that Bank F was not entitled to reimbursement acting as a nominated bank, because it had not negotiated or honored a complying presentation according to the terms of UCP 600; principally because of a delay in negotiation of more than five days after presentation, placing it outside the terms of UCP Article 14(b). This argument failed too.

Article 7(c) of UCP 600 states that "… an issuing bank undertakes to reimburse a nominated bank that has honored or negotiated a complying presentation and forwarded the documents to the issuing bank. Reimbursement… is due at maturity". The court held that this obligation to reimburse arises if, in fact, the nominating bank has negotiated or honored a complying presentation and forwarded the documents to the issuing bank. There was no doubt on the facts that Bank F had done so.

Questions

1. What is the role of an LC?

2. What is the function of the applicant?

3. What is the role of the beneficiary?

4. What is a discrepancy and why is there a discrepancy? What is a valid discrepancy and what is not a valid discrepancy?

5. What can a confirming bank do if there is a valid discrepancy?

6. Who will be liable for a valid discrepancy?

APPENDIX 1

Major Commodity Futures Agencies

Agencies for commodity risk hedge

ABN AMRO Futures Ltd

Address: 199 Bishopsgate, London EC2M 3XW

Website: www.aboamro.com/futures

Commodity products covered

- Futures: cocoa, robusta coffee, white sugar, feed wheat, milling wheat, rapeseed, corn

- Options: white sugar, feed wheat, milling wheat, rapeseed, corn

ADM Investor Services International Ltd

Address: 10th floor Temple Court, 11 Queen Victoria Street, London EC4N 4TJ

Website: www.admisi.com

Commodity products covered

- Futures: cocoa, robusta coffee, white sugar, feed wheat, milling wheat, rapeseed, corn

- Options: white sugar, feed wheat, milling wheat, rapeseed, corn

Bache Financial Ltd

Address: 9 Devonshire Square, London EC2M 4HP

Website: www.bachefin.com

Commodity products covered

- Futures: cocoa, robusta coffee, white sugar, feed wheat, milling wheat, rapeseed, corn

- Options: white sugar, feed wheat, milling wheat, rapeseed, corn

BNP Commodity Futures Ltd

Address: 10 Harewood Avenue, London NW1 6AA

Commodity products covered

- Futures: cocoa, robusta coffee, white sugar, feed wheat, milling wheat, rapeseed, corn
- Options: white sugar, feed wheat, milling wheat, rapeseed, corn

Calyon Financial SNC

Address: 119 Rue Reaumur, 75002 Paris France

Website: www.calyonfinancial.com

Commodity products covered

- Futures: cocoa, robusta coffee, white sugar, feed wheat, milling wheat, rapeseed, corn
- Options: white sugar, feed wheat, milling wheat, rapeseed, corn

Dienstencentrum Agrarische Markt BV

Address: Postbus 2298, 8203 AG Lelystad The Netherlands

Website: www.dca-markt.nl

Commodity products covered

- Futures: white sugar, feed wheat, milling wheat, rapeseed, corn
- Options: white sugar, feed wheat, milling wheat, rapeseed, corn

ED & F Man Commodity Advisers Ltd

Address: Cottons Centre, Hay's Lane, London SE1 2QE

Commodity product covered

- Futures: cocoa, robusta coffee, white sugar, feed wheat
- Options: cocoa, robusta coffee, white sugar, feed wheat

Fimat International Banque SA

Address: SG House, 41 Tower Hill, London EC3N 2SG

Website: www.imat.com

Commodity products covered

- Futures: cocoa, robusta coffee, white sugar
- Options: cocoa, robusta coffee, white sugar

Fimat SNC Paris

Address: 50 Boulevard Haussmann, 75439 Paris Cedex 09

Website: www.fimat.com

Commodity products covered

- Futures: milling wheat, rapeseed, corn
- Options: milling wheat, rapeseed, corn

Fortis Commodity Derivatives

Address: Camomile Court, 23 Camomile Street, London EC3A 7PP

Commodity products covered

- Futures: cocoa, robusta coffee, white sugar, feed wheat, milling wheat, rapeseed, corn
- Options: cocoa, robusta coffee, white sugar, feed wheat, milling wheat, rapeseed, corn

GNI Touch

Address: Sugar Quay, Lower Thames Street, London EC3R 6DU

Website: www.gnitouch.com

Commodity products covered

- Futures: cocoa, robusta coffee, white sugar, feed wheat, milling wheat
- Options: cocoa, robusta coffee, white sugar, feed wheat, milling wheat

J.P. Morgan Securities Ltd

Address: J.P. Morgan Securities Ltd, 125 London Wall, London EC2Y 5AJ

Website: www.jpmorgan.com

Commodity products covered

- Futures: cocoa, robusta coffee, white sugar, feed wheat, milling wheat, rapeseed, corn
- Options: cocoa, robusta coffee, white sugar, feed wheat, milling wheat, rapeseed, corn

Macquarie Bank Ltd

Address: Level 30 City Point, 1 Ropemaker Street, London EC2Y 9HD

Website: www.marquarie.com.au

Commodity products covered

- Futures: cocoa, robusta coffee, white sugar
- Options: cocoa, robusta coffee, white sugar

Man Financial Ltd

Address: Sugar Quay, Lower Thames Street, London, EC3R 6DU

Website: www.manfinancial.com

Commodity products covered

- Futures: cocoa, robusta coffee, white sugar, feed wheat, milling wheat, rapeseed, corn
- Options: cocoa, robusta coffee, white sugar, feed wheat, milling wheat, rapeseed, corn

Marex Carlton Ltd

Address: 25 Grosvenor Street, London WIK 4QN

Commodity products covered

- Futures: cocoa, robusta coffee, white sugar
- Options: cocoa, robusta coffee, white sugar

Maynard & Keynes BV

Address: Prins Hendrikkade, 48A 1012 AC, Amsterdam, The Netherlands

Website: www.maynardkeynes.com

Commodity products covered

- Futures: robusta coffee, white sugar, feed wheat
- Options: robusta coffee, white sugar, feed wheat

Natexis Commoditity Markets Ltd

Address: 3rd Floor Capital House, 85 King William Street, London EC4N 7BL

Website: www.natenxisscm.com

Commodity products covered

- Futures: cocoa, robusta coffee, white sugar, feed wheat, milling wheat, rapeseed, corn
- Options: cocoa, robusta coffee, white sugar, feed wheat, milling wheat, rapeseed, corn

Plantureux SA

Address: B.P. 86 16 Avenue Louison Bobet, 94123 Fontenay-sous-Bois Cedex France

Website: www.plantureux.com

Commodity products covered

- Futures: milling wheat, rapeseed, corn
- Options: milling wheat, rapeseed, corn

Rabo Securites NV

Address: Dam 27,1012 JS, Amsterdam, The Netherlands

Website: www.rabosecurites.nl

Commodity products covered

- Futures: cocoa, robusta coffee, white sugar, feed wheat, milling wheat, rapeseed, corn
- Options: cocoa, robusta coffee, white sugar, feed wheat, milling wheat, rapeseed, corn

Rand Financial Services Inc.

Address: 141 W. Jackson Boulevard, Suite 1950, Chicago, Illinoin IL 60604 USA

Website: www.randfinancial com

Commodity products covered

- Futures: cocoa, robusta coffee, white sugar, feed wheat
- Options: cocoa, robusta coffee, white sugar, feed wheat

Sigma Terme SNC

Address: 83 Avenue de la Grande Armee F-75 782 Paris Cedex 16

Website: www.invivo-group.com

Commodity products covered

- Futures: milling wheat, rapeseed, corn
- Options: milling wheat, rapeseed, corn

Sucden (UK) Ltd

Address: 5 London Bridge Street, London SE1 9SG

Website: www.sucden.co.uk

Commodity products covered

- Futures: cocoa, robusta coffee, white sugar, feed wheat
- Options: cocoa, robusta coffee, white sugar, feed wheat

TRX Futures Ltd

Address: Ground Floor, 3 Finsbury Square, London EC2A 1AE

Website: www.trxfutures.com

Commodity products covered

- Futures: cocoa, robusta coffee, white sugar
- Options: cocoa, robusta coffee, white sugar

UBS Ltd

Address: 1 Finsbury Avenue, London EC2M 2PP

Website: www.ubs.com

Commodity products covered

- Futures: cocoa, robusta coffee, white sugar, feed wheat, milling wheat, rapeseed, corn

- Options: cocoa, robusta coffee, white sugar, feed wheat, milling wheat, rapeseed, corn

APPENDIX 2

Major Commodity Flows for China During Peak Years

All tables in Appendix 2 are courtesy of International
Trade Centre – International Trade Statistics
(Calculations based on COMTRADE statistics)
www.trademap.org

Tradeflow main commodities 2006–2010

Crude petroleum oils: import

IMPORT	2006 Country	%	2007 Country	%	2008 Country	%	2009 Country	%	2010 Country	%
World	World	100.0	World	100.0	World	100.0	World	100.0	World	100.0
1	United States of America	22.9	United States of America	22.9	United States of America	22.9	United States of America	21.9	United States of America	20.1
2	Japan	9.7	Japan	9.4	Japan	9.4	China	9.4	China	9.0
3	China	6.5	China	7.2	China	7.2	Japan	7.8	Japan	8.0
4	Republic of Korea	5.5	Republic of Korea	5.5	India	5.5	India	5.2	Republic of Korea	6.5
5	Germany	5.1	Germany	5.0	Republic of Korea	5.0	Republic of Korea	5.2	Germany	5.1
6	India	4.7	India	4.9	Germany	4.9	Germany	4.8	Netherlands	4.3
7	Italy	3.9	Italy	4.1	France	4.1	America not elsewhere specified	3.6	Italy	3.7
8	France	3.9	France	3.9	Italy	3.9	Italy	3.5	France	3.4
9	Netherlands	2.8	Spain	2.8	America not elsewhere specified	2.7	France	3.2	Spain	3.2
10	Spain	2.7	Netherlands	2.7	Netherlands	2.7	Netherlands	2.5	United Kingdom	2.6
11	United Kingdom	2.6	Chinese Taipei	2.6	Spain	2.2	Spain	2.5	Chinese Taipei	2.3
12	Chinese Taipei	2.3	United Kingdom	2.3	United Kingdom	2.1	United Kingdom	2.3	Singapore	2.3
13	Canada	2.0	Canada	2.0	Singapore	2.0	Singapore	2.2	Thailand	2.0
14	Singapore	2.0	Singapore	2.0	Chinese Taipei	2.0	Chinese Taipei	2.0	Canada	2.0
15	Thailand	2.0	Thailand	2.0	Canada	1.8	Thailand	1.9	Belgium	1.9
16	Belgium	1.5	Belgium	1.5	Thailand	1.6	Canada	1.8	Australia	1.9
17	Turkey	1.1	Australia	1.1	Europe other than the Netherlands	1.1	LAIA not elsewhere specified	1.5	India	1.8
18	LAIA not elsewhere specified	1.0	Brazil	1.0	Belgium	1.1	Europe other than the Netherlands	1.5	Poland	1.6
19	Australia	1.0	Turkey	1.0	Brazil	1.1	Belgium	1.0	South Africa	1.5
20	South Africa	0.9	Europe other than the Netherlands	0.9	Turkey	1.0	South Africa	0.9	Greece	1.0
21	Brazil	0.9	South Africa	0.9	Australia	1.0	Australia	0.9	Sweden	0.9
22	Sweden	0.9	Poland	0.9	South Africa	0.9	Brazil	0.9	Brazil	0.9
23	Europe other than the Netherlands	0.9	Sweden	0.9	Poland	0.8	Poland	0.9	Turkey	0.8
24	Poland	0.8	Indonesia	0.8	LAIA not elsewhere specified	0.8	Indonesia	0.9	Indonesia	0.7
25	Greece	0.8	Greece	0.8	Sweden	0.8	Sweden	0.8	Belarus	0.6

Tradeflow main commodities 2006–2010

Crude petroleum oils: export

EXPORT	2006 Country	%	2007 Country	%	2008 Country	%	2009 Country	%	2010 Country	%
World	World	100.0	World	100.0	World	100.0	World	100.0	World	100.0
1	Saudi Arabia	17.5	Saudi Arabia	17.2	Saudi Arabia	16.5	Saudi Arabia	16.1	Saudi Arabia	15.7
2	Russian Federation	10.5	Russian Federation	10.9	Russian Federation	10.2	Russian Federation	10.6	Russian Federation	12.1
3	Venezuela	6.1	Iran (Islamic Republic of)	6.1	Iran (Islamic Republic of)	5.8	Iran (Islamic Republic of)	5.7	Nigeria	5.7
4	Nigeria	5.9	United Arab Emirates	5.7	United Arab Emirates	5.4	United Arab Emirates	5.3	Iran (Islamic Republic of)	5.2
5	Norway	5.5	Norway	5.2	Nigeria	5.0	Nigeria	4.8	United Arab Emirates	5.1
6	Iran (Islamic Republic of)	5.4	Nigeria	4.8	Norway	4.5	Norway	4.6	Canada	4.7
7	Kuwait	4.0	Libyan Arab Jamahiriya	3.7	Angola	4.4	Iraq	4.3	Norway	4.5
8	Libyan Arab Jamahiriya	3.8	Canada	3.7	Canada	4.3	Angola	4.3	Angola	4.4
9	Mexico	3.6	Kuwait	3.6	Venezuela	3.7	Canada	4.3	Iraq	4.0
10	Canada	3.3	Mexico	3.6	Iraq	3.6	Kuwait	4.0	Libyan Arab Jamahiriya	3.7
11	Algeria	3.1	Angola	3.4	Kuwait	3.6	Venezuela	3.9	Kuwait	4.1
12	Iraq	2.6	Iraq	3.2	Libyan Arab Jamahiriya	3.4	Libyan Arab Jamahiriya	3.7	Mexico	3.4
13	Kazakhstan	2.5	Algeria	3.0	Azerbaijan	3.2	Kazakhstan	3.0	Kazakhstan	3.0
14	United Kingdom	1.7	Kazakhstan	2.9	Kazakhstan	2.7	Mexico	2.9	Qatar	2.9
15	Qatar	1.6	United Kingdom	2.4	Mexico	2.4	Qatar	2.9	United Kingdom	2.5
16	Oman	1.0	Qatar	1.6	Algeria	1.8	Algeria	2.4	Algeria	2.4
17	Malaysia	0.9	Oman	1.0	United Kingdom	1.4	United Kingdom	2.1	Azerbaijan	2.2
18	Congo	0.9	Malaysia	0.9	Qatar	0.9	Oman	1.7	Oman	1.6
19	Vietnam	0.9	Indonesia	0.9	Oman	0.9	Azerbaijan	1.5	Brazil	1.4
20	Indonesia	0.9	Brazil	0.9	Brazil	0.9	Brazil	1.1	Netherlands	1.1
21	Equatorial Guinea	0.8	Equatorial Guinea	0.8	Malaysia	0.8	Colombia	0.9	Colombia	0.9
22	Ecuador	0.8	Ecuador	0.7	Indonesia	0.8	Indonesia	0.8	Indonesia	0.9
23	Brazil	0.7	Congo	0.6	Equatorial Guinea	0.7	Malaysia	0.8	Malaysia	0.8
24	Yemen	0.6	Australia	0.6	Congo	0.7	Sudan	0.7	Australia	0.8
25	Denmark	0.6			Ecuador	0.6	Congo	0.7	Congo	0.7

Tradeflow main commodities 2006–2010

Coffee: import

IMPORT	2006 Country	%	2007 Country	%	2008 Country	%	2009 Country	%	2010 Country	%
World	World	100.0	World	100.0	World	100.0	World	100.0	World	100.0
1	United States of America	21.4	United States of America	20.4	United States of America	19.4	United States of America	19.2	United States of America	19.9
2	Germany	15.6	Germany	15.2	Germany	15.2	Germany	14.2	Germany	14.9
3	Japan	6.8	France	6.3	France	6.3	France	7.1	France	7.1
4	France	6.1	Italy	6.1	Italy	5.8	Italy	6.1	Japan	6.0
5	Italy	5.8	Japan	6.0	Japan	5.5	Japan	5.7	Italy	5.5
6	Canada	4.2	Canada	3.8	Belgium	3.6	Belgium	4.9	Belgium	4.7
7	Belgium	3.8	Spain	3.4	Canada	3.5	Canada	3.9	Canada	4.1
8	Spain	3.2	Belgium	3.4	Spain	2.9	Spain	3.2	Spain	3.1
9	Netherlands	3.1	Netherlands	3.2	United Kingdom	2.1	United Kingdom	3.0	United Kingdom	2.9
10	United Kingdom	2.8	United Kingdom	2.7	Netherlands	2.1	Netherlands	2.5	Netherlands	2.5
11	Sweden	2.0	Austria	2.2	Austria	1.9	Switzerland	2.1	Switzerland	2.4
12	Switzerland	1.7	Sweden	1.9	Switzerland	1.9	Sweden	1.8	Sweden	2.1
13	Austria	1.7	Switzerland	1.8	Sweden	1.4	Austria	1.7	Austria	1.6
14	Poland	1.4	Algeria	1.2	Algeria	1.3	Poland	1.7	Poland	1.6
15	Finland	1.1	Poland	1.2	Republic of Korea	1.2	Republic of Korea	1.4	Republic of Korea	1.6
16	Republic of Korea	1.1	Republic of Korea	1.1	Poland	1.1	Russian Federation	1.2	Russian Federation	1.4
17	Algeria	1.0	Finland	1.1	Russian Federation	1.1	Algeria	1.2	Finland	1.2
18	Australia	0.9	Australia	1.0	Finland	1.0	Finland	1.1	Australia	1.1
19	Denmark	0.9	Russian Federation	1.0	Australia	1.0	Australia	1.1	Denmark	1.1
20	Russian Federation	0.8	Denmark	0.8	Portugal	0.8	Portugal	0.9	Portugal	0.9
21	Portugal	0.7	Portugal	0.8	Denmark	0.8	Denmark	0.8	Norway	0.9
22	Norway	0.7	Norway	0.7	Greece	0.7	Slovakia	0.7	Slovakia	0.8
23	Romania	0.7	Greece	0.7	Czech Republic	0.7	Greece	0.7	Romania	0.6
24	Luxembourg	0.6	Czech Republic	0.7	Norway	0.7	Norway	0.6	Greece	0.6
25	Czech Republic	0.6	Romania	0.6	Romania	0.6	Czech Republic	0.6	Czech Republic	0.6

Tradeflow main commodities 2006–2010

Coffee: export

EXPORT	2006 Country	%	2007 Country	%	2008 Country	%	2009 Country	%	2010 Country	%
World	World	100.0	World	100.0	World	100.0	World	100.0	World	100.0
1	Brazil	20.0	Brazil	19.2	Brazil	18.9	Brazil	19.0	Brazil	21.3
2	Colombia	10.0	Vietnam	10.8	Vietnam	9.6	Vietnam	8.7	Germany	7.9
3	Germany	8.3	Colombia	9.8	Colombia	8.7	Germany	8.4	Colombia	7.8
4	Vietnam	8.2	Germany	8.3	Germany	7.8	Colombia	7.9	Vietnam	7.3
5	Italy	4.5	Italy	4.6	Belgium	5.0	Switzerland	4.7	Switzerland	5.0
6	Indonesia	4.0	Indonesia	3.6	Indonesia	4.5	Belgium	4.5	Belgium	4.1
7	Peru	3.5	Guatemala	3.3	Italy	4.4	Italy	4.5	Italy	3.9
8	Belgium	3.3	United States of America	3.1	Switzerland	3.4	United States of America	4.1	Peru	3.6
9	United States of America	3.3	Belgium	3.0	Guatemala	2.9	Indonesia	3.0	Indonesia	3.3
10	Guatemala	3.1	Honduras	2.8	Peru	2.9	Peru	2.9	Ethiopia	3.2
11	Ethiopia	2.9	Switzerland	2.7	United States of America	2.8	Guatemala	2.9	Honduras	3.1
12	Honduras	2.6	Peru	2.4	Honduras	2.6	Honduras	2.6	United States of America	3.1
13	India	2.1	Ethiopia	2.4	Ethiopia	2.6	Ethiopia	1.9	Guatemala	2.9
14	Mexico	2.1	Mexico	2.0	Uganda	1.8	Mexico	1.8	Mexico	2.9
15	Costa Rica	1.6	India	1.7	India	1.8	Uganda	1.8	Nicaragua	1.6
16	Nicaragua	1.4	Uganda	1.5	Mexico	1.6	Netherlands	1.4	India	1.6
17	Austria	1.3	Costa Rica	1.5	Costa Rica	1.6	France	1.3	Netherlands	1.5
18	Uganda	1.3	Netherlands	1.3	Netherlands	1.3	India	1.3	Canada	1.4
19	El Salvador	1.3	Austria	1.2	Nicaragua	1.2	Nicaragua	1.2	France	1.3
20	Switzerland	1.1	Nicaragua	1.1	El Salvador	1.2	El Salvador	1.2	Uganda	1.3
21	Canada	1.0	El Salvador	1.1	Austria	1.1	Costa Rica	1.1	Costa Rica	1.2
22	Netherlands	1.0	Côte d'Ivoire	1.0	France	1.0	Canada	1.0	Papua New Guinea	1.1
23	Papua New Guinea	0.9	Kenya	0.9	Papua New Guinea	0.9	Poland	0.9	El Salvador	1.1
24	Kenya	0.9	Canada	0.9	Canada	0.9	Kenya	0.8	Kenya	0.9
25	France	0.8	France	0.8	Kenya	0.7	Papua New Guinea	0.7	Poland	0.8

Tradeflow main commodities 2006–2010

Petroleum gases: import

IMPORT	2006 Country	%	2007 Country	%	2008 Country	%	2009 Country	%	2010 Country	%
World	World	100.0	World	100.0	World	100.0	World	100.0	World	100.0
1	United States of America	15.4	Japan	15.0	Japan	15.0	Japan	16.9	Japan	16.2
2	Germany	14.2	United States of America	14.2	Germany	14.2	Germany	13.0	Germany	15.1
3	Japan	13.8	Germany	12.8	United States of America	12.8	Italy	11.0	Italy	11.2
4	France	7.0	France	6.9	Republic of Korea	6.9	United States of America	7.4	Republic of Korea	7.9
5	Republic of Korea	6.6	Republic of Korea	6.8	France	6.8	France	7.4	United States of America	7.8
6	Belgium	6.4	Belgium	4.6	Belgium	4.6	Republic of Korea	5.4	France	7.6
7	Spain	4.4	Spain	4.5	Spain	4.5	Spain	5.1	Belgium	4.8
8	Netherlands	3.4	United Kingdom	2.8	United Kingdom	2.8	Belgium	3.8	Spain	4.1
9	United Kingdom	2.3	Ukraine	2.8	Ukraine	2.8	Ukraine	2.8	United Kingdom	3.5
10	Ukraine	2.1	Chinese Taipei	2.1	Chinese Taipei	2.1	United Kingdom	2.3	Ukraine	3.4
11	Chinese Taipei	1.9	India	1.6	Mexico	1.9	Chinese Taipei	1.9	Chinese Taipei	2.1
12	Mexico	1.7	Canada	1.5	India	1.6	India	1.7	China	1.8
13	Hungary	1.5	Hungary	1.4	Hungary	1.5	Austria	1.6	Belarus	1.5
14	Austria	1.4	China	1.4	Canada	1.3	China	1.4	Czech Republic	1.5
15	China	1.4	Austria	1.2	Austria	1.3	Czech Republic	1.3	Brazil	1.4
16	India	1.2	Czech Republic	1.1	Czech Republic	1.2	Canada	1.3	Canada	1.4
17	Canada	1.1	Belarus	1.0	Brazil	1.0	Thailand	1.1	Mexico	1.3
18	Czech Republic	1.0	Brazil	0.9	Thailand	0.9	Hungary	1.1	Thailand	1.3
19	Thailand	0.9	Thailand	0.9	China	0.9	Mexico	0.9	Hungary	1.3
20	Slovakia	0.9	Turkey	0.8	Belarus	0.9	Belarus	0.8	Slovakia	1.2
21	Romania	0.8	Slovakia	0.8	Slovakia	0.8	Brazil	0.8	Morocco	1.0
22	Brazil	0.8	Portugal	0.7	Turkey	0.7	Slovakia	0.7	Turkey	1.0
23	Turkey	0.7	Netherlands	0.6	Portugal	0.7	Australia	0.7	Democratic People's Republic of Korea	0.8
24	Portugal	0.6	Romania	0.5	Romania	0.6	Portugal	0.6	Australia	0.7
25	Switzerland	0.5			Ireland	0.6	Turkey	0.6	Portugal	0.7

Tradeflow main commodities 2006–2010

Petroleum gases: export

EXPORT	2006 Country	%	2007 Country	%	2008 Country	%	2009 Country	%	2010 Country	%
World	World	100.0	World	100.0	World	100.0	World	100.0	World	100.0
1	Russian Federation	19.5	Russian Federation	18.6	Russian Federation	20.0	Russian Federation	18.1	Russian Federation	17.8
2	Canada	12.1	Canada	12.3	Norway	13.0	Norway	14.3	Norway	11.5
3	Norway	11.5	Norway	11.2	Canada	10.2	Algeria	7.9	Qatar	9.8
4	Algeria	8.6	Algeria	8.3	Algeria	8.7	Qatar	7.8	Algeria	7.6
5	Qatar	5.8	Qatar	7.2	Qatar	6.9	Canada	7.1	Canada	6.5
6	Indonesia	4.6	Indonesia	4.2	Malaysia	4.2	Malaysia	4.5	Indonesia	5.1
7	Belgium	3.6	Malaysia	4.1	Indonesia	3.9	Indonesia	4.0	Malaysia	5.0
8	Saudi Arabia	3.5	Saudi Arabia	3.8	Saudi Arabia	3.1	Australia	3.0	Australia	3.5
9	Malaysia	3.4	Belgium	2.3	Belgium	3.0	United Arab Emirates	2.3	United States of America	2.7
10	Trinidad and Tobago	2.1	Australia	2.2	Australia	2.6	Saudi Arabia	2.3	Belgium	2.7
11	Australia	2.0	Trinidad and Tobago	2.1	United States of America	1.9	Belgium	2.3	United Arab Emirates	2.7
12	Germany	2.0	Turkmenistan	2.1	Turkmenistan	1.8	United States of America	2.1	United Kingdom	1.9
13	Turkmenistan	1.8	United States of America	2.0	United Kingdom	1.8	Libyan Arab Jamahiriya	1.8	Germany	1.8
14	United Kingdom	1.6	Germany	1.8	Trinidad and Tobago	1.7	Trinidad and Tobago	1.7	Nigeria	1.8
15	United States of America	1.5	United Kingdom	1.6	Germany	1.6	Germany	1.7	Trinidad and Tobago	1.7
16	Oman	1.5	Oman	1.5	Brunei Darussalam	1.5	Brunei Darussalam	1.4	Oman	1.6
17	France	1.4	France	1.4	Oman	1.4	United Kingdom	1.4	Brunei Darussalam	1.5
18	Brunei Darussalam	1.0	United Arab Emirates	1.1	France	1.1	Nigeria	1.3	Saudi Arabia	1.4
19	Myanmar	0.9	Brunei Darussalam	1.0	Egypt	1.0	Oman	1.2	Libyan Arab Jamahiriya	1.3
20	Kuwait	0.8	Myanmar	0.9	Equatorial Guinea	0.9	France	1.0	Bolivia	1.0
21	Bolivia	0.7	Bolivia	0.8	Bolivia	0.8	Myanmar	0.9	Myanmar	1.0
22	Iran (Islamic Republic of)	0.7	Kuwait	0.7	Myanmar	0.8	Egypt	0.9	Iran (Islamic Republic of)	1.0
23	Argentina	0.7	Iran (Islamic Republic of)	0.7	Kuwait	0.8	Equatorial Guinea	0.8	Egypt	0.9
24	Kazakhstan	0.4	Argentina	0.4	Uzbekistan	0.6	Bolivia	0.7	France	0.8
25	Austria	0.3	Austria	0.3	Iran (Islamic Republic of)	0.5	Uzbekistan	0.6	Kuwait	0.7

Tradeflow main commodities 2006–2010

Gold: import

IMPORT	2006 Country	2006 %	2007 Country	2007 %	2008 Country	2008 %	2009 Country	2009 %	2010 Country	2010 %
World	World	100.0	World	100.0	World	100.0	World	100.0	World	100.0
1	India	24.7	India	25.9	India	19.8	India	21.4	United States of America	9.9
2	United States of America	9.6	United Arab Emirates	12.6	United Arab Emirates	13.2	United States of America	7.4	Thailand	6.6
3	Australia	8.1	Turkey	8.0	United States of America	8.2	Australia	6.7	Hong Kong, China	6.5
4	Turkey	7.4	Australia	7.6	Australia	8.0	Hong Kong, China	3.6	Canada	6.2
5	Italy	6.8	Italy	6.6	Thailand	7.6	Canada	3.6	Australia	5.3
6	Canada	4.2	United States of America	6.2	Turkey	6.6	Germany	3.5	India	5.1
7	Thailand	3.5	Canada	4.1	Italy	6.2	Thailand	3.5	Germany	4.3
8	Vietnam	3.5	Hong Kong, China	3.2	Hong Kong, China	5.0	Italy	3.2	Italy	3.8
9	Malaysia	3.0	Malaysia	3.1	Canada	4.1	Austria	2.5	Singapore	3.2
10	Singapore	2.8	Thailand	2.5	Germany	3.9	Singapore	2.2	Turkey	2.1
11	Chinese Taipei	2.4	Chinese Taipei	2.4	Vietnam	3.6	United Arab Emirates	2.1	Austria	1.9
12	Germany	2.0	Germany	2.3	Malaysia	3.1	Malaysia	1.6	Chinese Taipei	1.9
13	Hong Kong, China	1.6	Vietnam	2.0	Austria	2.7	Chinese Taipei	1.5	Malaysia	1.5
14	Republic of Korea	1.5	Republic of Korea	2.0	Chinese Taipei	2.5	Turkey	1.4	United Arab Emirates	1.4
15	Japan	1.3	Singapore	1.8	Singapore	2.1	Netherlands	1.3	Republic of Korea	1.3
16	Spain	0.9	Japan	1.1	Republic of Korea	2.0	Republic of Korea	1.3	Netherlands	1.3
17	Pakistan	0.9	Austria	1.0	Netherlands	1.8	Saudi Arabia	1.1	Cambodia	1.2
18	Saudi Arabia	0.8	Saudi Arabia	1.0	Saudi Arabia	1.7	Belgium	1.0	Belgium	0.7
19	Netherlands	0.7	Greece	0.7	Egypt	1.3	Japan	0.7	Japan	0.6
20	France	0.7	Netherlands	0.7	Japan	1.1	Lebanon	0.7	Nepal	0.5
21	Mexico	0.5	France	0.7	Ukraine	1.0	Vietnam	0.5	France	0.5
22	Philippines	0.4	Spain	0.7	Lebanon	0.9	France	0.5	Philippines	0.4
23	Austria	0.3	Mexico	0.6	Belgium	0.9	Europe other than the Netherlands	0.5	Switzerland	0.3
24	Belgium	0.3	Lebanon	0.4	France	0.7	Philippines	0.4	Ukraine	0.2
25	Lebanon	0.3	Philippines	0.3	Mexico	0.3	Switzerland	0.3	Vietnam	0.2

Tradeflow main commodities 2006–2010

Gold: export

EXPORT	2006		2007		2008		2009		2010	
	Country	%	Country	%	Country	%	Country	%	Country	%
World	World	100.0	World	100.0	World	100.0	World	100.0	World	100.0
1	United States of America	13.8	United States of America	17.8	United States of America	17.8	United States of America	16.6	United States of America	12.8
2	Australia	12.8	Australia	14.2	Australia	14.2	Australia	12.0	Canada	11.4
3	Hong Kong, China	9.3	Canada	8.3	United Arab Emirates	8.3	Hong Kong, China	7.9	Australia	10.8
4	Canada	8.8	United Arab Emirates	6.8	Canada	6.8	Canada	7.7	Peru	6.5
5	Peru	7.4	Hong Kong, China	6.6	Hong Kong, China	6.6	United Arab Emirates	7.2	Germany	5.9
6	Japan	5.5	Peru	6.3	Peru	6.3	Peru	5.5	Thailand	5.5
7	Singapore	2.7	Japan	5.4	Japan	5.4	Thailand	5.0	Japan	5.0
8	Germany	2.3	Mexico	2.4	Turkey	2.4	Turkey	3.6	Mexico	4.8
9	Mali	2.1	Thailand	2.3	Thailand	2.3	Japan	3.4	Italy	3.4
10	Ghana	2.1	Germany	2.3	Germany	2.3	Mexico	3.1	Singapore	3.2
11	Mexico	1.9	Ghana	2.2	Mexico	2.2	Italy	2.7	Republic of Korea	2.5
12	Italy	1.6	Singapore	1.9	Ghana	1.9	Germany	1.7	United Arab Emirates	1.8
13	Republic of Korea	1.5	Mali	1.6	Singapore	1.6	Republic of Korea	1.5	Colombia	1.8
14	Papua New Guinea	1.4	Italy	1.5	Mali	1.5	Singapore	1.4	Papua New Guinea	1.7
15	Brazil	1.2	Turkey	1.5	Papua New Guinea	1.5	Chinese Taipei	1.4	Turkey	1.7
16	Turkey	1.2	Papua New Guinea	1.3	Republic of Korea	1.3	Papua New Guinea	1.3	Brazil	1.5
17	United Republic of Tanzania	1.1	Brazil	1.2	Italy	1.2	Colombia	1.2	Chinese Taipei	1.5
18	Argentina	1.0	Indonesia	1.0	Chinese Taipei	1.0	Brazil	1.1	Hong Kong, China	1.4
19	Indonesia	1.0	Republic of Korea	1.0	Netherlands	1.0	Sudan	1.1	Netherlands	1.2
20	Chile	1.0	Chile	1.0	Brazil	0.9	Argentina	1.0	Indonesia	1.0
21	Thailand	1.0	Argentina	1.0	Colombia	0.8	Indonesia	0.9	Austria	1.0
22	Malaysia	0.9	United Republic of Tanzania	0.9	Indonesia	0.8	Egypt	0.8	Argentina	1.0
23	Saudi Arabia	0.9	Belgium	0.9	United Republic of Tanzania	0.8	Chile	0.8	Switzerland	0.9
24	Lebanon	0.8	Netherlands	0.8	Chile	0.7	Lebanon	0.7	Egypt	0.9
25	Belgium	0.8	Chinese Taipei	0.8	Argentina	0.7	Vietnam	0.7	Chile	0.9

Tradeflow main commodities 2006–2010

Petroleum oils, not crude: import

IMPORT	2006 Country	%	2007 Country	%	2008 Country	%	2009 Country	%	2010 Country	%
World	World	100.0	World	100.0	World	100.0	World	100.0	World	100.0
1	United States of America	14.8	United States of America	14.2	United States of America	14.2	United States of America	11.6	United States of America	11.0
2	Singapore	5.2	Singapore	5.5	Singapore	5.5	Singapore	6.5	Singapore	7.8
3	Germany	4.1	Netherlands	3.7	China	3.7	Netherlands	3.9	Netherlands	4.5
4	France	4.0	United Kingdom	3.5	Germany	3.5	Germany	3.6	Germany	4.1
5	United Kingdom	3.6	France	3.4	Netherlands	3.4	France	3.4	France	3.7
6	Japan	3.4	Germany	3.2	France	3.2	China	3.3	China	3.5
7	Netherlands	3.4	Japan	3.1	Belgium	3.1	Belgium	3.0	Japan	3.0
8	China	3.3	China	3.1	Japan	3.1	United Kingdom	3.0	Mexico	2.9
9	Belgium	3.1	Belgium	2.9	United Kingdom	2.9	Japan	3.0	United Kingdom	2.9
10	Spain	2.5	Spain	2.7	Mexico	2.7	Republic of Korea	2.7	Belgium	2.8
11	Indonesia	2.4	Mexico	2.5	Indonesia	2.5	Mexico	2.6	Indonesia	2.8
12	Mexico	2.0	Indonesia	2.4	Spain	2.3	Spain	2.4	Republic of Korea	2.8
13	Republic of Korea	2.0	Republic of Korea	2.0	Ship stores and bunkers	2.1	Indonesia	2.2	Hong Kong, China	2.3
14	Ship stores and bunkers	1.9	Ship stores and bunkers	1.9	Republic of Korea	1.9	Ship stores and bunkers	2.2	Spain	2.3
15	Hong Kong, China	1.7	Hong Kong, China	1.7	Australia	1.7	Hong Kong, China	1.6	Ship stores and bunkers	2.1
16	Italy	1.5	India	1.6	Chinese Taipei	1.6	Turkey	1.6	Chinese Taipei	1.8
17	Australia	1.4	Chinese Taipei	1.5	India	1.6	Australia	1.6	Brazil	1.8
18	Vietnam	1.3	Vietnam	1.4	Hong Kong, China	1.5	Italy	1.5	Turkey	1.7
19	India	1.3	Italy	1.3	Vietnam	1.4	Vietnam	1.5	Italy	1.5
20	Canada	1.3	Turkey	1.3	Turkey	1.3	United Arab Emirates	1.4	Canada	1.5
21	Malaysia	1.2	Australia	1.3	Italy	1.3	Chinese Taipei	1.3	Australia	1.4
22	Turkey	1.2	Canada	1.2	Canada	1.2	Canada	1.3	Malaysia	1.3
23	Austria	1.2	Malaysia	1.2	Brazil	1.1	Gibraltar	1.2	Gibraltar	1.2
24	Chinese Taipei	1.1	Brazil	1.1	Sweden	1.1	Pakistan	1.0	Pakistan	1.1
25	Switzerland	1.0	Austria	1.0	Malaysia	1.0	Austria	0.9	Vietnam	1.1

Tradeflow main commodities 2006–2010

Petroleum oils, not crude: export

EXPORT	2006 Country	%	2007 Country	%	2008 Country	%	2009 Country	%	2010 Country	%
World	World	100.0	World	100.0	World	100.0	World	100.0	World	100.0
1	Russian Federation	9.5	Russian Federation	9.5	Russian Federation	9.5	Russian Federation	10.1	Russian Federation	11.0
2	Singapore	7.3	Singapore	7.3	Singapore	7.3	Singapore	7.8	Singapore	8.8
3	Netherlands	6.8	Netherlands	7.0	Netherlands	7.0	United States of America	6.8	United States of America	8.5
4	United States of America	4.8	United States of America	4.9	United States of America	4.9	Netherlands	6.6	Netherlands	7.2
5	Republic of Korea	4.3	Republic of Korea	4.3	Republic of Korea	4.3	India	4.7	Republic of Korea	4.8
6	Saudi Arabia	3.9	India	4.2	India	4.2	Republic of Korea	4.0	India	4.6
7	India	3.7	Germany	3.5	Belgium	3.5	Venezuela	3.6	Belgium	3.8
8	Germany	3.6	Belgium	3.4	United Kingdom	3.4	Belgium	3.0	United Kingdom	3.2
9	Belgium	3.5	Kuwait	3.5	Germany	3.4	United Kingdom	3.0	Italy	2.9
10	United Kingdom	3.3	Saudi Arabia	3.3	United Arab Emirates	3.2	Saudi Arabia	2.9	China	2.7
11	Kuwait	3.1	Italy	3.1	Kuwait	3.1	China	2.9	United Arab Emirates	2.4
12	Italy	2.9	United Kingdom	2.9	Saudi Arabia	3.0	Germany	2.8	Canada	2.3
13	France	2.7	United Arab Emirates	2.7	Italy	3.0	Italy	2.7	Saudi Arabia	2.2
14	Canada	2.3	Chinese Taipei	2.3	France	2.4	United Arab Emirates	2.4	Chinese Taipei	2.2
15	Chinese Taipei	2.2	France	2.2	Chinese Taipei	2.4	Kuwait	2.3	France	2.0
16	Bahrain	2.0	Canada	2.0	Japan	2.3	Chinese Taipei	2.2	Germany	2.0
17	Spain	1.8	Bahrain	1.8	Canada	2.0	Canada	2.2	Japan	1.8
18	China	1.5	Spain	1.5	Venezuela	1.8	France	2.2	Kuwait	1.8
19	Sweden	1.5	China	1.5	Spain	1.7	Japan	1.9	Spain	1.6
20	Belarus	1.4	Japan	1.4	China	1.4	Spain	1.8	Nigeria	1.6
21	Norway	1.2	Belarus	1.2	Sweden	1.4	Belarus	1.5	Sweden	1.5
22	Malaysia	1.1	Sweden	1.1	Belarus	1.3	Sweden	1.4	Algeria	1.4
23	Sudan	1.0	Norway	1.0	Thailand	1.2	Malaysia	1.1	Malaysia	1.3
24	Japan	1.0	Malaysia	1.0	Malaysia	1.1	Bahrain	1.0	Thailand	1.2
25	Thailand	0.9	Algeria	0.9	Norway	1.0			Belarus	1.1

Tradeflow main commodities 2006–2010

Silver: import

IMPORT	2006 Country	%	2007 Country	%	2008 Country	%	2009 Country	%	2010 Country	%
World	World	100.0	World	100.0	World	100.0	World	100.0	World	100.0
1	United Kingdom	18.5	United States of America	18.4	United States of America	18.4	United Kingdom	18.8	United States of America	24.3
2	United States of America	17.6	Hong Kong, China	14.3	India	14.3	United States of America	13.4	United Kingdom	11.6
3	Hong Kong, China	15.0	United Kingdom	10.9	United Kingdom	10.9	Hong Kong, China	11.0	Japan	7.7
4	Germany	7.1	India	8.8	Hong Kong, China	8.8	Chinese Taipei	10.2	Canada	7.5
5	Japan	6.9	Germany	7.7	Japan	7.7	Germany	7.0	Germany	7.3
6	Italy	5.1	Japan	6.0	Germany	6.0	Japan	6.2	Hong Kong, China	6.9
7	Chinese Taipei	3.6	Italy	4.6	China	4.6	Canada	4.9	Chinese Taipei	6.1
8	Thailand	3.4	Thailand	3.9	Thailand	3.9	China	3.5	India	5.2
9	China	3.0	China	3.6	Chinese Taipei	3.6	India	3.4	China	4.3
10	Belgium	2.7	Chinese Taipei	3.3	Italy	3.3	Thailand	3.3	Thailand	4.2
11	Republic of Korea	2.3	Belgium	2.8	Belgium	2.8	Italy	3.0	Italy	3.4
12	France	2.0	France	1.9	Canada	1.9	Belgium	2.2	France	2.5
13	Canada	1.4	Republic of Korea	1.9	Republic of Korea	1.9	Republic of Korea	2.1	Republic of Korea	1.9
14	India	1.2	Canada	1.4	Austria	1.4	Austria	1.6	Austria	1.6
15	Spain	0.9	Brazil	1.2	France	1.2	France	1.4	Brazil	1.1
16	Brazil	0.9	United Arab Emirates	0.9	Singapore	1.1	Brazil	1.0	Netherlands	1.0
17	Netherlands	0.9	Singapore	0.9	Brazil	1.0	Australia	0.9	Australia	0.8
18	Singapore	0.8	Spain	0.8	Australia	0.8	United Arab Emirates	0.9	Belgium	0.7
19	Australia	0.5	Netherlands	0.8	Netherlands	0.8	Singapore	0.8	Singapore	0.4
20	Austria	0.5	Austria	0.6	Spain	0.6	Netherlands	0.6	Spain	0.4
21	Mexico	0.4	Mexico	0.6	Mexico	0.6	Poland	0.6	Malaysia	0.4
22	Turkey	0.4	Czech Republic	0.5	United Arab Emirates	0.5	Spain	0.5	United Arab Emirates	0.3
23	Czech Republic	0.4	Australia	0.4	Czech Republic	0.5	Mexico	0.5	Mexico	0.3
24	Sweden	0.3	Turkey	0.4	Turkey	0.4	Czech Republic	0.3	Czech Republic	0.3
25	Israel	0.3	Israel	0.3	Israel	0.3	Malaysia	0.2	Nepal	0.3

Tradeflow main commodities 2006–2010

Silver: export

EXPORT	2006		2007		2008		2009		2010	
	Country	%	Country	%	Country	%	Country	%	Country	%
World	World	100.0	World	100.0	World	100.0	World	100.0	World	100.0
1	China	15.2	China	15.6	United Kingdom	15.6	China	15.4	Mexico	14.1
2	Mexico	11.3	Mexico	11.0	China	13.5	Hong Kong, China	13.5	Germany	10.2
3	Hong Kong, China	9.8	Hong Kong, China	8.5	Mexico	10.9	United States of America	10.9	United States of America	9.8
4	United States of America	9.6	Germany	8.0	Hong Kong, China	8.0	Germany	8.3	Canada	9.5
5	Germany	8.9	United Kingdom	6.8	Germany	7.5	Japan	7.5	United Kingdom	9.0
6	Canada	5.4	United States of America	6.1	United States of America	6.2	Republic of Korea	6.2	Japan	5.6
7	Peru	4.5	Canada	4.9	Canada	4.3	Canada	4.3	Republic of Korea	5.4
8	Poland	4.2	Peru	4.2	Republic of Korea	4.3	Chinese Taipei	4.3	China	5.3
9	Republic of Korea	4.1	Japan	4.1	Japan	4.2	Poland	4.2	Poland	4.3
10	Japan	3.7	Republic of Korea	4.0	Peru	3.9	United Kingdom	3.9	Chinese Taipei	4.0
11	United Kingdom	3.2	Poland	3.7	Poland	3.5	Belgium	3.5	Belgium	2.7
12	Belgium	3.0	Chile	3.6	Chile	2.1	Chile	2.1	Hong Kong, China	2.0
13	Kazakhstan	2.6	Belgium	3.6	Belgium	2.0	Kazakhstan	2.0	Chile	2.0
14	Chile	2.3	Kazakhstan	2.4	Kazakhstan	2.0	Sweden	2.0	Morocco	1.8
15	Australia	1.5	Singapore	1.4	Sweden	1.3	Peru	1.3	Sweden	1.4
16	Singapore	1.3	Australia	1.4	Australia	1.1	Australia	1.1	Italy	1.4
17	Sweden	1.3	Italy	1.3	Chinese Taipei	1.0	Argentina	1.0	Australia	1.2
18	Italy	1.2	Sweden	1.2	Italy	1.0	Italy	1.0	Argentina	1.2
19	Chinese Taipei	0.8	United Arab Emirates	1.1	Singapore	1.0	Morocco	1.0	Peru	1.0
20	Morocco	0.7	Philippines	0.9	Morocco	0.7	Netherlands	0.7	Kazakhstan	0.8
21	Spain	0.7	Chinese Taipei	0.7	Netherlands	0.7	India	0.7	Netherlands	0.7
22	France	0.6	Morocco	0.7	France	0.6	Turkey	0.6	New Zealand	0.7
23	Netherlands	0.6	France	0.6	Spain	0.5	Singapore	0.5	Bolivia	0.6
24	Czech Republic	0.4	Spain	0.6	Argentina	0.5	France	0.5	France	0.6
25	Austria	0.4	Netherlands	0.4	Czech Republic	0.4			Turkey	0.5

Tradeflow main commodities 2006–2010

Sugar: import

IMPORT	2006 Country	%	2007 Country	%	2008 Country	%	2009 Country	%	2010 Country	%
World	World	100.0	World	100.0	World	100.0	World	100.0	World	100.0
1	United States of America	10.5	United States of America	8.7	United States of America	9.2	United States of America	8.9	United States of America	9.3
2	United Kingdom	5.6	United Kingdom	6.0	United Kingdom	6.1	Germany	5.2	United Kingdom	3.9
3	Germany	4.8	Germany	5.2	Germany	5.9	United Kingdom	5.1	Germany	3.8
4	Russian Federation	4.3	Russian Federation	4.6	Russian Federation	3.8	Italy	3.4	Russian Federation	3.6
5	Belgium	3.9	France	3.9	France	3.6	France	3.4	India	3.1
6	France	3.0	Indonesia	3.0	Italy	3.3	Belgium	3.0	Indonesia	3.0
7	Italy	2.7	Italy	2.7	Belgium	2.9	India	2.8	Republic of Korea	2.8
8	Canada	2.7	Belgium	2.7	Netherlands	2.8	Canada	2.7	Italy	2.7
9	Republic of Korea	2.5	Netherlands	2.5	Spain	2.7	Republic of Korea	2.6	Canada	2.6
10	Japan	2.4	Canada	2.5	Canada	2.6	Spain	2.6	China	2.5
11	Pakistan	2.2	Japan	2.4	Republic of Korea	2.5	United Arab Emirates	2.4	Mexico	2.4
12	Spain	2.2	Spain	2.2	Japan	2.5	Russian Federation	2.3	France	2.3
13	Indonesia	2.1	Republic of Korea	2.2	Egypt	2.2	Netherlands	2.3	Japan	2.3
14	China	2.0	Mexico	2.1	Saudi Arabia	1.8	Japan	2.2	Belgium	2.2
15	Netherlands	1.7	United Arab Emirates	2.0	Mexico	1.8	Mexico	2.1	Malaysia	2.1
16	Mexico	1.6	Malaysia	1.7	Malaysia	1.7	Indonesia	2.1	Netherlands	2.1
17	Saudi Arabia	1.5	China	1.6	Indonesia	1.6	Malaysia	2.0	United Arab Emirates	2.0
18	Malaysia	1.5	Saudi Arabia	1.5	Austria	1.5	Algeria	1.7	Pakistan	2.0
19	Algeria	1.3	Iran (Islamic Republic of)	1.5	Bangladesh	1.5	Saudi Arabia	1.5	Spain	1.8
20	Austria	1.1	Algeria	1.3	Algeria	1.4	China	1.4	Iran (Islamic Republic of)	1.7
21	Bangladesh	1.0	Austria	1.1	China	1.3	Bangladesh	1.4	Saudi Arabia	1.7
22	Chinese Taipei	1.0	Portugal	1.0	Sudan	1.3	Morocco	1.3	Algeria	1.5
23	Kazakhstan	1.0	Denmark	1.0	Portugal	1.3	Poland	1.3	Morocco	1.4
24	Denmark	1.0	Syrian Arab Republic	1.0	Denmark	1.2	Nigeria	1.2	Syrian Arab Republic	1.4
25	Syrian Arab Republic	0.9	Ireland	0.9	Ireland	1.1	Portugal	1.1	Egypt	1.2

Tradeflow main commodities 2006–2010

Sugar: export

EXPORT	2006		2007		2008		2009		2010	
	Country	%	Country	%	Country	%	Country	%	Country	%
World	World	100.0	World	100.0	World	100.0	World	100.0	World	100.0
1	Brazil	21.5	Brazil	17.5	Brazil	17.4	Brazil	25.0	Brazil	30.6
2	France	8.3	France	8.6	France	8.3	France	7.4	France	5.8
3	Belgium	5.7	Germany	5.5	Germany	5.7	Thailand	5.9	Thailand	5.6
4	Germany	5.5	Thailand	4.6	Thailand	5.0	Germany	5.8	Germany	4.8
5	Netherlands	3.6	United States of America	3.6	India	4.8	United States of America	3.5	United States of America	4.1
6	United States of America	3.5	Belgium	3.5	Belgium	4.4	Belgium	3.3	Netherlands	3.1
7	Thailand	3.0	Netherlands	3.0	United States of America	4.3	Netherlands	3.3	Belgium	3.0
8	Mexico	2.9	India	2.9	Netherlands	3.5	Mexico	3.2	Mexico	3.0
9	Canada	2.4	United Kingdom	2.4	Mexico	2.6	China	3.1	China	2.5
10	India	2.3	Canada	2.3	Canada	2.5	Canada	2.3	Canada	2.0
11	United Kingdom	2.3	Mexico	2.3	United Kingdom	2.0	United Kingdom	2.5	Guatemala	1.9
12	Colombia	1.9	China	1.9	China	1.9	Colombia	2.1	Colombia	1.6
13	Spain	1.8	Spain	1.8	Spain	1.8	Guatemala	1.8	United Kingdom	1.6
14	Poland	1.6	Colombia	1.6	Poland	1.6	Spain	1.5	Spain	1.4
15	China	1.6	Poland	1.6	Guatemala	1.5	Denmark	1.4	Poland	1.2
16	Italy	1.4	United Arab Emirates	1.4	Denmark	1.4	Poland	1.4	Egypt	1.2
17	South Africa	1.3	Guatemala	1.3	United Arab Emirates	1.4	Argentina	1.3	Argentina	1.2
18	Mauritius	1.2	Italy	1.2	Colombia	1.3	South Africa	1.2	Denmark	1.0
19	Guatemala	1.2	Denmark	1.2	Italy	1.2	United Arab Emirates	1.1	Republic of Korea	0.9
20	Argentina	1.2	South Africa	1.2	Cuba	1.0	Italy	1.1	Turkey	0.9
21	Denmark	1.1	Mauritius	1.1	Turkey	1.0	Hungary	1.1	Hungary	0.9
22	Czech Republic	1.0	Turkey	1.0	Czech Republic	1.0	Turkey	1.0	Belarus	0.9
23	Swaziland	1.0	Slovakia	1.0	Hungary	1.0	Cuba	1.0	Slovakia	0.8
24	Turkey	0.9	Saudi Arabia	0.9	Mauritius	1.0	Czech Republic	0.8	India	0.8
25	Austria	0.9	Cuba	0.9	Austria	0.8	Republic of Korea	0.8	Italy	0.8

Tradeflow main commodities 2006–2010

Maize (corn): import

IMPORT	2006 Country	%	2007 Country	%	2008 Country	%	2009 Country	%	2010 Country	%
World	World	100.0	World	100.0	World	100.0	World	100.0	World	100.0
1	Japan	19.5	Japan	18.6	Japan	20.5	Japan	19.0	Japan	18.1
2	Republic of Korea	9.5	Republic of Korea	8.9	Republic of Korea	10.4	Republic of Korea	8.3	Republic of Korea	9.1
3	Spain	8.6	Spain	7.7	Mexico	8.8	Mexico	7.2	Mexico	7.2
4	Mexico	5.7	Mexico	7.5	Spain	6.0	Chinese Taipei	4.8	Egypt	5.8
5	Chinese Taipei	5.6	Chinese Taipei	4.6	Chinese Taipei	4.7	Spain	4.7	Chinese Taipei	5.6
6	Netherlands	3.5	Netherlands	4.3	Egypt	4.4	Egypt	4.2	Spain	4.4
7	Colombia	3.5	Colombia	3.3	Netherlands	3.6	Netherlands	3.6	Colombia	3.7
8	Germany	3.3	Germany	3.2	Colombia	3.4	Colombia	3.4	Malaysia	3.5
9	Malaysia	3.0	Italy	3.0	Italy	3.2	Germany	3.1	Netherlands	3.1
10	Algeria	2.5	Malaysia	2.7	Germany	3.0	Iran (Islamic Republic of)	2.9	Germany	2.7
11	Italy	2.4	Iran (Islamic Republic of)	2.5	Algeria	2.7	Malaysia	2.9	Italy	2.3
12	Indonesia	2.1	Algeria	2.5	Malaysia	2.5	Italy	2.5	Peru	2.1
13	Chile	1.9	Saudi Arabia	2.3	Iran (Islamic Republic of)	2.3	Kenya	2.4	Syrian Arab Republic	1.9
14	United Kingdom	1.9	Canada	2.2	Canada	2.2	Algeria	2.3	Indonesia	1.7
15	Canada	1.9	Morocco	2.2	Saudi Arabia	2.2	Canada	2.1	China	1.7
16	Portugal	1.8	Portugal	2.0	Morocco	2.0	Saudi Arabia	2.0	United States of America	1.6
17	Morocco	1.7	United Kingdom	2.0	Portugal	2.0	Morocco	1.8	Portugal	1.5
18	Peru	1.7	Chile	1.8	United States of America	1.8	France	1.7	Canada	1.5
19	Saudi Arabia	1.6	France	1.8	Chile	1.7	Syrian Arab Republic	1.6	Iran (Islamic Republic of)	1.5
20	United States of America	1.6	United States of America	1.7	Belgium	1.6	Vietnam	1.6	Saudi Arabia	1.4
21	Syrian Arab Republic	1.4	Belgium	1.6	Peru	1.5	Peru	1.5	France	1.2
22	Israel	1.3	Turkey	1.4	Turkey	1.4	United States of America	1.4	United Kingdom	1.2
23	Belgium	1.2	Syrian Arab Republic	1.3	United Kingdom	1.2	Venezuela	1.3	Dominican Republic	1.1
24	Dominican Republic	1.1	Israel	1.2	Venezuela	1.1	Portugal	1.3	Morocco	1.0
25	France	1.1	Greece	1.1	France	1.0	United Kingdom	1.0	Israel	1.0

Tradeflow main commodities 2006–2010

Maize (corn): export

EXPORT	2006 Country	%	2007 Country	%	2008 Country	%	2009 Country	%	2010 Country	%
World	World	100.0	World	100.0	World	100.0	World	100.0	World	100.0
1	United States of America	55.0	United States of America	49.0	United States of America	51.1	United States of America	45.8	United States of America	46.2
2	France	9.9	Argentina	10.9	Argentina	13.0	France	9.3	Argentina	10.7
3	Argentina	9.5	Brazil	9.3	France	8.6	Argentina	8.1	Brazil	10.1
4	Brazil	3.6	France	7.4	Brazil	5.2	Brazil	6.6	France	8.4
5	China	3.1	Hungary	5.4	Hungary	3.6	Hungary	5.1	Hungary	4.0
6	Hungary	3.0	China	4.2	India	3.4	Ukraine	4.2	Ukraine	3.6
7	Germany	1.5	India	1.5	Ukraine	2.5	India	2.5	Romania	2.4
8	Serbia	1.4	Paraguay	1.4	South Africa	1.3	South Africa	1.9	Serbia	1.5
9	Ukraine	1.3	Germany	1.3	Canada	1.0	Romania	1.0	South Africa	1.4
10	Paraguay	1.2	Ukraine	1.2	Germany	0.8	Serbia	0.9	Canada	1.1
11	South Africa	1.1	Austria	1.1	Thailand	0.7	Thailand	0.8	Paraguay	1.1
12	Slovakia	0.8	Canada	0.8	Belgium	0.6	Paraguay	0.7	India	0.9
13	India	0.8	Belgium	0.8	Austria	0.6	Germany	0.7	Germany	0.9
14	Chile	0.8	Chile	0.8	Romania	0.6	Chile	0.7	Bulgaria	0.9
15	Austria	0.7	Slovakia	0.7	Chile	0.5	Russian Federation	0.6	Mexico	0.7
16	Thailand	0.5	Thailand	0.5	Paraguay	0.5	Austria	0.6	Chile	0.7
17	Belgium	0.5	Romania	0.5	Netherlands	0.5	Slovakia	0.5	Thailand	0.6
18	Netherlands	0.4	Malawi	0.4	Serbia	0.5	Bulgaria	0.5	Austria	0.5
19	Canada	0.4	Serbia	0.4	Slovakia	0.4	Canada	0.3	Slovakia	0.5
20	Romania	0.4	Netherlands	0.4	Spain	0.4	Netherlands	0.3	Spain	0.4
21	Spain	0.3	Mexico	0.3	China	0.3	Mexico	0.3	Netherlands	0.4
22	Czech Republic	0.3	Italy	0.3	Italy	0.3	Czech Republic	0.3	Italy	0.4
23	Mexico	0.3	Zambia	0.3	Czech Republic	0.3	Turkey	0.2	Czech Republic	0.2
24	Poland	0.3	Spain	0.3	Myanmar	0.3	Belgium	0.2	Belgium	0.2
25	Turkey	0.3	Bulgaria	0.3	Zambia	0.2	Croatia	0.2	Croatia	0.2

Tradeflow main commodities 2006–2010

Wheat and meslin: import

IMPORT	2006		2007		2008		2009		2010	
	Country	%	Country	%	Country	%	Country	%	Country	%
World	World	100.0	World	100.0	World	100.0	World	100.0	World	100.0
1	Italy	6.7	Nigeria	7.1	Japan	7.3	Algeria	5.7	Egypt	6.8
2	Nigeria	6.6	Italy	6.1	Algeria	7.1	Italy	5.4	Italy	5.8
3	Japan	6.2	Japan	5.4	Italy	5.1	Egypt	4.9	Japan	5.2
4	Algeria	4.8	Algeria	4.6	Egypt	4.7	Japan	4.5	Brazil	4.7
5	Brazil	4.8	Brazil	4.6	Indonesia	4.4	Spain	4.3	Indonesia	4.4
6	Spain	4.2	India	4.2	Brazil	4.2	Indonesia	4.1	Morocco	3.5
7	Indonesia	4.0	Indonesia	3.9	Pakistan	3.6	Brazil	3.8	Republic of Korea	3.3
8	Mexico	3.3	Morocco	3.7	Morocco	3.6	Nigeria	3.4	Spain	3.3
9	Netherlands	3.3	Netherlands	3.6	Netherlands	3.4	Netherlands	3.0	Algeria	3.3
10	Republic of Korea	3.2	Spain	3.2	Iran (Islamic Republic of)	3.1	Iran (Islamic Republic of)	3.0	Netherlands	3.0
11	Belgium	2.8	Belgium	3.0	Turkey	3.0	Republic of Korea	2.9	Germany	2.9
12	Philippines	2.6	Mexico	2.8	Spain	2.8	Germany	2.8	Mexico	2.8
13	Iraq	2.1	Republic of Korea	2.7	Republic of Korea	2.7	Turkey	2.6	Nigeria	2.6
14	Bangladesh	1.9	Yemen	2.2	Mexico	2.2	Philippines	2.6	Belgium	2.6
15	Yemen	1.9	Iraq	2.0	Belgium	2.0	Belgium	2.5	Bangladesh	2.5
16	Germany	1.8	Germany	2.0	United States of America	2.0	Yemen	2.4	Turkey	2.3
17	Morocco	1.7	Bangladesh	1.9	Iraq	1.9	Mexico	2.3	United States of America	2.0
18	United States of America	1.6	Tunisia	1.9	Yemen	1.9	United States of America	2.1	Yemen	1.8
19	Sudan	1.6	Turkey	1.9	Germany	1.9	Iraq	2.0	Philippines	1.6
20	India	1.5	United States of America	1.7	Tunisia	1.7	Morocco	1.8	Viet Nam	1.4
21	Venezuela	1.5	Philippines	1.4	Venezuela	1.4	Bangladesh	1.6	Thailand	1.4
22	Malaysia	1.4	United Kingdom	1.4	Philippines	1.4	Venezuela	1.6	Peru	1.3
23	Colombia	1.3	Malaysia	1.2	Nigeria	1.2	United Kingdom	1.5	Iraq	1.3
24	Peru	1.3	Colombia	1.2	United Kingdom	1.2	Sudan	1.3	Tunisia	1.3
25	Portugal	1.3	Greece	1.2	Peru	1.2	Peru	1.3	Libyan Arab Jamahiriya	1.2

Tradeflow main commodities 2006–2010

Wheat and meslin: export

EXPORT	2006 Country	%	2007 Country	%	2008 Country	%	2009 Country	%	2010 Country	%
World	World	100.0	World	100.0	World	100.0	World	100.0	World	100.0
1	United States of America	20.5	United States of America	20.5	United States of America	27.4	United States of America	25.2	United States of America	16.7
2	Canada	15.6	Canada	15.6	Canada	14.4	Canada	14.7	France	16.4
3	France	13.0	Russian Federation	13.0	France	11.8	France	12.5	Canada	11.7
4	Australia	12.3	France	12.3	Australia	11.6	Australia	7.1	Australia	11.6
5	Argentina	7.1	Argentina	7.1	Russian Federation	6.6	Russian Federation	6.4	Russian Federation	8.5
6	Russian Federation	6.6	Australia	6.6	Argentina	5.3	Germany	5.7	Germany	6.8
7	Germany	5.0	Kazakhstan	5.0	Germany	3.8	Ukraine	5.6	Argentina	5.5
8	Ukraine	2.9	Germany	2.9	Ukraine	3.8	Argentina	3.6	Ukraine	3.1
9	Kazakhstan	2.5	China	2.5	Kazakhstan	1.6	Kazakhstan	3.2	United Kingdom	2.0
10	United Kingdom	1.7	United Kingdom	1.7	United Kingdom	1.5	United Kingdom	1.7	Kazakhstan	1.5
11	Hungary	1.5	Hungary	1.5	Hungary	1.4	Romania	1.5	Romania	1.3
12	Syrian Arab Republic	0.9	Belgium	0.9	Mexico	0.8	Poland	1.3	Bulgaria	1.2
13	Bulgaria	0.8	Spain	0.8	Romania	0.7	Hungary	1.2	Hungary	1.0
14	China	0.8	Denmark	0.8	Bulgaria	0.7	Belize	1.1	Uruguay	1.0
15	Belgium	0.8	Czech Republic	0.8	Belgium	0.7	Bulgaria	0.9	Denmark	0.9
16	Czech Republic	0.7	Syrian Arab Republic	0.7	Spain	0.7	Czech Republic	0.8	Lithuania	0.9
17	Spain	0.7	Ukraine	0.7	Lithuania	0.6	Denmark	0.8	Paraguay	0.9
18	Denmark	0.6	Austria	0.6	Czech Republic	0.6	Mexico	0.6	Czech Republic	0.9
19	Romania	0.6	Mexico	0.6	Italy	0.5	Lithuania	0.6	Latvia	0.8
20	Austria	0.5	Sweden	0.5	Austria	0.4	Uruguay	0.5	Brazil	0.8
21	Poland	0.5	Lithuania	0.5	Netherlands	0.4	Latvia	0.5	Austria	0.7
22	Turkey	0.5	Netherlands	0.5	Latvia	0.4	Belgium	0.5	Poland	0.6
23	Sweden	0.4	Italy	0.4	Brazil	0.4	Greece	0.5	Turkey	0.6
24	Greece	0.4	Croatia	0.4	Sweden	0.3	Spain	0.4	Belgium	0.5
25	Mexico	0.4	Iran (Islamic Republic of)	0.4	Paraguay	0.3	Paraguay	0.4	Italy	0.4

The 2010 % column values (rank 1–25): 16.7, 16.4, 11.7, 11.6, 8.5, 6.8, 5.5, 3.1, 2.0, 1.5, 1.3, 1.2, 1.0, 1.0, 0.9, 0.9, 0.9, 0.9, 0.8, 0.8, 0.7, 0.6, 0.6, 0.5, 0.5

The far-right % column values (rank 1–25): 20.9, 14.4, 14.0, 11.6, 6.4, 6.1, 3.0, 2.8, 2.2, 2.1, 1.5, 1.4, 1.3, 1.2, 1.0, 0.8, 0.8, 0.7, 0.7, 0.7, 0.6, 0.6, 0.6, 0.6, 0.4

Tradeflow main commodities 2006–2010

Cotton: import

IMPORT		2006		2007		2008		2009		2010	
		Country	%	Country	%	Country	%	Country	%	Country	%
World		World	100.0	World	100.0	World	100.0	World	100.0	World	100.0
	1	China	17.7	China	14.8	China	14.1	China	14.7	China	20.1
	2	Hong Kong, China	9.6	Hong Kong, China	9.3	Hong Kong, China	7.9	Hong Kong, China	8.2	Hong Kong, China	6.8
	3	Turkey	4.1	Turkey	5.4	Bangladesh	4.6	Turkey	5.0	Turkey	6.4
	4	Italy	3.9	Italy	4.1	Turkey	4.4	Bangladesh	4.6	Bangladesh	4.2
	5	United States of America	3.1	Bangladesh	3.1	Indonesia	3.8	Vietnam	3.6	Indonesia	4.2
	6	Mexico	2.7	United States of America	2.7	Italy	3.8	Indonesia	3.5	Vietnam	3.5
	7	Republic of Korea	2.5	Germany	2.6	Vietnam	2.9	Italy	3.3	Italy	3.4
	8	Germany	2.5	Republic of Korea	2.3	Republic of Korea	2.5	Republic of Korea	2.9	Republic of Korea	3.3
	9	Bangladesh	2.4	Vietnam	2.1	Germany	2.4	Germany	2.9	Germany	2.5
	10	Thailand	1.7	Mexico	2.1	United States of America	2.3	Mexico	2.3	Mexico	2.5
	11	Romania	1.6	Tunisia	2.0	Pakistan	2.3	Benin	2.1	United States of America	2.1
	12	France	1.6	Indonesia	1.8	Mexico	2.3	Tunisia	2.1	Thailand	2.1
	13	Tunisia	1.6	Pakistan	1.8	Nigeria	2.2	United States of America	2.1	Benin	1.7
	14	Japan	1.6	France	1.7	Benin	2.1	Thailand	1.7	Pakistan	1.6
	15	Vietnam	1.5	Thailand	1.7	Thailand	2.0	Egypt	1.6	Honduras	1.5
	16	Indonesia	1.5	Romania	1.6	Tunisia	2.0	France	1.5	Egypt	1.4
	17	Spain	1.4	Morocco	1.5	France	1.5	Morocco	1.3	Tunisia	1.4
	18	Portugal	1.3	Japan	1.5	Japan	1.5	Japan	1.2	Japan	1.3
	19	Morocco	1.3	Spain	1.5	Morocco	1.5	Spain	1.2	Morocco	1.2
	20	Poland	1.2	Benin	1.4	India	1.4	Portugal	1.2	France	1.2
	21	Belgium	1.0	Portugal	1.3	Romania	1.3	Pakistan	1.2	Spain	1.2
	22	Sri Lanka	1.0	Poland	1.1	Egypt	1.3	Romania	1.2	Portugal	1.2
	23	Chinese Taipei	1.0	Belgium	1.0	Spain	1.1	Sri Lanka	1.1	Brazil	1.1
	24	Dominican Republic	0.9	Sri Lanka	1.0	Portugal	1.0	Poland	1.2	Chinese Taipei	1.1
	25	India	0.9	India	1.0	Poland	1.0	Belgium	1.2	Sri Lanka	1.1

Tradeflow main commodities 2006–2010

Cotton: export

EXPORT	2006		2007		2008		2009		2010	
	Country	%	Country	%	Country	%	Country	%	Country	%
World	World	100.0	World	100.0	World	100.0	World	100.0	World	100.0
1	China	17.3	China	18.0	China	20.2	China	22.9	China	24.7
2	United States of America	12.6	United States of America	12.2	United States of America	12.6	United States of America	11.7	United States of America	14.3
3	Hong Kong, China	9.9	Hong Kong, China	9.4	India	8.6	Hong Kong, China	8.5	India	10.0
4	Pakistan	7.0	India	8.5	Hong Kong, China	8.1	Pakistan	7.6	Pakistan	7.6
5	India	6.8	Pakistan	6.6	Pakistan	6.8	India	7.6	Italy	4.2
6	Italy	6.2	Italy	6.4	Italy	5.7	Italy	4.9	Turkey	2.7
7	Germany	2.9	Turkey	3.1	Turkey	3.1	Germany	3.1	Germany	2.6
8	Uzbekistan	2.8	Germany	2.8	Germany	2.7	Turkey	3.0	Uzbekistan	2.5
9	Turkey	2.6	Uzbekistan	2.8	Brazil	1.8	Brazil	2.0	Brazil	1.9
10	Japan	2.0	Spain	1.9	Spain	1.7	Japan	1.6	Australia	1.8
11	Spain	1.8	Japan	1.8	Japan	1.6	Spain	1.6	Spain	1.4
12	France	1.7	France	1.7	Uzbekistan	1.6	France	1.4	Indonesia	1.4
13	Australia	1.6	Brazil	1.6	France	1.5	Greece	1.4	Thailand	1.4
14	Indonesia	1.5	Indonesia	1.3	Togo	1.3	Uzbekistan	1.3	Republic of Korea	1.3
15	Bangladesh	1.4	Republic of Korea	1.3	Syrian Arab Republic	1.3	Thailand	1.3	Hong Kong, China	1.3
16	Republic of Korea	1.4	Belgium	1.2	Indonesia	1.3	Indonesia	1.2	Japan	1.3
17	Brazil	1.3	Chinese Taipei	1.2	Belgium	1.2	Chinese Taipei	1.2	Greece	1.3
18	Chinese Taipei	1.3	Thailand	1.1	Republic of Korea	1.1	Republic of Korea	1.2	Vietnam	1.2
19	Belgium	1.3	Australia	0.9	Thailand	0.9	Belgium	1.1	Egypt	1.1
20	Greece	1.2	Greece	0.9	Greece	0.9	Australia	1.0	Chinese Taipei	1.1
21	Thailand	1.0	Syrian Arab Republic	1.0	Chinese Taipei	0.6	Vietnam	1.0	France	1.1
22	Syrian Arab Republic	0.7	Czech Republic	0.7	Australia	0.6	Netherlands	0.7	Nigeria	1.0
23	United Kingdom	0.7	Turkmenistan	0.7	Netherlands	0.6	Dominican Republic	0.7	Belgium	0.9
24	Austria	0.6	Netherlands	0.6	Egypt	0.6	Czech Republic	0.7	Turkmenistan	0.8
25	Netherlands	0.5	United Kingdom	0.5	Czech Republic	0.6	Egypt	0.7	Syrian Arab Republic	0.8

Tradeflow main commodities 2006–2010

Organic chemicals: import

IMPORT	2006 Country	%	2007 Country	%	2008 Country	%	2009 Country	%	2010 Country	%
World	World	100.0	World	100.0	World	100.0	World	100.0	World	100.0
1	United States of America	15.0	United States of America	15.0	United States of America	13.4	United States of America	14.5	United States of America	14.9
2	China	10.0	China	10.0	China	11.1	China	10.7	China	11.8
3	Belgium	9.5	Belgium	9.5	Germany	9.3	Belgium	8.7	Belgium	8.6
4	Germany	8.2	Germany	8.2	Belgium	8.8	Germany	8.2	Germany	8.4
5	France	5.1	United Kingdom	5.1	France	5.2	France	5.0	France	5.0
6	United Kingdom	4.9	France	4.9	Italy	5.2	Japan	4.6	Netherlands	4.6
7	Italy	4.9	Italy	4.9	Netherlands	4.9	Italy	4.5	Japan	4.5
8	Netherlands	4.2	Netherlands	4.2	United Kingdom	4.3	United Kingdom	4.4	United Kingdom	4.4
9	Japan	4.1	Japan	4.1	Japan	3.8	Netherlands	4.2	Italy	3.7
10	Chinese Taipei	3.3	Switzerland	3.3	Republic of Korea	3.1	Republic of Korea	3.0	Republic of Korea	2.9
11	Spain	3.0	Chinese Taipei	3.0	Spain	3.0	Switzerland	2.9	Switzerland	2.8
12	Republic of Korea	3.0	Spain	3.0	Switzerland	2.9	India	2.9	Chinese Taipei	2.8
13	Switzerland	2.7	Republic of Korea	2.7	Chinese Taipei	2.9	Spain	2.7	India	2.7
14	Canada	2.3	India	2.3	India	2.2	Chinese Taipei	2.4	Spain	2.3
15	Mexico	2.0	Canada	2.0	Brazil	2.1	Brazil	2.3	Brazil	2.3
16	India	1.9	Mexico	1.9	Mexico	2.0	Mexico	2.2	Mexico	2.1
17	Brazil	1.6	Brazil	1.6	Canada	1.8	Canada	2.0	Canada	1.8
18	Singapore	1.5	Singapore	1.5	Indonesia	1.4	Indonesia	1.4	Singapore	1.5
19	Thailand	1.3	Thailand	1.3	Singapore	1.2	Singapore	1.4	Indonesia	1.4
20	Turkey	1.2	Turkey	1.2	Thailand	1.2	Turkey	1.3	Thailand	1.3
21	Indonesia	1.2	Indonesia	1.2	Turkey	1.1	Thailand	1.2	Turkey	1.2
22	Ireland	1.0	Ireland	1.0	Australia	0.9	Austria	0.9	Austria	1.0
23	Australia	0.9	Australia	0.9	Poland	0.9	Ireland	0.9	Ireland	0.9
24	Austria	0.8	Malaysia	0.8	Ireland	0.9	Australia	0.9	Malaysia	0.9
25	Malaysia	0.8	Austria	0.8	Argentina	0.8	Sweden	0.8	Australia	0.9

Tradeflow main commodities 2006–2010

Organic chemicals: export

EXPORT	2006 Country	%	2007 Country	%	2008 Country	%	2009 Country	%	2010 Country	%
World	World	100.0	World	100.0	World	100.0	World	100.0	World	100.0
1	United States of America	11.3	United States of America	10.9	United States of America	10.3	United States of America	10.0	United States of America	10.8
2	Germany	9.2	Belgium	9.1	Germany	9.7	Belgium	9.0	China	8.3
3	Belgium	9.0	Germany	8.6	Belgium	8.5	Ireland	8.2	Belgium	8.3
4	Ireland	7.5	Ireland	8.2	China	7.9	China	7.9	Ireland	7.0
5	Japan	6.2	Netherlands	6.5	Ireland	7.6	Germany	7.8	Germany	6.8
6	Netherlands	5.9	Japan	6.0	Netherlands	6.1	Japan	6.2	Netherlands	6.5
7	China	5.2	China	6.0	Japan	5.5	Netherlands	5.7	Japan	5.9
8	United Kingdom	5.2	United Kingdom	4.6	United Kingdom	4.4	Switzerland	5.3	Switzerland	4.6
9	Switzerland	4.7	Republic of Korea	4.4	Republic of Korea	4.3	United Kingdom	5.0	Republic of Korea	4.5
10	Singapore	4.7	Switzerland	4.3	Switzerland	4.3	Republic of Korea	4.3	Singapore	3.9
11	Republic of Korea	4.3	Singapore	4.1	France	4.2	Singapore	3.8	United Kingdom	3.9
12	France	4.3	France	4.0	Singapore	3.1	France	3.8	France	3.5
13	Italy	2.1	Chinese Taipei	2.6	Chinese Taipei	2.9	Chinese Taipei	2.6	Chinese Taipei	3.0
14	Chinese Taipei	2.0	Italy	2.0	India	2.1	India	2.3	Saudi Arabia	2.9
15	India	1.9	India	1.9	Italy	1.9	Italy	1.9	India	2.6
16	Saudi Arabia	1.7	Saudi Arabia	1.6	Saudi Arabia	1.6	Saudi Arabia	1.6	Italy	1.8
17	Canada	1.6	Spain	1.5	Canada	1.4	Spain	1.4	Spain	1.3
18	Spain	1.4	Canada	1.5	Spain	1.5	Canada	1.4	Canada	1.1
19	Russian Federation	1.0	Russian Federation	1.1	Russian Federation	1.1	Thailand	1.1	Thailand	1.0
20	Malaysia	0.9	Malaysia	0.9	Iran (Islamic Republic of)	0.9	Malaysia	1.0	Malaysia	1.0
21	Thailand	0.9	Thailand	0.8	Malaysia	0.8	Brazil	0.9	Brazil	0.8
22	Brazil	0.7	Brazil	0.8	Brazil	0.8	Iran (Islamic Republic of)	0.8	Russian Federation	0.8
23	Indonesia	0.6	Indonesia	0.7	Thailand	0.7	Panama	0.8	Iran (Islamic Republic of)	0.8
24	Mexico	0.5	Mexico	0.5	Mexico	0.5	Russian Federation	0.5	Indonesia	0.7
25	Austria	0.5	Iran (Islamic Republic of)	0.5	Indonesia	0.5	Indonesia	0.5	Sweden	0.6

Tradeflow main commodities 2006–2010

Inorganic chemicals: import

IMPORT	2006 Country	%	2007 Country	%	2008 Country	%	2009 Country	%	2010 Country	%
World	World	100.0	World	100.0	World	100.0	World	100.0	World	100.0
1	United States of America	15.4	United States of America	14.8	United States of America	14.5	United States of America	13.8	United States of America	13.2
2	China	7.7	Japan	6.9	China	7.2	Germany	8.6	China	8.7
3	Germany	6.8	Germany	6.6	Germany	6.9	France	7.4	Germany	7.7
4	Japan	6.7	China	6.4	Japan	6.7	China	7.3	Japan	7.0
5	France	5.9	France	6.0	France	5.3	Japan	6.4	France	5.8
6	United Kingdom	5.3	United Kingdom	5.8	United Kingdom	4.3	United Kingdom	5.2	Republic of Korea	4.3
7	Belgium	4.2	Belgium	3.9	Republic of Korea	4.0	Republic of Korea	4.4	United Kingdom	4.2
8	Canada	4.1	Netherlands	3.9	Belgium	3.8	Belgium	3.9	Netherlands	3.4
9	Republic of Korea	3.5	Republic of Korea	3.7	India	3.8	India	3.8	Canada	3.3
10	Netherlands	3.4	Canada	3.7	Canada	3.3	Canada	3.5	Belgium	3.2
11	India	3.1	Russian Federation	2.8	Netherlands	3.3	Netherlands	3.2	Chinese Taipei	2.8
12	Russian Federation	2.9	India	2.8	Russian Federation	2.6	Russian Federation	2.5	Russian Federation	2.4
13	Italy	2.2	Italy	2.1	Chinese Taipei	2.2	Chinese Taipei	2.5	India	2.4
14	Chinese Taipei	2.1	Chinese Taipei	2.1	Spain	2.1	Spain	2.3	Italy	2.2
15	Spain	2.1	Spain	2.0	Italy	2.0	Italy	2.1	Spain	2.1
16	Norway	1.8	Sweden	1.8	Brazil	2.0	Brazil	1.9	Brazil	1.6
17	Brazil	1.4	Norway	1.6	Thailand	1.7	Norway	1.6	Sweden	1.6
18	Mexico	1.4	Brazil	1.4	Norway	1.6	Sweden	1.6	Norway	1.5
19	Sweden	1.3	Thailand	1.3	Sweden	1.5	Mexico	1.5	Mexico	1.3
20	Thailand	1.3	Austria	1.3	Turkey	1.3	Turkey	1.3	Turkey	1.3
21	Austria	1.2	Mexico	1.2	Mexico	1.2	Australia	1.2	Indonesia	1.2
22	South Africa	1.2	Switzerland	1.2	Australia	1.1	Indonesia	1.2	Thailand	1.2
23	Turkey	1.1	South Africa	1.1	Indonesia	1.1	Thailand	1.1	Singapore	1.2
24	Malaysia	1.0	United Arab Emirates	1.0	Austria	1.1	Malaysia	1.1	Malaysia	1.0
25	Switzerland	1.0	Turkey	1.0	United Arab Emirates	1.1	Switzerland	1.1	Austria	1.0

Tradeflow main commodities 2006–2010

Inorganic chemicals: export

EXPORT	2006 Country	2006 %	2007 Country	2007 %	2008 Country	2008 %	2009 Country	2009 %	2010 Country	2010 %
World	World	100.0	World	100.0	World	100.0	World	100.0	World	100.0
1	United States of America	12.2	United States of America	11.5	United States of America	10.7	United States of America	12.8	United States of America	11.3
2	China	9.3	China	9.6	China	10.4	Germany	9.3	China	10.3
3	Germany	8.7	Germany	8.6	Germany	8.6	China	9.1	Germany	7.9
4	Australia	6.0	Canada	5.9	France	6.1	France	6.6	Russian Federation	5.7
5	Canada	4.9	United Kingdom	5.6	Australia	4.6	United Kingdom	5.1	France	5.2
6	France	4.9	France	5.6	United Kingdom	4.3	Australia	4.7	United Kingdom	4.7
7	United Kingdom	4.8	Australia	5.5	Netherlands	4.1	Netherlands	4.5	Netherlands	4.6
8	Netherlands	4.2	Netherlands	4.6	Canada	4.0	Japan	4.1	Australia	4.5
9	Japan	4.2	Japan	4.1	Japan	4.0	Canada	4.1	Japan	3.9
10	Belgium	3.5	Belgium	3.6	Belgium	3.6	Belgium	2.8	Canada	3.8
11	Russian Federation	2.8	Russian Federation	2.6	Russian Federation	2.9	Russian Federation	2.6	Belgium	3.2
12	Brazil	2.1	Brazil	2.0	Morocco	2.3	Kazakhstan	2.5	Republic of Korea	2.6
13	Kazakhstan	1.7	Italy	1.7	Brazil	2.0	Brazil	2.4	Brazil	2.4
14	Ukraine	1.3	Kazakhstan	1.6	Italy	1.9	Republic of Korea	2.4	Kazakhstan	2.0
15	Italy	1.3	Republic of Korea	1.2	Republic of Korea	1.8	Italy	1.6	Trinidad and Tobago	1.8
16	South Africa	1.3	Trinidad and Tobago	1.2	Kazakhstan	1.8	Spain	1.2	Italy	1.6
17	Jamaica	1.3	Ukraine	1.1	South Africa	1.4	Chinese Taipei	1.2	Morocco	1.2
18	Morocco	1.2	South Africa	1.1	Trinidad and Tobago	1.4	Morocco	1.2	Chinese Taipei	1.2
19	Republic of Korea	1.2	Chile	1.1	Chile	1.3	South Africa	1.2	Chile	1.1
20	Chile	1.2	Jamaica	1.1	Ukraine	1.3	Chile	1.1	Ukraine	1.1
21	Trinidad and Tobago	1.1	Morocco	1.1	Spain	1.2	India	1.1	South Africa	1.0
22	Spain	1.1	Chinese Taipei	1.0	Chinese Taipei	1.1	Israel	1.0	Spain	0.9
23	India	1.0	Spain	1.0	Jamaica	1.1	Ukraine	0.9	Israel	0.8
24	Chinese Taipei	1.0	Austria	0.8	India	1.0	Finland	0.8	Turkey	0.8
25	Austria	0.8	Finland	0.8	Tunisia	0.9	Turkey	0.7	Austria	0.8

Tradeflow main commodities 2006–2010

Soya beans: import

IMPORT	2006 Country	%	2007 Country	%	2008 Country	%	2009 Country	%	2010 Country	%
World	World	100.0	World	100.0	World	100.0	World	100.0	World	100.0
1	China	46.5	China	50.2	China	62.1	China	56.8	China	61.8
2	Japan	8.0	Japan	7.3	Japan	6.7	Japan	5.3	Japan	4.5
3	Netherlands	6.4	Netherlands	5.8	Netherlands	5.5	Germany	4.4	Mexico	3.9
4	Germany	5.9	Germany	5.4	Germany	5.3	Mexico	4.3	Netherlands	3.9
5	Mexico	5.7	Mexico	5.1	Mexico	5.1	Spain	3.9	Germany	3.7
6	Chinese Taipei	3.9	Spain	4.2	Spain	4.9	Netherlands	3.7	Spain	3.4
7	Spain	3.5	Chinese Taipei	3.5	Argentina	3.8	Chinese Taipei	3.1	Chinese Taipei	2.9
8	Belgium	2.7	Argentina	2.7	Chinese Taipei	3.4	Thailand	2.1	Indonesia	2.1
9	Italy	2.5	Belgium	2.5	Thailand	2.8	Egypt	2.0	Thailand	2.0
10	Thailand	2.3	Thailand	2.3	Italy	2.5	Indonesia	1.9	Turkey	1.8
11	Republic of Korea	2.0	Italy	2.0	Republic of Korea	2.3	Italy	1.8	Egypt	1.7
12	Indonesia	1.9	Indonesia	1.9	Indonesia	2.0	Republic of Korea	1.3	Italy	1.7
13	Portugal	1.7	Portugal	1.7	Turkey	1.8	Russian Federation	1.3	Republic of Korea	1.4
14	Turkey	1.6	Republic of Korea	1.6	Portugal	1.8	Turkey	1.3	Russian Federation	1.2
15	United Kingdom	1.4	Turkey	1.4	Egypt	1.5	United Kingdom	1.2	Free Zones	1.2
16	Malaysia	1.0	United Kingdom	1.0	United Kingdom	1.2	Iran (Islamic Republic of)	1.2	United Kingdom	1.0
17	Israel	1.0	Iran (Islamic Republic of)	1.0	Belgium	0.9	Portugal	0.9	Portugal	0.9
18	Argentina	0.9	Malaysia	1.0	Russian Federation	0.9	Free Zones	0.9	Malaysia	0.8
19	Cayman Islands	0.9	Morocco	0.9	Iran (Islamic Republic of)	0.9	Argentina	0.9	Argentina	0.7
20	Free Zones	0.7	Israel	0.7	Malaysia	0.9	Belgium	0.9	Belgium	0.7
21	Norway	0.7	Free Zones	0.7	Free Zones	0.8	France	0.8	France	0.6
22	Morocco	0.7	Norway	0.7	France	0.7	Malaysia	0.7	United States of America	0.6
23	France	0.6	France	0.7	Norway	0.7	Syrian Arab Republic	0.7	Israel	0.6
24	Colombia	0.6	Cayman Islands	0.6	United States of America	0.6	United States of America	0.6	Norway	0.5
25	Greece	0.6	United Arab Emirates	0.6	Greece	0.6	Norway	0.6	Syrian Arab Republic	0.4

Tradeflow main commodities 2006–2010

Soya beans: export

EXPORT	2006 Country	2006 %	2007 Country	2007 %	2008 Country	2008 %	2009 Country	2009 %	2010 Country	2010 %
World	World	100.0	World	100.0	World	100.0	World	100.0	World	100.0
1	United States of America	43.0	United States of America	43.8	United States of America	44.2	United States of America	49.8	United States of America	45.9
2	Brazil	35.2	Brazil	29.3	Brazil	31.2	Brazil	34.6	Brazil	27.2
3	Argentina	11.0	Argentina	15.0	Argentina	13.0	Argentina	5.1	Argentina	14.1
4	Paraguay	2.6	Paraguay	3.8	Paraguay	4.2	Canada	2.9	Paraguay	3.9
5	Canada	2.6	Canada	2.8	Canada	2.5	Paraguay	2.4	Canada	3.4
6	Netherlands	1.9	Netherlands	1.8	Netherlands	1.5	Netherlands	1.5	Uruguay	1.8
7	China	0.9	Uruguay	0.9	China	1.0	Uruguay	1.0	Netherlands	1.4
8	Uruguay	0.9	China	0.9	Uruguay	0.9	China	0.9	Ukraine	0.4
9	Belgium	0.5	Ukraine	0.4	Belgium	0.4	Ukraine	0.3	China	0.3
10	Ukraine	0.4	Belgium	0.4	Ukraine	0.4	Belgium	0.2	Belgium	0.2
11	Italy	0.2	Italy	0.2	Slovenia	0.2	South Africa	0.2	Slovenia	0.2
12	Bolivia	0.1	Austria	0.1	Italy	0.1	Italy	0.2	Italy	0.2
13	Austria	0.1	Bolivia	0.1	Bolivia	0.1	Bolivia	0.1	South Africa	0.1
14	France	0.1	Germany	0.1	Austria	0.1	Austria	0.1	India	0.1
15	Romania	0.1	France	0.1	Germany	0.0	India	0.1	Austria	0.1
16	Germany	0.1	Ireland	0.1	Romania	0.0	Chile	0.1	Chile	0.1
17	United Kingdom	0.0	Malaysia	0.0	Portugal	0.0	India	0.1	Serbia	0.1
18	Republic of Moldova	0.0	Zambia	0.0	Malaysia	0.0	Cambodia	0.0	Cambodia	0.1
19	Ireland	0.0	Romania	0.0	India	0.0	Germany	0.0	Bolivia	0.0
20	Hong Kong, China	0.0	Europe other than the Netherlands	0.0	France	0.0	Croatia	0.0	France	0.0
21	Slovenia	0.0	Republic of Moldova	0.0	Republic of Moldova	0.0	Malaysia	0.0	Romania	0.0
22	Croatia	0.0	Portugal	0.0	Hungary	0.0	France	0.0	Germany	0.0
23	Portugal	0.0	United Kingdom	0.0	Croatia	0.0	Hungary	0.0	Croatia	0.0
24	Malaysia	0.0	Spain	0.0	Europe other than the Netherlands	0.0	Slovakia	0.0	Republic of Moldova	0.0
25	Kenya	0.0	Russian Federation	0.0	Chile	0.0	Malawi	0.0	Portugal	0.0
							Republic of Moldova	0.0		

Tradeflow main commodities 2006–2010

Iron and steel: import

IMPORT	2006 Country	%	2007 Country	%	2008 Country	%	2009 Country	%	2010 Country	%
World	World	100.0	World	100.0	World	100.0	World	100.0	World	100.0
1	United States of America	9.3	Germany	9.3	Germany	8.3	China	10.1	Germany	7.8
2	Germany	8.1	Italy	8.1	Republic of Korea	6.9	Germany	7.8	China	6.7
3	Italy	6.8	United States of America	6.8	United States of America	6.4	Republic of Korea	6.7	Republic of Korea	6.6
4	China	6.1	Republic of Korea	6.1	Italy	5.4	Italy	4.8	United States of America	5.9
5	Republic of Korea	5.1	China	5.1	China	5.4	United States of America	4.7	Italy	5.1
6	France	4.8	France	4.8	Turkey	4.7	France	4.3	Turkey	4.3
7	Belgium	4.0	Belgium	4.0	France	4.4	Turkey	4.2	France	3.8
8	Spain	4.0	Spain	4.0	Belgium	4.0	Belgium	3.4	Netherlands	3.4
9	Turkey	3.5	Turkey	3.5	Spain	3.8	India	3.1	Belgium	3.3
10	Netherlands	2.8	Netherlands	2.8	Chinese Taipei	2.9	Spain	2.7	Chinese Taipei	3.0
11	Chinese Taipei	2.8	Thailand	2.8	Netherlands	2.9	Netherlands	2.7	Thailand	2.9
12	Canada	2.4	Chinese Taipei	2.4	Thailand	2.7	Thailand	2.5	Spain	2.8
13	United Kingdom	2.2	United Kingdom	2.2	United Arab Emirates	2.3	Chinese Taipei	2.4	India	2.7
14	Thailand	2.1	India	2.1	Japan	2.0	Vietnam	2.2	Japan	2.2
15	Mexico	2.1	Japan	2.1	India	1.9	Mexico	1.9	Canada	2.0
16	Japan	1.9	Poland	1.9	Poland	1.9	Poland	1.8	Mexico	1.9
17	India	1.7	Canada	1.7	United Kingdom	1.8	Japan	1.8	Vietnam	1.7
18	Poland	1.6	Sweden	1.6	Canada	1.8	Canada	1.7	Poland	1.7
19	Sweden	1.4	Iran (Islamic Republic of)	1.4	Mexico	1.6	Iran (Islamic Republic of)	1.7	United Kingdom	1.7
20	Czech Republic	1.3	Mexico	1.3	Indonesia	1.6	United Kingdom	1.6	Indonesia	1.7
21	Malaysia	1.3	Czech Republic	1.3	Vietnam	1.4	Indonesia	1.6	Malaysia	1.4
22	Austria	1.1	Russian Federation	1.1	Czech Republic	1.3	Czech Republic	1.3	Czech Republic	1.4
23	Russian Federation	1.1	Malaysia	1.1	Sweden	1.3	Malaysia	1.3	Iran (Islamic Republic of)	1.3
24	Finland	1.1	Vietnam	1.1	Malaysia	1.3	Egypt	1.3	Sweden	1.3
25	Hong Kong, China	1.1	United Arab Emirates	1.1	Austria	1.3	Russian Federation	1.2	Russian Federation	1.3

Tradeflow main commodities 2006–2010

Iron and steel: export

EXPORT	2006 Country	%	2007 Country	%	2008 Country	%	2009 Country	%	2010 Country	%
World	World	100.0	World	100.0	World	100.0	World	100.0	World	100.0
1	Germany	8.6	China	9.4	China	10.3	Japan	10.3	Japan	10.3
2	Japan	7.8	Germany	8.4	Germany	7.6	Germany	7.6	Germany	8.5
3	China	7.6	Japan	7.1	Japan	7.5	Republic of Korea	7.5	China	5.6
4	Belgium	6.1	Belgium	6.1	Russian Federation	5.5	United States of America	5.5	Republic of Korea	5.6
5	Russian Federation	5.4	Russian Federation	5.4	Belgium	5.4	Russian Federation	5.4	United States of America	5.4
6	France	5.1	France	5.0	United States of America	4.6	Belgium	4.6	Russian Federation	5.3
7	Republic of Korea	4.2	United States of America	4.8	Ukraine	4.4	China	4.4	Belgium	4.9
8	Ukraine	3.9	Ukraine	4.0	France	4.3	France	4.3	France	4.8
9	Italy	3.9	Italy	4.0	Republic of Korea	3.6	Ukraine	4.1	Netherlands	3.7
10	United States of America	3.8	Republic of Korea	3.9	Italy	3.9	Italy	3.6	Ukraine	3.3
11	Netherlands	3.5	Netherlands	3.9	Netherlands	3.4	Netherlands	2.9	Italy	3.3
12	United Kingdom	2.9	United Kingdom	3.4	Turkey	2.9	Chinese Taipei	2.9	Chinese Taipei	2.9
13	Chinese Taipei	2.8	Chinese Taipei	2.9	United Kingdom	2.6	Turkey	2.6	United Kingdom	2.8
14	Brazil	2.7	Sweden	2.6	Brazil	2.3	United Kingdom	2.5	Spain	2.5
15	Spain	2.1	Spain	2.3	Spain	2.3	Brazil	2.3	Turkey	2.4
16	Sweden	2.1	Brazil	2.3	Chinese Taipei	2.2	Spain	2.2	Brazil	2.4
17	Turkey	1.9	Turkey	2.2	Sweden	2.0	Austria	1.9	South Africa	2.1
18	Austria	1.7	Austria	1.9	Austria	1.9	South Africa	1.9	Sweden	2.0
19	South Africa	1.7	South Africa	1.8	South Africa	1.8	Sweden	1.7	Canada	1.8
20	Canada	1.7	Finland	1.7	Canada	1.5	Canada	1.6	Austria	1.7
21	Finland	1.6	Canada	1.5	India	1.4	India	1.6	India	1.6
22	India	1.6	India	1.4	Poland	1.4	Finland	1.2	Finland	1.3
23	Czech Republic	1.1	Czech Republic	1.1	Kazakhstan	1.1	Slovakia	1.2	Finland	1.2
24	Slovakia	1.0	Poland	1.0	Finland	1.1	Kazakhstan	1.2	Czech Republic	1.1
25	Mexico	0.9	Slovakia	0.9	Czech Republic	0.9	Poland	1.2	Poland	1.0

Tradeflow main commodities 2006–2010

Iron ores: import

IMPORT	2006 Country	%	2007 Country	%	2008 Country	%	2009 Country	%	2010 Country	%
World	World	100.0	World	100.0	World	100.0	World	100.0	World	100.0
1	China	63.3	China	82.3	China	90.8	China	88.4	China	69.3
2	Japan	21.7	Japan	21.5	Japan	19.8	Japan	15.3	Japan	13.4
3	Germany	8.3	Germany	7.9	Republic of Korea	7.2	Republic of Korea	6.2	Republic of Korea	5.8
4	Republic of Korea	7.2	Republic of Korea	7.0	Germany	6.7	Germany	5.0	Germany	4.7
5	Italy	3.5	Chinese Taipei	3.3	Chinese Taipei	2.8	Chinese Taipei	1.9	Netherlands	3.8
6	France	3.4	Italy	3.2	Italy	2.7	Turkey	1.6	Chinese Taipei	2.2
7	Chinese Taipei	3.2	United Kingdom	3.2	United Kingdom	2.6	France	1.5	France	1.7
8	United Kingdom	3.0	France	3.1	France	2.5	Italy	1.3	Bahrain	1.6
9	United States of America	2.1	Netherlands	2.2	Saudi Arabia	1.7	United Kingdom	1.3	Italy	1.4
10	Netherlands	2.0	Austria	1.9	Belgium	1.7	Saudi Arabia	1.2	United Kingdom	1.2
11	Austria	1.9	Russian Federation	1.8	Netherlands	1.7	Austria	1.1	Saudi Arabia	1.2
12	Belgium	1.9	United States of America	1.6	Czech Republic	1.6	Russian Federation	1.1	Belgium	0.8
13	Czech Republic	1.8	Turkey	1.6	Russian Federation	1.6	Netherlands	0.9	Turkey	0.8
14	Canada	1.8	Poland	1.5	United States of America	1.5	Egypt	0.8	Canada	0.8
15	Turkey	1.6	Belgium	1.5	Canada	1.5	Czech Republic	0.8	Argentina	0.7
16	Saudi Arabia	1.6	Czech Republic	1.5	Austria	1.4	United States of America	0.7	Qatar	0.7
17	Argentina	1.5	Saudi Arabia	1.4	Argentina	1.4	Spain	0.7	United States of America	0.7
18	Russian Federation	1.4	Canada	1.4	Poland	1.2	Belgium	0.5	Czech Republic	0.6
19	Poland	1.4	Trinidad and Tobago	1.2	Turkey	1.1	Slovakia	0.5	Spain	0.6
20	Slovakia	1.2	Argentina	1.2	Spain	1.0	Argentina	0.5	Slovakia	0.5
21	Romania	1.1	Romania	1.1	Egypt	0.9	Poland	0.5	Poland	0.5
22	Spain	1.0	Slovakia	1.0	Slovakia	0.8	Canada	0.5	Trinidad and Tobago	0.5
23	Malaysia	0.8	Spain	1.0	Malaysia	0.8	Malaysia	0.4	Egypt	0.4
24	Finland	0.8	Malaysia	0.8	Romania	0.8	Qatar	0.4	Russian Federation	0.4
25	Mexico	0.7	Australia	0.7	Trinidad and Tobago	0.7	Bahrain	0.4	Malaysia	0.4

Tradeflow main commodities 2006–2010

Iron ores: export

EXPORT	2006 Country	%	2007 Country	%	2008 Country	%	2009 Country	%	2010 Country	%
World	World	100.0	World	100.0	World	100.0	World	100.0	World	100.0
1	Australia	33.0	Australia	32.4	Australia	37.9	Australia	41.6	Australia	38.8
2	Brazil	27.1	Brazil	25.7	Brazil	24.7	Brazil	23.4	Brazil	25.3
3	India	11.4	India	11.2	India	8.4	India	9.3	India	10.4
4	Canada	5.1	Canada	4.4	Canada	4.4	South Africa	5.5	South Africa	4.7
5	South Africa	4.1	South Africa	3.9	South Africa	3.6	Canada	5.2	Netherlands	2.8
6	Sweden	3.5	Sweden	3.7	Sweden	3.3	Sweden	2.3	Canada	2.7
7	Russian Federation	2.7	Russian Federation	3.2	Russian Federation	3.0	Ukraine	2.2	Sweden	2.2
8	Ukraine	2.4	Ukraine	2.3	Ukraine	3.0	Kazakhstan	1.7	Ukraine	2.2
9	Kazakhstan	2.0	Kazakhstan	1.9	Kazakhstan	1.9	Russian Federation	1.6	Russian Federation	1.6
10	United States of America	1.9	United States of America	1.8	United States of America	1.8	Mauritania	1.4	Iran (Islamic Republic of)	1.6
11	Chile	1.0	Mauritania	1.0	Iran (Islamic Republic of)	1.4	Iran (Islamic Republic of)	1.1	Mauritania	1.1
12	Peru	0.8	Iran (Islamic Republic of)	0.8	Mauritania	1.3	Chile	1.0	Kazakhstan	1.1
13	Netherlands	0.5	Chile	0.5	Chile	1.0	United States of America	0.6	Bahrain	1.0
14	Philippines	0.5	Trinidad and Tobago	0.5	Venezuela	0.8	Peru	0.5	Chile	1.0
15	Bahrain	0.4	Peru	0.4	Trinidad and Tobago	0.7	Bahrain	0.5	United States of America	1.0
16	Iran (Islamic Republic of)	0.3	Netherlands	0.3	Peru	0.5	Trinidad and Tobago	0.4	Peru	0.5
17	Bosnia and Herzegovina	0.2	Bahrain	0.2	Mexico	0.5	Venezuela	0.3	Mexico	0.2
18	Democratic People's Republic of Korea	0.2	Philippines	0.2	Democratic People's Republic of Korea	0.4	Mexico	0.3	Mongolia	0.2
19	Mexico	0.2	Indonesia	0.2	Mongolia	0.2	Indonesia	0.2	Democratic People's Republic of Korea	0.2
20	Indonesia	0.1	Democratic People's Republic of Korea	0.1	Indonesia	0.2	Democratic People's Republic of Korea	0.2	Indonesia	0.2
21	Norway	0.1	Mexico	0.1	Philippines	0.2	Philippines	0.2	Vietnam	0.1
22	Vietnam	0.1	Bosnia and Herzegovina	0.1	Thailand	0.2	Mongolia	0.2	Venezuela	0.1
23	Trinidad and Tobago	0.1	Thailand	0.1	Norway	0.1	Norway	0.1	Argentina	0.1
24	Libyan Arab Jamahiriya	0.1	Norway	0.1	Bosnia and Herzegovina	0.1	Vietnam	0.1	Philippines	0.1
25	Republic of Korea	0.0	Libyan Arab Jamahiriya	0.0	Vietnam	0.1	Thailand	0.1	Norway	0.1

APPENDIX 3

Top Commodity Trading Companies Worldwide

Arcadia

Arcadia Petroleum Limited is engaged in the source, supply, blending, and marketing of physical oils.

www.arcadiapet.com

Archer Daniels Midland

ADM Company manufactures and sells protein meal, vegetable oil, corn sweeteners, flour, biodiesel, ethanol, and other value-added food and feed ingredients. It has a subsidiary in Singapore, Archer Daniels Midland Singapore Pte Ltd.

www.adm.com

Bunge

Bunge Limited engages in the agriculture and food businesses worldwide, with integrated operations from farming to retail.

www.bunge.com

Cargill

Cargill is an international producer and marketer of food, agricultural, financial and industrial products and services.

www.cargill.com

Glencore

Glencore has worldwide activities in the production, sourcing, processing, refining, transporting, storage, financing and supply of metals and minerals, energy products and agricultural products.

www.glencore.com

Gunvor International

Gunvor International B.V. engages in the trade, transport, and storage of oil and petroleum products internationally. It has a subsidiary in Singapore, Gunvor Singapore Pte Ltd.

gunvorgroup.com

Hin Leong Trading Pte Ltd

Hin Leong is involved in oil trading, bunkering, lubricants blending and sales, diesel retailing, logistics support and storage support.

www.hinleong.com.sg

Koch Industries

Koch companies are involved in refining, chemicals and biofuels; forest and consumer products; fertilizers; polymers and fibers; process and pollution control equipment and technologies; commodity trading and services; minerals; ranching; and investments.

www.kochind.com

Louis Dreyfus

Louis Dreyfus Commodities B.V. processes and trades agricultural products, and engages in merchandising a range of commodities.

www.ldc.com

Mabanaft

Mabanaft is the trading arm of Marquard & Bahls AG, a leading independent petroleum company that engages in the wholesale and import of petroleum products in Europe, North America, South America, Africa, and Asia.

www.mabanaft.com

Mercuria

Mercuria's core business is sourcing, supplying and trading crude oil and refined petroleum products.

www.mercuria.com

Noble Group

Noble Group provides supply chain management services for agricultural, industrial, and energy products worldwide.

www.thisisnoble.com

Olam

Olam International is a global integrated supply chain manager and processor of agricultural products and food ingredients.

olamgroup.com

Trafigura

Trafigura Beheer B.V. engages in the sourcing and trading of crude oil, petroleum products, renewable energies, metals, metal ores, coal, and concentrates for industrial consumers worldwide.

www.trafigura.com

Vitol

The company engages in the extraction, trade, refining, storage, and transport of energy. Vitol Asia Pte Ltd is headquartered in Singapore.

www.vitol.com

Wilmar

Wilmar International Limited operates through seven segments: Palm and Laurics, Oilseeds and Grains, Consumer Products, Plantations and Palm Oil Mills, Sugar Milling, Sugar Merchandising and Processing, and Others. Wilmar International Limited was founded in 1991 and is headquartered in Singapore.

www.wilmar-international.com

Source: Reuters: updated 2018

Bibliography

Atkin, Michael, *The International Grain Trade*, Woodhead Publishing Ltd. UK 2010

Browning, J., Lambrecht, B., Norrish, K., Smith, D., 'Metals View: Where Next?', *LME Week Supplement*, October 2010

Burger, Markus, Graeber, Bernhard and Schindlmayr, Gero, Managing Energy Risk – *An Integrated View on Power and other Energy Markets*, John Wiley & Sons 2007

Chatrath, A. and Song F., 'Futures Commitments and Commodity Price Jumps', *The Financial Review* 34:95 – 112. 1999.

Collinson, etc., *Financial Products: A Survival Guide*, Euromoney 1996

Cook, S. and Philcox, R., 'The Physical Challenge', *Commodities Now*, Vol. 14–4, 2010, available at: http://content.yudu.com/A1q88f/ComNowDec2010/resources/60.htm

Desai, A. Mihir, *International Finance: A Case Book*, John Wiley & Sons 2004

Economist *Pocket World in Figures 2012 Edition*, Profile Books Ltd, London, 2012

Fung, King Tak, *Leading Court Cases on Letters of Credit*, ICC Publishing SA 2004

Garcia, P., Leuthold, R. M. and Zapata, H., 'Lead-Lag Relationships between Trading Volume and Price Variability: New Evidence', *Journal of Futures Markets* 6(1):1–10, 1986

Haigh, M., Hranaiova, J. and Overdahl, J., 'Hedge Funds, Volatility, and Liquidity Provision in Energy Futures Markets', *Journal of Alternative Investments* 9(4):10–38, 2007

Interagency Agricultural Projections Committee, USDA Agricultural Projections to 2020, February 2011, available at: http://www.usda.gov/oce/commodity/archive_projections/USDAAgriculturalProjections2020.pdf

Irwin, S.H. and Yoshimaru, S., 'Managed Futures, Positive Feedback Trading and Futures Price Volatility', *Journal of Futures Markets* 19(7):759–78, 1999

Isherwood, G., 'Food Prices Reaching Crisis Levels?' *Commodities Now*, Vol. 14–4, 2010, available at: http://content.yudu.com/A1q88f/ComNowDec2010/resources/60.htm

Jones, G. and Hollands, P., 'Copper The New Fundamentals', 2011, available at http://www.amebc.ca/documents/roundup/2011/Presentations/Thurs_415_Jones%20%5BCompatibility%20Mode%5D.pdf

McNamara, John, *Structured Trade and Commodity Finance*, Woodhead Publishing Ltd 2010

Moors, Emmanuelle, *Structured Commodity Finance*, Euromoney, 2003

Kneen, Brewster, *Invisible Giant – Cargill and its Transnational Strategies*, Pluto Press USA 2002

Ordons News Team, 'WORLD OIL OUTLOOK 2010: World energy trends, an overview of the Reference Case', December 2010, available at: http://www.ordons.com/reports-a-analisis/energy-analisis/9176-world-oil-outlook-2010-world-energy-trends-an-overview-of-the-reference-case.html

Park, Murray, *The Fertilizer Industry*, Woodhead Publishing Ltd UK 2010

Roche, Julian, *The International Cocoa Trade*, Woodhead Publishing Ltd UK 2010

Roche, Julian, *The International Cotton Trade*, Woodhead Publishing Ltd UK 2010

Roche, Julian, *The International Rice Trade*, Woodhead Publishing Ltd UK 2010

Barros, Rodolfo, etc., *Agribusiness and Commodity Risk: Strategies and Management*, Risk Books, London 2003

Rowe, Michael, *Counter Trade*, Euromoney Publications PLC, London 1989

Sahi, G. S. and Raizada, G., 'Commodity Futures Market Efficiency in India and Effect on Inflation', 2006, available at: http://ssrn.com/abstract=949161

Schofield, Neil C., *Commodity Derivatives*, John Wiley & Sons 2010

USDA Economic Research Service, *Sugar and Sweeteners Outlook*, January 2003

Van Genus, Orlando and Weaver, A. B., *Practices of International Product Trade*, ICC

Wolter, Eelco and Barendregt, Reijer, Solid Reporting, Sustainable Results_ *Risk Management and Financial reporting for Commodities*, KPMG 2008

World Energy Outlook: 2010; Global Energy to 2035, *Commodities Now*, Vol. 14–4, 2010, and available at http://content.yudu.com/A1q88f/ComNowDec2010/resources/60.htm

http://www.fao.org

http://www.oxan.com

Index

Note: Page numbers in *italic* refer to Figures;
Page numbers in **bold** refer to Tables

Africa 5, 15, 26, 186
  Ethiopia 34–38, 41–43
  micro-financial institutions 39, 40
agri-products (agricultural products) 4, 5, 7, 9,
24–25, 27–28, 50–51, 85, 139, 197, 208
applicant-paid usance letters of credit 117,
118, 121, 122–24
Asia 15, 26, 27, 33, 186, 206, 207, 217, 224
Australia 5, 26, 113

back-to-back finance 58–59, 143, **144**
bad debts 166, 167, 171–72
bank credit limits 110–11, 112, 179, 198, 200
bank guarantees 29, 60, 109, 159, 196
bank risk 99, 100, 101, 102–3, 107–12,
126–27, 129, 197
banking capital regulations 15, 70, 78, 205
banks 110–11, 161, 175–76, 219 *see also*
commodity finance banks
base metals 5
Basel II 15, 70
Basle Committee lists 109
bills of exchange 50, 55–56
bills of lading (BLs) 50, 141, 155, 186,
187–88, 241–42
bonded warehouses 153–54
borrowers 15, 19, 79, 101, 139–40
  pre-export finance 63–64, 66, 68–69
  supply chain finance 90–91
  warehouse finance 76, 77
  see also commodity trading companies
Brazil 23, 26, 113
BRIC countries (Brazil, Russia, India and
China) 23, 207

Canada 5
cash and carry 75, *76*
caustic washing 220–21

CCOs *see* commodity collateralized
obligations (CCOs)
CFCs *see* common fund for
commodities (CFCs)
chemicals, China **277, 278, 279, 280**
Chicago Board of Trade (CBOT) 9,
10, 191, 212
China 23–24, 26, 50, 206, 207, 209, 210, 224
  commodities trade **257–64, 265–72,**
273–80, 281–86
cocoa export ban, Côte d'Ivoire 208
Cocobod *see* Haana Cocoa Board (Cocobod)
coffee 26, 31, 37–38
  China **259, 260**
collaboration 34
collateral 133, 147, 152, 167, 176
collateral management 147–48, 152–56, 184
Collateral Management Agreements 156
collateral risk 147
collateral value 156, 183–84
commitment to negotiation (CTN) 114–15
commodities 3–5, 6–8, 14, 23, 44–51, 100,
175, 205, 216 *see* also commodity traders;
commodity trading companies
Commodities Research Board Index
(CRB) *207*, 212
commodity collateralized obligations
(CCOs) 213–14
commodity contracts 4, 15, 44–51
commodity exchanges 3, 4, 6, 9, **10–**
13, 14, 17, 191
commodity finance 6, 13, 14–20, 24, 55–56,
175–76, 189, 194–95, 205, 224–26
  common fund for commodities 32–34
  Ethiopia 37–38, 43
  least-developed countries 28, 29–30
  micro-financial institutions 39, 40
  see also structured commodity
  finance (SCF)
commodity finance banks 13, 15, 16–20, 55–56,
62, 63, 175–80, 194–95, 216, 223–26, 231–32

back-to-back finance 58, 59, 143
bank credit limits 110–11, 112, 179, 198, 200
bank risk 101, 102–3, 107–12, 127, 129
collateral management 147–48, 184
commodity price risk 135, 180, 190
corporate social responsibility
72, 138, 223–24
country risk 92, 100, 101, 102–7, 179, 210
fraud risk 161–64, 165–66, 239
letters of credit 56–57, 111, 114–18, 127, 128,
129, 196, 197–98
ownership-based finance 70–72, 78
risk 83, 84, 89, 134, 135, 195–97
risk management 137–41, 142, 143–44, 157–
60, 166–70, 177, 200–201
supply chain finance 85–90, 91, 92, 93–95
warehouse finance 152, 153, 154–55
see also correspondent banks
commodity futures agencies 247–53
commodity investment 211, 212–14, 215–16, 224
see also institutional investors
commodity markets 3, 4, 5, 6, 8–9, 17, 18,
206, 217, 222
commodity price risk 135, 180, 190, 191–94
commodity prices 3, 5, 7, 8, 14, 44, 45–46,
48–49, 69, 129, 205, 206–10, 215–16
commodity quality 3, 129, 155
commodity repurchase agreements
(commodity REPOs) 72–73, 74
commodity supply chain see supply chain
commodity supply chain finance see supply
chain finance (SCF)
Commodity Support Group
(CSG) 178, 181–84
commodity swaps 212–13
commodity traders 6, 16, 17, 18, 44–51, 84, 190
letters of credit 127–28, 130
commodity trading companies 5, 14, 16, 62,
189, 216, 218–19, 289–91
back-to-back finance 58–59
risk 134, 135
risk management 137–41
supply chain finance 86, 89–90, 91–92
commodity-for-interest swaps 212
commodity-related shares 213
common fund for commodities (CFCs) 32–34
compliance risk 136
confirmation of letters of credit 114–15
cooperative unions 40–41
Copenhagen Accord 220
copper 7, 93–95
corn see maize (corn)

corporate social responsibility (CSR) 72, 138,
179, 221–22, 223–24
correspondent banks 110, 122, 126, 198–99
Côte d'Ivoire
    cocoa export ban 208
    toxic waste dumping 220–21
cotton, China **275, 276**
countertrade 160
country limits 100, 103–7, 200
country risk 18, 31, 69, 92–93, 99–107, 134,
135–36, 179, 210
CRB see Commodities Research
Board Index (CRB)
credit 145, 183, 195, 218, 224
credit analysts 177
credit approval 111–12, 178
credit limits see bank credit limits
credit risk 133–34, 144, 145, 184–85, 198
credit-enhancement 145
crude oil 8, 27, 85, 223
    China **257, 258**
CSG see Commodity Support Group (CSG)
CSR see corporate social responsibility (CSR)
CTN see commitment to negotiation (CTN)

debt collection 171, 172
debt sales 171
debts 6, 15, 102–3, 106, 166, 167, 171–72
Deepwater Horizon oil spill 220, 221–22, 223
defaults 166, 167, 171–72
derivatives 5, 105, 107, 190, 225
developing countries 23, 100, 217
discrepancies 44, 117, 167–69, 170
    letters of credit 127–29, 167, 186
disputes 44, 49, 50, 107, 118, 135, 136, 167–69
documentary department 185–86
documents
    bills of lading 50, 141, 155, 186,
    187–88, 241–42
    fraud 239
    letters of indemnity 187–88
    trust receipts 186–87
    warehouse warrants 188
    see also legal documentation; letters of credit
    (LCs); title documents

ECA cover see export credit
agency (ECA) cover
EFTs see exchange traded funds (ETFs)
electricity 4–5, 7
emerging markets 15, 16, 18, 23–24, 26–30, 99,
100, 126–27, 206, 207, 210
    country risk 134, 135–36

lending arrangements 172
letters of credit 113
risk management 145, 160
structured commodity finance 62
supply chain finance 86–87, 89
warehouse finance 152, 155–56
energy and climate change legislation 222–23
energy commodities 4–5, 8, 13, 14, **25**, 27, 85,
138–39, 210, 224
standby credit 60–61
environment pollution penalty cases
Deepwater Horizon oil spill 220, 221–22
toxic waste dumping 220–21
environmental protection 219–24
Ethiopia 34–38, 41–43
micro-financial institutions 39, 40
Europe 16, 26, 38, 217, 222, 226
event risk 69
exchange traded funds (ETFs) 213, 214
export credit agency (ECA) cover 101, 157–58
export receivables finance 63–65, *66*
exporting restrictions 208
external credit rating 110–11

Federation of Oils, Seeds and Fats
Associations (FOSFA) 51
field warehouses 153
financial assets 7, 55, 210, 215
financial engineering 212
financial institutions 178, 179, 198–200, 201
fixed-floating swaps 212
foreign exchange products 189, 190
forfaiting 133, 157
forward contracts 191
FOSFA *see* Federation of Oils, Seeds and Fats
Associations (FOSFA)
fraud 133, 238–41
sugar fraud case 162, 166, 238, 240
fraud risk 136, 161–64, 165–66, 239
front-to-back finance 59–60, 143
futures contracts 191–93
futures markets 3, 212

GAFTA regulations see Grain and Feed Trade
Organization (GAFTA) regulations
gas 224
China **261, 262**
Ghana Cocoa Board case 144
global commodity markets 190, 206, 218
gold 5
China **263, 264**
Goldman Sachs Commodities Index
(GSCI) 5, 212

Grain and Feed Trade Organization (GAFTA)
regulations 50–51
guarantee funds 28–30

Haana Cocoa Board (Cocobod) 233–35
hard commodities 5, 13, **25**, 114, 138
holding certificates 156

ICC *see* International Chamber of
Commerce (ICC)
Incoterms 2000 see International Commercial
Terms (Incoterms 2000)
index funds 213
India 23, 24, 113, 207
industry research 179, 180–81
institutional banks see correspondent banks
institutional investors 212–14, 215–16, 224
insurance 28, 78, 80, 82, 156, 158–59
International Chamber of
Commerce (ICC) 128
International Commercial Terms
(Incoterms 2000) 7, 49
International Petroleum Exchange (IPE) 8, 9
iron, China **283, 284**
iron ore 181
China **285, 286**
IT systems 184–85, 217–18, 224

Latin America 15, 33, 206, 224
LCs see letters of credit (LCs)
least-developed countries (LDCs) 27, 28, 33
legal action 168, 169–71, 172
legal department 178–79
legal documentation 156, 178, 211, 218
legal registration 80–81
legal risk 136
lending arrangements 84, 100, 101, 145–46,
147–48, 156–57, 172, 185, 225
pledge agreements 148, 149–52, 157
see also pre-export finance
letters of credit (LCs) 17, 19–20, 56–61, 101–2,
107, 109–10, 111, 112–21, 122–30, 167, 188, 196,
197–98, 200, 224
case study 242–43
letters of indemnity (LOIs) 187–88
leverage finance 17
limited recourse 118
liquidity 82–83, 101, 102–3, 126–27,
145, 197, 218
litigation *see* legal action
LOIs see letters of indemnity (LOIs)
London International Financial Futures and
Options Exchange (LIFFE) 9, **11**

London Metal Exchange (LME) 5, 9, **11**, 51

maize (corn) 5, 208
   China **271, 272**
managed futures funds 213
Marché à Terme International de France
(MATIF) 9, **11**
maritime bills of lading 186
maritime letters of indemnity 187
market risk 134
maximum country risk (MCR) 103–4, 105
metals 4, 5, 7, **25**, 51, 138, 210, 224
Mexico 5
micro-financial institutions 39, 40
Middle East 27, 186, 206
minor metals 5
Minton Report 221

New York Board of Trade (NYBOT) 9
New York Mercantile Exchange
(NYMEX) 8, 9, **10**
non-bonded warehouses 153, 154
non-ferrous metals 5

OBF see ownership-based finance (OBF)
off balance sheet items (OBIs) 105
oil 3, 5, 114, 208, 216, 222–23, 224
   China **265, 266**
   Deepwater Horizon oil spill 220, 221–22, 223
   letters of credit 196
   letters of indemnity 187
OPEC 187
open confirmation letters of credit 57
operational risk 135
option contracts 193–94
over the counter (OTC) markets 5, 6, 190
ownership liability 79–80
ownership-based finance (OBF) 70–79
   risks 79–84

palm oil 142, *143*
pay at sight usance letters of credit (UPAS) 121
payment systems 162, 164
payments 236–37
performance risk 69, 92, 106
perishable goods 83–84
Peru 5
plain vanilla trade finance 55
platinum 5
pledge agreements 148, 149–52, 157
political insurance 133, 158–59
political risk 101, 158–60, 211
population growth 208

portfolio management 200
post-finance letters of credit 124–26
precious metals 5
pre-export finance 62, 63–65, 66–69,
146, 196, 229–30
   borrowers 63–64, 66, 68–69
prepayment finance 63, 66, *67*
presentation period (letters of credit) 113–14
price risk 28, 58, 68, 69, 71, 80, 135, 180, 214
processed goods 83, 93
product risk 135
public warehouses 153

railway bills 186, 241–42
refinance, letters of credit 121
regional development banks 18, 159, 160
relationship management 177, 189, 200
repurchase agreement transactions 107
reputation risk 136
risk 69, 83–84, 89, 106–7, 133–37, 195–97, 224
   ownership-based finance 79–84
   supply chain finance 89, 91, 92–93
risk management 133, 137–41, 142–44, 157–60,
166–70, 177, 194, 200–201
   collateral management 147–48, 149–52
   fraud risk 161–64, 165–66
   structured commodity finance
142, 144, 145–46
   supply chain 142–46
   warehouse finance 154–57
Russia 5, 23, 26–27, 47, 208

SCF *see* structured commodity finance (SCF)
SCF *see* supply chain finance (SCF)
secured lending 62
shipping guarantees 187
sight letters of credit 121
silent confirmation letters of credit 57, 116–17
silver 5
   China **267, 268**
soft commodities 4, 13, 14, **24–25**, 138, 224
solar energy 7, 208
South Africa 5, 26
South America 26, 156
soya beans 5
   China **281, 282**
speculation 214, 215–16
standby credit 60–61
steel, China 283, 284
stock finance 152
structured commodity finance (SCF) 28,
30–32, 43, 62–63, 217, 218
   risk management 142, 144, 145–46

structured letters of credit 118, *119*, 120, 121
structured pre-export finance 68–69
sugar 26–27, 239, 240–41
   China **269, 270**
   sugar fraud case 162, 166, 238, 240
sugar long futures hedge 192–93
sugar prices 7, *8*
supply chain 6, 7, 16, 18–20, 85–90, 142–46, 175, 216–18
   palm oil 142, *143*
supply chain finance (SCF) 68, 85–92
   commodity finance banks 91, 92, 93–95
   commodity trading companies 89–90, 91–92
   copper 93–95
   risks 89, 91, 92–93
support group 181–84
synthetic letters of credit 118, 119, 120

technological development 208
tenor 113–14, 134, 196, 200
three-party agreement 74, *75*
title documents 136, 147, 186
   fraud risk 161–64
   warehouse warrants 188
tolling 65, *66*, 94, *95*
toxic waste dumping 220–21
trade finance see commodity finance
trade service department 185–86, 188–89
transaction risk 142
transfer risk 106
transferable letters of credit 58
transportation 7, 49–51, 135
true sales 81–82
trust receipts 186–87

Uniform Customs and Practice (UCP) 162
   UCP 500 116, 117
   UCP 600 56, 57, 108, 117, 120, 242, 243
unprocessed goods 83, 93
unsecured lending 62, 147–48
UPAS *see* pay at sight usance letters of
credit (UPAS)
USA 5, 9, 26, 38, 99, 211, 222
usance letters of credit 117–18, 121, 122–24

warehouse finance 76–77
collateral management 152–56
emerging markets 152, 155–56
risk management 154–57
warehouse warrants 188
wheat, China **273, 274**
wheat prices 208, *209*